THE ARTISTIC CS

EDITED BY W. R. LETHABY

WRITING & ILLUMINATING,& LETTERING

BY

EDWARD JOHNSTON

WITH

DIAGRAMS & ILLUSTRATIONS

BY THE AUTHOR & NOEL ROOKE

A SCRIPTORIUM

This drawing [about two-fifths of the linear size of the original] is made from a photograph of a miniature painted in an old MS. (written in 1456 at the Hague by Jean Mielot, Secretary to Philip the Good, Duke of Burgundy), now in the Paris National Library (MS. Fonds francais 9,198).

It depicts Jean Mielot himself writing his collection of Miracles of Our Lady in French. His parchment appears to be held steady by a weight and also by (? the knife or filler in) his left hand — compare Fig. 41 in this book. Above there is a sort of reading desk, holding MSS. for copying or reference.

EDITOR'S PREFACE

In issuing these volumes of a series of Handbooks Editor's on the Artistic Crafts, it will be well to state what Preface are our general aims.

In the first place, we wish to provide trustworthy textbooks of workshop practice, from the points of view of experts who have critically examined the methods current in the shops, and putting aside vain survivals, are prepared to say what is good workmanship, and to set up a standard of quality in the crafts which are more especially associated with design. Secondly, in doing this, we hope to treat design itself as an essential part of good workmanship. During the last century most of the arts, save painting and sculpture of an academic kind, were little considered, and there was a tendency to look on "design" as a mere matter of appearance.

Such "ornamentation" as there was usually obtained by following in a mechanical way a drawing provided by an artist who often knew little of the technical processes involved in production.

With the critical attention given to the crafts by Editor's Ruskin and Morris, it came to be seen that it was Preface impossible to detach design from craft in this way, and that, in the widest sense, true design is an inseparable element of good quality, involving as it does the selection of good and suitable material, contrivance for special purpose, expert workmanship, proper finish, and so on, far more than mere ornament, and indeed, that ornamentation itself was rather an exuberance of fine workmanship than a matter of merely abstract lines. Workmanship when separated by too wide a gulf from fresh thought — that is, from design — inevitably decays, and, on the other hand, ornamentation, divorced from workmanship, is necessarily unreal, and quickly falls into affectation. Proper ornamentation may be defined as a language addressed to the eye; it is pleasant thought expressed in the speech of the tool. In the third place, we would have this series put artistic craftsmanship before people as furnishing reasonable occupations for those who would gain a livelihood. Although within the bounds of academic art, the competition, of its kind, is so acute that only a very few per cent, can fairly hope to succeed as painters and sculptors: yet, as artistic craftsmen, there is every probability that nearly everyone who would pass through a sufficient period of apprenticeship to workmanship and design would reach a measure of success.

In the blending of handwork and thought in such arts as we propose to deal with, happy careers Editor's may be found as far removed from the dreary Preface routine of hack labour as from the terrible uncertainty of academic art. It is desirable in every way that men of good education should be brought back into the productive crafts: there are more than enough of us "in the city," and it is probable that more consideration will be given in this century than in the last to Design and Workmanship.

Of all the Arts, writing, perhaps, shows most clearly the formative force of the instruments, used. In the analysis which Mr. Johnston gives us in this volume, nearly all seems to be explained by the two factors, utility and masterly use of tools. No one has ever invented a form of script, and herein lies the wonderful interest of the subject; the forms used have always formed themselves by a continuous process of development.

The curious assemblages of wedge-shaped indentations which make up Assyrian writing are a direct outcome of the clay cake, and the stylus used to imprint little marks on it. The forms of Chinese characters, it is evident, were made by quickly representing with a brush earlier pictorial signs. The Roman characters, which are our letters today, although their earlier forms have only come down to us cut in stone, must have been formed by incessant practice with a flat, stiff Editor's brush, or some such tool. The disposition of the Preface thicks-and-thins, and the exact shape of the curves, must have been settled by an instrument used rapidly; I suppose, indeed, that most of the great monumental inscriptions were designed in situ by a master writer, and only cut in by the mason, the cutting being merely a fixing, as it were, of the writing, and the cut inscriptions must always have been intended to be completed by painting.

The "Rustic letters" found in stone inscriptions of the fourth century are still more obviously cursive, and in the Catacombs, some painted inscriptions of this kind remain which perfectly show that they were rapidly written. The ordinary "lower case" type with which this page is printed is, in its turn, a simplified cursive form of the Capital letters. The Italic is a still more swiftly written hand, and comes near to the standard for ordinary handwriting.

All fine monumental inscriptions and types are but forms of writing modified according to the materials to which they are applied. The Italian type-founders of the fifteenth century sought out fine examples of old writing as models, and for their capitals studied the monumental Roman inscriptions. Roman letters were first introduced into English inscriptions by Italian artists. Torrigiano, on the tombs he made for Henry VII. in Westminster Abbey and for Dr. Editor's Young at the Rolls Chapel, designed probably preface the most beautiful inscriptions of this kind to be found in England.

This volume is remarkable for the way in which its subject seems to be developed inevitably. There is here no collection of all sorts of lettering, some sensible and many eccentric, for us to choose from, but we are shown the essentials of form and spacing, and the way is opened out to all who will devote practice to it to form an individual style by imperceptible variations from a fine standard.

Writing is for us the most universal of the Arts, and most craftsmen have to deal with lettering of a more formal kind. It is a commonplace of historical criticism to point out how much the Italian artists owed to the general practice amongst them of goldsmith's work, a craft which required accuracy and delicacy of hand. We cannot go back to that, but we do need a basis of training in a demonstrably useful art, and I doubt if any is so generally fitted for the purpose of educating the hand, the eye, and the mind as this one of writing.

W. R. LETHABY.

October 1906.

"We must set up the strong present tense against all the rumours of wrath, past or to come. So many things are unsettled which it is of the first importance to settle, — and, pending their settlement, we will do as we do . . . Expediency of literature, reason of literature, lawfulness of writing down a thought, is questioned; much is to say on both sides, and, while the fight waxes hot, thou, dearest scholar, stick to thy foolish task, add a line every hour, and between whiles add a line. Right to hold land, right of property is disputed, and the conventions convene, and before the vote is taken, dig away in your garden, and spend your earnings as a waif or godsend to all serene and beautiful purposes. Life itself is a bubble and a scepticism, and a sleep within a sleep. Grant it, and as much more as they will, — but thou, God's darling! heed thy private dream: thou wilt not be missed in the scorning and scepticism: there are enough of them: stay there in thy closet, and toil, until the rest are agreed what to do about it. Thy sickness, they say, and thy puny habit, require that thou do this or avoid that, but know that thy life is a flitting state, a tent for a night, and do thou, sick or well, finish that stint. Thou art sick, but shalt not be worse, and the universe, which holds thee dear, shall be the better."— Emerson.

"I began to think that if I should discover how to make enamels, I could make earthen vessels and other things very prettily, because God had gifted me with some knowledge of drawing. And thereafter, regardless of the fact that I had no knowledge of drugs, I began to seek for the enamels as a man gropes in the dark"— Palissy.

"... in that communion only, beholding beauty with the eye of the mind, he will be enabled to bring forth, not images of beauty, but realities {for he has hold not of an image but of a reality), and bringing forth and nourishing true virtue to become the friend of God and be immortal, if mortal man may."— Plato.

AUTHOR'S PREFACE

The arts of WRITING, ILLUMINATING, & LETTERING offer a wide field for the ingenious and careful craftsman and open the way to a number of delightful occupations. Beyond their many uses — some of which are referred to below — they have a very great educational value. This has long been recognized in the teaching of elementary design, and the practice of designing Alphabets and Inscriptions is now common in most Schools of Art. Much would be gained by substituting, generally, writing for designings writing because writing being the medium by which nearly all our letters have been evolved from the Roman Capital (See p. 1), the use of the pen — essentially a letter-making tool — gives a practical insight into the construction of letters attainable in no other way. The most important use of letters is in the making of books, and the foundations of typography and book decoration may be mastered — as they were laid — by the planning, writing, and illuminating of MSS. in book form.

Of this a modern printer (See also p. 368) says:

"In the making of the Written Book, the adjustment of letter to letter, of word to word, of picture to text and of text to picture, and of the whole to the subject matter and to the page, admits of great nicety and perfection. The type is fluid, and the letters and words, picture, text, and page are conceived of as one and are all executed by one hand, or by several hands all working together without intermediation on one identical page and with a view to one identical effect. In the Printed Book this adjustment is more difficult . . . Yet in the making of the printed book, as in the making of the written book, this adjustment is essential, and should be specially borne in mind, and Calligraphy and immediate decoration by hand and the unity which should be inseparably associated therewith would serve as an admirable discipline to that end."

And though calligraphy is a means to many ends, a fine MS. has a beauty of its own that — if two arts may be compared — surpasses that of the finest printing. This in itself would justify the transcribing and preservation of much good literature in this beautiful form (besides the preparation of "Illuminated Addresses," Service Books, Heraldic and other MSS.) and make the practice of formal writing desirable. And furthermore, as the old-fashioned notion that a legible hand is a mark of bad breeding dies out, it may be that our current handwriting will take legibility and beauty from such practice. And even the strict utilitarian could not fail to value the benefits that might someday come to men, if children learnt to appreciate beauty of form in their letters and in their writing the beauty of carefulness.

Illuminating

Of the practice of illuminating — properly associated with writing — it may be observed that, among various ways of acquiring a knowledge of the elements of design & decoration it is one of the most simple and complete. Moreover, a fine illumination or miniature has a beauty of its own that may surpass the finest printed book-decoration. And pictures in books may be as desirable as pictures on the wall — even though like the beautiful household gods of the Japanese they are kept in safe hiding and displayed only now and then.

Magnificent as are the dreams of a fine Decoration based on lettering, the innumerable practical applications of lettering itself (See Chap. XVI.) make the study of Letter-Craft not only desirable but imperative. And perhaps I may here be permitted to quote from The Athenteum of Feb. 3, 1906, which says of "the new school of scribes and designers of inscriptions":

"These have attacked the problem of applied design in one of its simplest and most universal applications, and they have already done a great deal to establish a standard by which we shall be bound to revise all printed and written lettering. If once the principles they have established could gain currency, what a load of ugliness would be lifted from modern civilization ! If once the names of streets and houses, and, let us hope, even the announcements of advertisers, were executed in beautifully designed and well-spaced letters, the eye would become so accustomed to good proportion in these simple and obvious things that it would insist on a similar gratification in more complex and difficult matters."

Yet *Ordinary Writing* and even scribbling has had, and still might have, a good influence on the art of the Letter maker, and at least the common use of pen, ink, & paper makes it a simple matter for anyone to essay a formal or 'book' hand. A broad nib cut to give clean thick and thin strokes (without appreciable variation of pressure) will teach anyone who cares to learn, very clearly and certainly. And though much practice goes to the making of a perfect MS., it is easier than people suppose to make really beautiful things by taking a little pains. As "copy book" hands simple, primitive pen-forms — such as the Uncial & Half-Uncial (pp. 3, 35) — afford the best training and permit the cultivation of the freedom which is essential in writing: they prepare the way for the mastery of the most practical characters — the ROMAN CAPITAL, roman small-letter, & Italic — and the ultimate development of a lively and personal penmanship.

Modern development of writing & illuminating

Developing, or rather redeveloping, an art involves the tracing in one's own experience of a process resembling its past development. And it is by such a course that we, who wish to revive Writing & Illuminating, may renew them, evolving new methods and traditions for ourselves, till at length we attain a modern and beautiful technique. And if we would be more than amateurs, we must study and practise the making of beautiful THINGS and thereby gain experience of Tools, Materials, and Methods. For it is certain that we must teach ourselves how to make beautiful things, and must have some notion of the aim and bent of our work, of what we seek and what we do.

Early illuminated MSS. and printed books with woodcuts (or good facsimiles) may be studied with advantage by the would-be Illuminator, and he should if possible, learn to draw from hedgerows and from country gardens. In his practice he should begin as a scribe making MS. books and then decorating them with simple pen & colour work. We may pass most naturally from writing to the decoration of writing, by the making and placing of initial letters. For in seeking first a fine effectiveness we may put readableness before "looks:" and, generally, make a text to read smoothly, broken only by its natural division into paragraphs, chapters, and the like. But these divisions, suggesting that a pause in reading is desirable, suggest also that a mark is required — as in music — indicating the "rest": this a large capital does most effectively.

A technical division of illumination into Colour-work, Pen-work, and Draughtsmanship is convenient (See Chap. XL). Though these are properly combined in practice, it is suggested that, at first, it will be helpful to think of their effects as distinct so that we may attain quite definitely some mastery of pure, bright, colours & simple colour effects, of pen nourishing and ornament, and of drawing — whether plain or coloured, that will go decoratively with writing or printing. This distinction makes it easier to devise definite schemes of illumination that will be within our power to carry out at any stage of our development. And while the penman inevitably gains some power of pen decoration it is well for him as an illuminator to practise in bright colours and gold; for illumination may be as brilliant and splendid in its own way as stained glass, enamels, and jewellery are in theirs.[1] At first, at any rate, hues that have the least suspicion of being dull or weak are to be avoided as though they were plainly "muddy "or "washed-out." The more definite we make our work the more definitely will our materials instruct us: and such service must precede mastery.

Referring again to good lettering: the second part of this book deals with some of its Qualities, Forms — the Roman Capitals their important pen-derivatives — and Uses. It is written largely from the penman's point of view,[2] but a Preface chapter on inscriptions in stone has been added and various types and modes of letter making are discussed. The essential qualities of Lettering are legibility, beauty, and character, and these are to be found in numberless inscriptions and writings of the last two thousand years. But since the traditions of the early scribes and printers and carvers have decayed, we have become so used to inferior forms and arrangements that we hardly realize how poor the bulk of modern lettering really is. In the recent "revival" of printing and book decoration, many attempts have been made to design fine alphabets and beautiful books — in a number of cases with notable success. But the study of Palaeography and Typography has hitherto been confined to a few specialists, and these attempts to make "decorative" books often shew a vagueness of intention, which weakens their interest and an ignorance of Letter-craft which makes the poorest, ordinary printing seem pleasant by comparison. The development of Letters was a purely natural process in the course of which distinct and characteristic types were evolved and some knowledge of how these came into being will help us in understanding their anatomy and distinguishing good and bad forms. A comparatively little study of old manuscripts and inscriptions will make clear much of the beauty and method of the early work. And we may accustom ourselves to good lettering by carefully studying such examples as we can find, and acquire a practical knowledge of it by copying from them with a pen or chisel or other letter-making tool. A conscientious endeavour to make our lettering readable, and models[3] and methods chosen to that end, will keep our work straight: and after all the problem before us is fairly simple — To make good letters and

---

[1] See Chap. XVI. "Of Colour" in "Stained Glass Work" by C. W. Whall, in this Series, and the illuminator might profit by the suggestion (ibid., p. 232) of playing with a homemade kaleidoscope.

[2] Dealing with the practical and theoretical knowledge of letter-making and arrangement which may be gained most effectually by the use of the pen.

[3] In making choice of a model we seek an essentially legible character, remembering that our personal view of legibility is apt to favour custom and use unduly, for a quite bad, familiar writing may seem to us more readable than one that is far clearer in itself but unfamiliar.

to arrange them well. To make good letters is not necessarily to "design" them — they have been designed long ago — but it is to take the best letters we can find, and to acquire them and make them our own. To arrange letters well requires no great art, but it requires a practical knowledge of letter-forms and of the rational methods of grouping these forms to suit every circumstance.

The Scope of this Handbook

Generally, this book has been planned as a sort of "guide" to models and methods for Letter-craftsmen and Students — more particularly for those who cannot See the actual processes of Writing, Illuminating, &c. carried out, and who may not have access to collections of MSS. Much of, if not all, the explanation is of the most obvious, but that, I hope, gives it more nearly the value of a practical demonstration. In describing methods and processes I have generally used the present tense — saying that they "are —": this is to be taken as meaning that they are so in early MSS. and inscriptions, and in the practice of the modern school of scribes who found their work on them.

Regarding the copying of early work (See pp. 195, 323, &c.) it is contended that to revive an art one must begin at the beginning, and that, in an honest attempt to achieve a simple end, one may lawfully follow a method[4] without imitating a style. We have an excellent precedent in the Italian scribes who went back 300 years for a model and gave us the Roman small-letter as a result (See p. 47). The beginner's attitude is largely, and necessarily, imitative, and at this time we should have much to hope from a school of Artist-Beginners who would make good construction the only novelty in their work. We have almost as much — or as little — to be afraid of in Originality as in imitation, and our best attitude towards this problem is that of the Irishman with a difficulty — "to look it boldly in the face and pass on" — making an honest attempt to achieve a simple end. Perhaps we trouble too much about what we "ought to do" & "do": it is of greater moment to know what we are doing & trying to do. In so far as tradition fails to bound or guide us we must think for ourselves and in practice make methods and rules for ourselves: endeavouring that our work should be effective rather than have

---

[4] Much remains to be found out and done in the matter of improving tools & materials & processes, and it would be preferable that the rediscovery of simple, old methods should precede new & complex inventions. We still find the Quill — for its substance & for shaping it and keeping it sharp — is a better tool than a modern gold or metal pen (see p. 60). The old parchment, paper, ink, gilding-size & colours are all much better than those now obtainable (see pp. 51, 167, 173, 178-179). I should greatly appreciate any advice from illuminators and letter-craftsmen as to materials and methods, and should endeavour to make such information available to others. — E. J.

"a fine effect" — or be, rather than appear, good — and following our craft rather than making it follow us. For all things — materials, tools, methods — are waiting to serve us and we have only to find the "spell" that will set the whole universe a-making for us.

Endeavouring to attain this freedom we may make Rules and Methods serve us (See p. 221), knowing that Rules are only Guides and that Methods are suggested by the work itself: from first to last our necessary equipment consists in good models, good tools, & a good will. Within the limits of our craft we cannot have too much freedom ; for too much fitting & planning makes the work lifeless, and it is conceivable that in the finest work the Rules are concealed, and that, for example, a MS. might be most beautiful without ruled lines and methodical arrangement (See p. 343). But the more clearly we realize our limitations the more practical our work. And it is rather as a stimulus to definite thought — not as an embodiment of hard and fast rules — that various methodical plans & tables of comparison & analysis are given in this book. It is well to recognize at once, the fact that mere taking to pieces, or analysing, followed by "putting together," is only a means of becoming acquainted with the mechanism of construction, and will not reproduce the original beauty of a thing: it is an education for work, but all work which is honest and straight-forward has a beauty and freshness of its own.

The commercial prospects of the student of Writing & Illuminating — or, indeed, of any Art or Craft — are somewhat problematical, depending largely on his efficiency & opportunities. There is a fairly steady demand for Illuminated Addresses: but the independent craftsman would have to establish himself by useful practice, and by seizing opportunities, and by doing his work well. Only an attempt to do practical work will raise practical problems, and therefore useful practice is the making of real or definite things. In the special conditions attaching to work which the craftsman is commissioned to do for another person, there is a great advantage. And the beginner by setting himself specific tasks (for example: making a MS. book for a specific purpose — See p. 100) should give reality to his work. As a craftsman in Lettering he might get work in some of the directions mentioned in pp. 337-341.

Although the demand for good work is at present limited, the production of good work will inevitably create a demand; and, finally, the value of Quality is always recognized — sooner or later, but inevitably — and whatever "practical" reasons we may hear urged in favour of Quantity, the value of Quality is gaining recognition every day in commerce and even in art, and there or here, sooner or later we shall know that we can afford the best.

—EDWARD JOHNSTON
October 1906

ACKNOWLEDGEMENTS

My thanks are due to Mr. T. J. Cobden-Sanderson, to Mr. Emery Walker, and to Mr. George Allen for quotations: to Mr. Graily Hewitt, to Mr. Douglas Cockerell, to Mr. A. E. R. Gill, to Mr. C. M. Firth, and to Mr. G. Loumyer, for special contributions on gilding, binding, and inscription-cutting: to Mr. S. C. Cockerell for several of the plates: to Mr. W. H. Cowlishaw, to the Rev. Dr. T. K. Abbott, to Dr. F. S. Kenyon of the New Palaeographical Society, to the Vicar of Holy Trinity Church, Hastings, to the Secretary of the Board of Education, S. Kensington, to Mr. H. Yates-Thompson, to Mr. G. H. Powell, and to others, for permission to reproduce photographs, &c.: and to Mr. Noel Rooke and G. J. H. for assistance with the illustrations and many other matters: I should like, moreover, to acknowledge my indebtedness to Mr. W. R. Lethaby and Mr. S. C. Cockerell for encouragement and advice in years past.

—E. J.

ADDENDA & CORRIGENDA

P. 17. Beginners practising large writing may more easily use a thin, or diluted, ink; in small writing this does not show up the faults with sufficient clearness.

P. 24. Quills often have a sort of skin (which tends to make a ragged nib), this should be scraped off the back.

P. 28. Until the simple pen-stroke forms are mastered, the pen should be used without appreciable pressure. With practice one gains sleight of hand (pp. 48, 236), and slightly changing pressures & quick movements on to the corners, or points, of the nib are used. The forms in the best MSS. shew such variations: e.g. the Uncials in Fig. 5 appear to have been made with varying pressure (perhaps with a soft reed) & their fine finishing-strokes with the nib-point (comp. forms in Fig. 146). Versals likewise shew varying, and sometimes uncertain, structures that suggest a form consisting of strokes other than definite pen strokes.

P. 28. A nib may be sharpened several times, before it is re-cut, by paring it underneath (Fig. a).

Pp. 39 & 45. The thin finishing-strokes of j & F, G, J, N, are made with the point of the nib — See note p. 63 above.

P. 60. The plan of a paper scale is shown in Fig. b.

P. 67. The dots for lines were often pricked through the edges of the book-sheets which were cut off after ruling (Fig. c).

P. 76. The spread or wedge-shaped thin stroke, sometimes very strongly marked, is common in early forms (Fig. d).

P. 97. $\bar{V}$ & R: better (pen) forms of these are shown in Fig. e.

P. 149. Ornamental Letter forms may consist of flourishes, patterns, leaves, flowers, &c. (See Fig. f).

Pp. 155-56. Diapering generally means the variegation, figuring, or flowering, of a plain or patterned surface, with a finer pattern (See Fig. 191a). Some diagrams of simple patterns (g-g^2 from modern cantagalli ware) are shown in Fig. g. Note: the more solid penwork line-fillings in Figs. 87, 126, make effective framing borders (See Fig. h).

Pp. 158-59. Note: the principle of breaking straight or long lines, mentioned in regard to background edges (p. 190), and illustrated in the line-finishings (Fig. 126) and flourishes (Fig. 79), is related to branching out and is re-creative, whereas the prolonged line is tiresome (See Figs. k, k^1 & comp. k^2).

P. 185. The B & D should be round-shouldered — See note p. 212 below.

Pp. 203-207.

Pp. 212-218;

P. 193. It is sometimes better to make narrow forms than to combine wide ones — example Fig. 1.

Pp. 203-207, Pp. 212-218. The large types — "Old Face "(founded on Caslon Type) and "Old French" (modern) respectively — are used in these pages as reference or index letters (not as models).

P. 212. Generally round-shouldered letters have finer and more stable forms than square-shouldered, and generally emphasis should be laid on the strong thick stroke running obliquely down from left to right (\), while the weak, thin stroke (/) is rather to be avoided (See Fig. m). The writing used in the diagrams in this book, considered as a formal hand, shows a little too much of the thin stroke (See p. 373).

P. 248. Commonly letters are made more slender in proportion as they are made larger, and it is generally not desirable (or possible) in practical work to have exactly similar proportions in large and small lettering.

P. 249. g from Fig. 173 inaccurate — comp. Fig. 173 & See Fig. n.

P. 253. Ornamental letters — See note p.149 above.

P. 365. A small writing is often the most practical — in the matter of speed in reading and less bulk in the MS., besides speed in the writing of it — but it is more difficult for the beginner to write it well and it is apt to lose some of the virtues of formal penmanship (See Fine-pen writing pp. 19, 49, 237, 248, 367).

P. 373. Oblique thin stroke — See note p. 149 above.

TABLE OF CONTENTS

A SCRIPTORIUM i
EDITOR'S PREFACE ii
AUTHOR'S PREFACE vi
ACKNOWLEDGEMENTS xiii
ADDENDA & CORRIGENDA xiv
CHAPTER I THE DEVELOPMENT OF WRITING 1
CHAPTER II ACQUIRING A FORMAL HAND: TOOLS 15
CHAPTER III ACQUIRING A FORMAL HAND: METHODS 27
CHAPTER IV ACQUIRING A FORMAL HAND: MODELS 35
CHAPTER V ACQUIRING A FORMAL HAND: PRACTICE 49
CHAPTER VI MANUSCRIPT BOOKS 61
CHAPTER VII VERSAL LETTERS & COLOURED CAPITALS 73
CHAPTER VIII BLACK & RED 85
CHAPTER IX LAYING & BURNISHING GOLD 103
CHAPTER X THE USE OF GOLD & COLOURS IN INITIAL LETTERS & SIMPLE ILLUMINATION 125
CHAPTER XI A THEORY OF ILLUMINATION 143
CHAPTER XII THE DEVELOPMENT OF ILLUMINATION 151
CHAPTER XIII "DESIGN" IN ILLUMINATION 161
CHAPTER XIV GOOD LETTERING SOME METHODS OF CONSTRUCTION & ARRANGEMENT 181
CHAPTER XV THE ROMAN ALPHABET & ITS DERIVATIVES .. 209
CHAPTER XVI SPECIAL SUBJECTS 269
BIBLIOGRAPHY, &C. 309
CHAPTER XVII INSCRIPTIONS IN STONE 313
COLLOTYPE PLATES AND NOTES 327

FIGS. a to n, illustrating Addenda & Corrigenda

PART I
WRITING & ILLUMINATING

FIG. I.

CHAPTER I
THE DEVELOPMENT OF WRITING

Nearly every type of letter with which we are familiar is derived from the Roman Capitals, and has come to us through the medium, or been modified by the influence, of the pen. And, therefore, in trying to revive good Lettering, we cannot do better than make a practical study of the best pen-forms, and learn at the same time to appreciate the forms of their magnificent archetypes as preserved in the monumental Roman inscriptions.

The development and the relations of the principal types of letters are briefly set out in the accompanying "family tree" — Fig. I. When the student has learnt to cut and handle a pen, he can trace this development practically by trying to copy a few words from each example given below.

THE ROMAN ALPHABET — The Alphabet, as we know it, begins with the ROMAN CAPITALS[5] (See Fig. 2). Their fine monumental forms were evolved by the use of the chisel — probably under the influence of writing — and had reached full development about 2000 years ago (See Plates I., II., and Chapter XV.).

FIG. 2.

FORMAL WRITING — the "book-hand" or professional writing of the scribes — comes of the careful writing of the Roman Capitals (See also footnote, p. 3, on the beginnings of fine penmanship). It was the —

---

[5] "The alphabet which we use at the present day has been traced back, in all its essential forms, to the ancient hieratic writing of Egypt of about the twenty-fifth century before Christ. It is directly derived from the Roman alphabet; the Roman, from a local form of the Greek; the Greek, from the Phoenician; the Phoenician, from the Egyptian hieratic ... We may without exaggeration ... carry back the invention of Egyptian writing to six or seven thousand years before Christ." — Sir Edivard Maunde Thompson, "Greek and Latin Paleography," pp. 1-2.

"literary hand, used in the production of exactly written MSS., and therefore a hand of comparatively limited use. By its side, and of course of far more extensive and general use, was the cursive hand of the time"[6]

In early cursive writing — the running-hand or ordinary writing of the people — *"The Letters are nothing more than the old Roman letters written with speed, and thus undergoing certain modifications in their forms, which eventually developed into the minuscule hand"*[7] (See Fig. 3.)

FIG. 3.

Here it is sufficient to trace the history of the formal Latin "hands," but the continual, modifying influence exerted on them by the ordinary cursive writing should be borne in mind. Notable results of this influence are seen in Half- Uncials and Italics.

SQUARE CAPITALS were formal, pen-made Roman Capitals, of the monumental type: they were used (perhaps from the second) till about the end of the fifth century for important books (See Plate III.).

---

[6] Ibid., p. 196.

[7] "G. & L. Paleography," p. 204. (Minuscules = "small letters." Half-Uncials are sometimes distinguished as "round minuscules" — p. 302.)

RUSTIC CAPITALS were probably a variety of the "Square Capitals," and were in use till about the end of the fifth century (Fig. 4 ; See also p. 224).

SCALAELAILROVISO
DISCVRRVNTALIIAD
LERRVALAIIITORQV
ILSEINTERPRIMOSL
AENEASALAGNAQV

FIG. 4.—Æneid, on vellum, third or fourth century.

ROMAN UNCIALS were fully developed by the fourth century, and were used from the fifth till the eighth century for the finest books (Fig. 5).

Uncials are true pen-forms[8] — more quickly written than the "Square," and clearer than the "Rustic" Capitals — having the characteristic, simple strokes and beautiful, rounded shapes which flow from the rightly handled reed or quill. The typical Uncial letters are the round D, E, H, M, U (or V), and A and Q (See p. 228).

ROMAN HALF-UNCIALS — or Semi-Uncials Writing — (Fig. 6) were mixed Uncial and Cursive forms adopted by the scribes for ease and quickness in writing. Their evolution marks the formal change from Capitals to "Small-Letters."

---

[8] It is possible that their forms were influenced by the use of the brush in painting up public notices and the like. The introduction of the use of vellum — a perfect writing material — in the making of books, led to such a great advance in the formality and finish of the book-hands (especially of the Uncial character) that, practically, it may be said to mark the beginning of penmanship as a "fine "art. This change may be assigned to any time between the first and the third centuries (paleographical dates before the fifth century must generally be regarded as approximate).

They were first used as a book-hand for the less important books about the beginning of the sixth century.

INOMI
CONFITEB
INDIRE
INEOQ
JUSTITI
JUSTIFICA
CUSTO
NONMEC

FIG. 5.—Psalter, fifth century.

FIG. 6.—S. Augustine: probably French sixth century.

IRISH HALF-UNCIALS were founded on the Roman Half-Uncials (probably brought to Ireland by Roman missionaries in the sixth century). As a beautiful writing, they attained in the seventh century a degree of perfection since unrivalled (See Plate VI.).

They developed in the eighth and ninth centuries into a "pointed "writing, which became the Irish national hand.

ENGLISH HALF-UNCIALS (Fig. 7) were modelled on the Irish Half-Uncials in the seventh century. They also developed in the eighth and ninth centuries into a "pointed" writing.

FIG. 7.—"Durham Book": Lindisfarne, about A.D. 700.
(See also Plate VII.)

5

CAROLINE (or CARLOVINGIAN) WRITING — While English and Irish writing thus came from Roman Half-Uncial, the Continental hands were much influenced by the rougher Roman Cursive, and were, till near the end of the eighth century, comparatively poor.

"The period of Charlemagne is an epoch in the history of the handwritings of Western Europe. With the revival of learning naturally came a reform of the writing in which the works of literature were to be made known. A decree of the year 789 called for the revision of church books; and this work naturally brought with it a great activity in the writing schools of the chief monastic centres of France. And in none was there greater activity than at Tours, where, under the rule of Alcuin of York, who was abbot of St. Martin's from 796 to 804, was specially developed the exact hand which has received the name of the Caroline Minuscule." [9]

The influence of the Caroline hands (See Fig. 8) The presently spread throughout Europe. The letters in our modern copy-books may be regarded as their merit of direct, though degenerate, descendants.

---

[9] "Greek and Latin Palaeography," p. 233.

ucescaeci excolantesculicem camelum
autem gluttentes:
Uae uobis scribae et pharisaei hipocritae
quia mundatis quod deforis est calicis
et parabsidis intus autem pleni sunt
rapina et inmunditia. Pharisaee cae-
ce munda prius quod intus est calicis
et parabsidis ut fiat et id quod

FIG. 8.—British Museum: Harl. MS. 2790.
Caroline MS. *first half of* 9th century.
(See also fig. 171 & p. 305.)

SLANTED-PEN or TILTED WRITING — The forms of the letters in early writing indicate an easily held pen — slanted away from the right shoulder. The slanted pen naturally produced oblique thick strokes and thin strokes, and the letters were "tilted" (See Fig. 9).

FIG. 9.

FIG. 10.

In the highly finished hands — used from the sixth to the eighth centuries — such as the later Uncials and the Roman, Irish, and English Half-Uncials, the pen was manipulated or cut so that the thin strokes were approximately horizontal, and the thick strokes vertical (Fig. 10). The earlier and easier practice came into fashion again in the eighth and ninth centuries, and the round Irish and English hands became "pointed "as a result of slanting the pen.

FIG. 11.

The alteration in widths and directions of pen strokes, due to the use of the "slanted pen," had these effects on the half-uncial forms (See Fig. 11):—

1. The thin strokes taking an oblique (upward) direction (a) (giving a sharp angle with the verticals (d, a)) led to angularity and narrower forms(a^1), and a marked contrast between thick and thin strokes — due to the abrupt change from one to the other (a^2).

9

2. The thick strokes becoming oblique (b) caused a thickening of the curves below on the left (b¹), and above on the right (b²), which gave heavy shoulders and feet.
3. The horizontal strokes becoming thicker (c) gave stronger and less elegant forms.
4. The vertical strokes becoming thinner (d) (with oblique or pointed ends — not square ended) increased the tendency to narrow letters.

It is to be noted that the Caroline letters — though written with a "slanted pen"— kept the open, round appearance of the earlier forms.

TENTH, ELEVENTH, AND TWELFTH CENTURY WRITING — The easy use of the merit of slanted pen, and the lateral compression of the letters which naturally followed, resulted in a valuable economy of time and space in the making of books. This lateral compression is strongly marked in the tenth century (See Fig. 12), and in the eleventh and twelfth centuries it caused curves to give place to angles, and writing to become "Gothic" in character (See Plate XI).

FIG. 12.—Psalter: English tenth century.
(See also Plate VIII.)

THIRTEENTH, FOURTEENTH, AND FIFTEENTH CENTURY WRITING — The tendency to compression continued, and a further economy of space was effected in the thirteenth and fourteenth centuries by the general use of much smaller writing (See Fig. 13). In the fifteenth century writing grew larger and taller again, but the letters had steadily become narrower, more angular, and stiffer, till the written page consisted of rows of perpendicular thick strokes with heads and feet connected by oblique hair-lines — which often look as if they had been

FIG. 13.—*Colophon* of English MS., dated 1254.

dashed in after with a fine pen — all made with an almost mechanical precision (See Plate XVII.).

ITALIAN WRITING — In Italy alone the roundness of the earlier hands was preserved, and though in course of time the letters were affected by the "Gothic" tendency, they never lost the curved forms or acquired the extreme angularity which is seen in the writings of Northern Europe (Compare Plates X. and XI.).

At the time of the Renaissance the Italian scribes remodeled their "hands" on the beautiful Italian writing of the eleventh and twelfth centuries (See Plates X. and XVIII., XIX., XX.). The early Italian printers followed after the scribes and modelled their types on these round clear letters. And thus, the fifteenth century Italian formal writing became the foundation of the "Roman" small letters, which have superseded all others for the printing of books.

ITALICS — The Roman Letters, together with the cursive hand of the time, gave rise to "Italic" letters (See Fig. I, & pp. 238, 340, 369).

ORNAMENTAL LETTERS originated in the simple written forms, which were developed for special purposes, and were made larger or written in colour (See Versals, &c., Figs. 1, 189).

Their first object was to mark important words, or the beginnings of verses, chapters, or books. As *Initial Letters* they were much modified and embellished, and so gave rise to the art of Illumination (See pp. 78, 79).

CHAPTER II
ACQUIRING A FORMAL HAND: TOOLS

Tools and &c.

The simplest way of learning how to make letters is to acquire a fine formal hand. To this end a legible and beautiful writing (See p. 35) should be chosen, and be carefully copied with a properly cut pen.

For learning to write, the following tools and materials are required:

- Desk
- Writing-paper
- Ink and filler
- Pens (Reed and Quill) with "springs"
- Pen-knife, sharpening-stone, and cutting-slab.
- Magnifying glass
- Two-foot (preferably three-foot) rule, and pencil
- Linen pen-wiper

FIG. 14.

The desk

An ordinary desk or drawing-board can be used, but the best desk is made by hinging a drawing-board ("Imperial" size) to the edge of a table. The board may be raised and supported at any desired angle by a hinged support,

FIG. 15.

or by a round tin set under it (Fig. 14). For a more portable desk two drawing-boards may be similarly hinged together and placed on a table (Fig. 15).

A tape or string is tightly stretched — horizontally — across the desk to hold the writing-paper (which, as a rule, is not pinned on). The lower part of the writing-paper is held and protected by a piece of stout paper or vellum

FIG. 16.

fixed tightly, with drawing-pins, across and over it (Fig. 16). Under the writing-paper there should be a "writing-pad" consisting of one or two sheets of blotting-paper, or some other suitable substance.[10]

It is a good plan to have the lower, front edge of the desk beveled or rounded, so that the tail part of a deep sheet, which may hang below the table, does not become accidentally creased by being pressed against it. A curved piece of cardboard fixed on the edge will answer the same purpose.

Paper & ink

I.
FIG. 17.

II.
FIG. 18.

cutting
back
slab

III.
FIG. 19.

For "practice" any smooth — not glazed — paper will do. For careful work a smooth hand-made paper is best (pp. 63, 68).

A good, prepared, liquid (carbon) ink is best. It should be as black as possible, without being too thick. A jet-black ink will test the quality of the writing by "showing up" all the faults; "pale" or "tinted" inks rather conceal the faults, and lend a false appearance of excellence (p. 246). A thin ink greatly adds to the ease of writing (See Addenda, p. 14). Waterproof inks, as a rule, are too thick or gummy, and do not flow freely enough.

The ink-bottle is kept corked when not in use, to keep the ink clean and prevent evaporation. Thick or muddy ink should be put away: it is not worth while trying to use it.

A small brush is used for filling the pen.

---

[10] Some Eastern scribes use a "pad" of fur. This, or a piece of springy cloth, or other elastic substance, would probably be helpful, and experiments should be made in this direction.

Pens: The Reed

A Reed or Cane pen is best for very large writing — over half an inch in height — and therefore it is of great use in studying pen strokes and forms.

A Quill is best for smaller writing, and is used for all ordinary MS. work (pp. 19-24).

The **REED**[11] pen should be about 8 inches long.

I. One end is cut off obliquely (Fig. 17)

II. The soft inside part is shaved away by means of a knife laid flat against it, leaving the hard-outer shell (Fig. 18).

III. The nib is laid, back up, on the slab (p. 25), and — the knife-blade being vertical — the tip is cut off at right angles to the shaft (Fig. 19).

IV. A short longitudinal slit (a-b) is made by inserting the knife-blade in the middle of the tip (Fig. 20).

V. A pencil or brush-handle is held under the nib, and is gently twitched upwards to lengthen the slit (Fig. 21). An ordinary reed should have a slit about ¾ inch long. A very stiff pen may have in addition a slit on either side of the centre.

The left thumb nail is pressed against the back of the pen — about 1 inch from the tip — to prevent it splitting too far up (See also Fig. 27).

FIG. 20.

FIG. 21.

FIG. 22.

---

[11] The ordinary "Reed pen" of the artists' colourman is rather soft and weak for formal writing. The reeds used by the native scribes in India and Egypt, and some of the harder English reeds, are excellent. A fine, hollow cane also makes a very good pen.

VI. The nib is laid, back up, on the slab, and — the knife-blade being vertical — the tip is cut off at an angle of about 70° to the shaft, removing the first rough slit a-b (Fig. 22).

VII. A strip of thin metal (very thin tin, or a clock spring with the "temper" taken out by heating and slowly cooling) is cut the width of the nib and about 2 inches long. This is folded into a "spring" (Fig. 23).

VIII. The spring is inserted into the pen (Fig. 24).

The loop *a-b-c* is "sprung" into place, and holds the spring in the right position. The loop *c-d*, which should be rather flat, holds the ink in the

FIG. 23.

FIG. 24.

pen. The point *d* should be about $1/8$ inch from the end of the nib.

THE QUILL — A Turkey's Quill is strong, and suitable for general writing. As supplied by the stationers it consists of a complete wing-feather, about 12 inches long, having the quill part cut for ordinary use. For careful writing it should be re-made thus: —

I. The quill should be cut down to 7 or 8 inches (Fig. 25) ; the long feather if left is apt to be in the way.

FIG. 25.

II. The "barbs" or filaments of the feather are stripped off the shaft (Fig. 26).

III. The nib already has a slit usually about ¼ inch long. This is sufficient in a fairly pliant pen; in a very stiff pen (See p. 24) the slit may be lengthened to $3/8$ inch. This may be done with care by holding a half-nib between the forefinger and thumb of each hand, but the safest way is to twitch the slit open (Fig. 27), using the end of another pen (or a brush-handle) as explained under Reed, V. (See p. 18).

stripping the shaft

II

FIG. 26.

lengthening the slit of the nib

III.

FIG. 27.

IV. The sides of the nib are pared till the width across the tip is rather less than the width desired[12] (Fig. 28).

shape of ordinary nib.

shape of pared nib.

FIG. 28.

V. The nib is laid, back up, on the glass slab, and the extreme tip is cut off obliquely to the slit, the knife blade being slightly sloped, and its edge forming an angle of about 70° with the line of the shaft (Fig. 29; See also Fig. 36).

The shaft rests lightly in the left hand (not gripped and not pressed down on slab at all), and the knife blade is entered with a steady pressure.

If the nib is then not wide enough it may be cut again; if too wide, the sides may be pared down.

Cut very little at a time off the tip of the nib; a heavy cut is apt to force the pen out of shape and spoil the edge of the nib.

VI. The nib should then be examined with the magnifying glass. Hold the pen, back down, over a sheet of white paper, and See that the ends of the two half-nibs are in the same straight line *a-b* (Fig. 30)

---

[12] The width of the cut nib corresponds exactly with the width of the thickest stroke which the pen will make in writing.

The nib should have an oblique chisel-shaped tip, very sharply cut (Fig. 31).

A magnifying glass is necessary for examining a fine pen; a coarse pen may be held up against the light from a window — a finger-tip being held just over the nib to direct the eye (Fig. 32).

A nib in which the slit does not quite close may be bent down to bring the two parts together (Fig. 33).

Uneven or blunt nibs (Fig. 34) must be carefully re-cut.

VII. The Spring (See Reed, VII.) (about $3/32$ inch by 1½ inches) is placed so that the point is about $1/16$ inch from the end of the nib. The long loop should be made rather flat to hold plenty of ink (A, Fig. 35) — neither too much curved (B: this holds only a drop), nor quite flat (C: this draws the ink up and away from the nib).

FIG. 29.

FIG. 30.

end of
NIB
magnified

VI.a.
FIG. 31.

VI b.
FIG. 32.

under. under. back
VI.d
typical nibs requiring recutting.

VI.c.
FIG. 33.

FIG. 34.

A.
B.
C.
VII.
FIG. 35.

The Quills—Of Quills Generally

For ordinary use the nib may be cut with a fairly steep angle, as shown (magnified) at *(a)* (Fig. 36).

But it is better for fine, sharp writing that the angle be made very sharp: the knife blade is laid back (much flatter than is shown in Fig. 29) and the quill is cut quite thin; the knife blade is then held vertical and the extreme tip of the nib is cut off sharp and true (b, Fig. 36).

For large writing, the curved inside of the quill is pared flat (c, d Fig. 36) to give full strokes. If the nib be left curved and hollow underneath (e), it is apt to make hollow strokes.

The pen may be made more pliant by scraping it till it is thinner, or by cutting the "shoulder" (a-b, Fig. 29) longer, or stiffer by cutting the nib back until the "shoulder" is short.

Goose and Crow Quills (See p. 121)

The main advantages of a quill over a metal pen are, that the former may be shaped exactly as the writer desires, and be re-cut when it becomes blunt.

A metal pen may be sharpened on an oilstone, but the process takes so much longer that there is no saving in time: it is not easily cut to the exact shape, and it lacks the pleasant elasticity of the quill.

A gold pen is probably the best substitute for a quill, and if it were possible to have a sharp, "chisel-edged" iridium tip on the gold nib, it would be an extremely convenient form of pen.

A "fountain pen" might be used with thin ink.

Pen-Knife, Cutting-Slab, &c.

THE KNIFE — Quill makers use a special knife. A surgical scalpel makes an excellent pen-knife. The blade should be fairly stout, as the edge of a thin blade is easily damaged. It should be ground almost entirely on the right side of the blade (Fig. 37) and kept very sharp.

FIG. 37.

THE SLAB — A piece of glass (preferably white) may be used for fine quills: hard wood, a bone, or celluloid for reed and cane pens.

SHARPENING STONE — A "Turkey"(fine) or "Washita" (fine or coarse grained) stone.

MAGNIFYING GLASS — A magnifying glass (about 1 inch in diameter) is necessary for examining fine pen nibs to See if they are "true." A "pocket" glass is the most suitable for general use, and for the analysis of small writing, &c.

RULE — A 2, or 3-foot wood rule having brass strips let in to protect the edges, or a metal rule.

LINEN PEN-WIPER — A piece of an old linen handkerchief may be used to keep the pen clean.

CHAPTER III
ACQUIRING A FORMAL HAND: METHODS

Position Of The Desk

Always write at a slope. This enables you to sit up comfortably at your work, and to See the MS. clearly as though it were on an easel — and, by the resulting horizontal position of the pen, the ink is kept under control. It may be seen from ancient pictures that this was the method of the scribes (See Frontispiece). Never write on a flat table; it causes the writer to stoop, the MS. is seen foreshortened, and the ink flows out of the pen too rapidly.

The slope of the desk may be about, or rather less than, 45° to begin with: as the hand becomes accustomed to it, it may be raised to about 60° (Fig. 38).

The "heel" of the right hand may be tired at first, but it soon grows used to the position. A rest for the left arm, if necessary, can be attached to the left side of the board.

LIGHTING — The desk is placed very near to a window, so that a strong light falls on it from the left. Direct sunlight may be cut off by fixing a sheet of thin white paper in the window. Careful work should be done by daylight. Work done by artificial light always appears faulty and unsatisfactory when viewed by day.

The Writing Level

Each penman will find for himself the writing level along which his pen will move most naturally and conveniently (See Figs. 39 and 16). The paper guard should be pinned on about 1 inch below the writing level: the tape is fixed across about 3 inches above the guard. In the case of very a large writing the space between the tape and the guard is greater, and in the case of a very small MS. it is less.

FIG. 38.

FIG. 39.

The writing level is kept constant. When one line has been written, the writing paper — which is placed behind the tape and the guard — is pulled up for another line.

Use Of The Pen

For the practical study of pen-forms use a cane or a reed pen — or a quill cut very broad — giving a broad, firm, thick stroke. It is the chisel edge (p. 22) of the nib which gives the "clean cut" thick and thin strokes and the graduated curved strokes characteristic of good writing (Fig. 40).

FIG. 40.

Therefore, set the nib glide about on the surface with the least possible pressure, making natural pen-strokes the thickness of which is only varied by the different directions in which the nib moves (See [Addenda](), p. 14).

It is very important that the nib be cut "sharp," and as often as its edge wears blunt it must be re-sharpened. It is impossible to make "clean cut" strokes with a blunt pen (See [Addenda](), p. 25).

When the nib is cut back, the "shoulder" should be cut back to preserve the elasticity of the pen (p. 24).

Holding The Pen

THE HAND holds the pen lightly and easily. A good method is to loop the thumb and forefinger over, and slightly gripping, the shaft of the pen, and support the shaft from below with the second finger. The third and fourth fingers are tucked, out of the way, into the palm (Figs. 41, 45).

The pen should be so lightly held that the act of writing should draw the edge of the nib into perfect contact with the paper, both the half nibs touching the surface. (To make sure that the contact is perfect, make experimental thick strokes on a scrap of paper — pinned at the right-hand side of the desk — and See that they are "true," i.e. that they are of even width, with "clean cut" edges and ends.)

The writer should be able to feel what the nib is doing. If the pen be gripped stiffly the edge of the nib cannot be felt on the paper; and it will inevitably be forced out of shape and prematurely blunted.

A thin slip of bone — a "folder" or the handle of the pen-knife will do — is commonly held in the left hand to keep the paper flat and steady (See Fig. 41).

THE CUSTOM ART MANNER — The ancient scribe probably held his pen in the manner most convenient to himself; and we, in order to write with freedom, should hold the pen in the way to which, by long use, we have been accustomed; provided that, for writing an upright round-hand, the pen be so manipulated and cut as to make fine horizontal thin strokes and clean vertical thick strokes (See Fig. 40, & footnote, p. 229).

SLANTED SHAFT, &c. — Most people are accustomed to holding a pen slanted away from the right shoulder. The nib therefore is cut at an oblique angle[13] to the shaft, so that, while the shaft is slanted, the edge of the

FIG. 41.

nib is parallel with the horizontal line of the paper, and will therefore produce a horizontal thin stroke and a vertical thick stroke.

For example: if the shaft is held slanted at an angle of 70° with the horizontal, the nib is cut at an angle of 70° with the shaft (Fig. 42). The angle

---

[13] If the edge of the nib were cut at right angles to the shaft, obviously the horizontal stroke would not be thin, and the true thick and thin strokes would be oblique (see slanted pen writing — Figs. 9 & 11).

of the nib with the shaft may vary from 90° (at right angles) to about 70°, according to the slant at which the shaft is held (Fig. 43).

If the writer prefers an extremely slanted shaft, to cut the nib correspondingly obliquely would weaken it, so it is better to counteract the slant by slightly tilting the paper (Fig. 44).

To produce the horizontal thin stroke, therefore:

The slant at which the shaft is held,
The angle at which the nib is cut, and
The tilt which may be given to the paper:

must be so adjusted, one to another, that the chisel edge of the nib is parallel to the horizontal line of the paper.

Before writing, make trial strokes on a scrap of paper to see that this is so: the vertical thick strokes should be square ended and the full width of the nib, the horizontal strokes as fine as possible.

HORIZONTAL SHAFT, &c. — The pen shaft is held approximately horizontal. This will be found the natural position for it when the slope of the desk is about 50° or 60°. It gives complete control of the ink

The desk is shewn here, with a slope of about 45°

FIG. 45.

in the pen, which can be made to run faster or slower by slightly elevating or depressing the shaft (Fig. 45).

30

The writing-board may be slightly lowered or raised with the object of elevating or depressing the pen shaft (Fig. 46 & p.73).

The pen makes a considerable angle with the writing surface, so that the ink, which is held in the hollow of the nib, comes in contact with the paper at the very extremity of the nib, making very fine strokes (a, Fig. 47).

The spring is adjusted carefully, the tip being approximately $1/16$ inch from the tip of the nib. The nearer the spring is to the end of the nib, the faster the ink flows. The loop must be kept flattish in order to hold the ink well (See Fig. 35).

Filling the Pen, &c.

It is convenient to stand the ink, &c., beside the desk on the left, and for this purpose a little cup-shaped bracket or clip may be attached to the edge of the writing-board. The filling-brush stands in the ink-bottle (p. 51) or pot of colour (p. 124), and is taken up in the left hand; the pen, retained in the right hand, being brought over to the left to be filled.

The back of the nib is kept dry (a, Fig. 48). A very convenient and perfectly clean method, when care is taken, of removing any ink on the back of the pen is to draw it across the back of the left forefinger.

In careful work the pen should be tried, on a scrap of paper, almost every time it is filled (to See that it is not too full and that the ink is flowing rightly).

The nib is kept clean. A carbon ink (p. 51), through gradual evaporation, is apt to clog the nib (especially in hot weather); therefore, every

normal (a.)

board lowered: pen elevated. (b.)

board raised: pen depressed (c.)

FIG. 46.

Slopes of Desk *pen shaft*
NORMAL ANGLES
(a)

(b.) *angle too acute: (ink marks thickly)*

(c.) *Angle too great: (pen works stiffly)*

FIG. 47.

Right: (a.)
Ink kept below can only follow the sharp nib and give sharp strokes

&

Wrong: (b.)
Ink occurring on back of nib forms a drop with ink below, so that you write with a drop and cannot make sharp strokes.

FIG. 48.

now and then, while the nib is in use, the spring is taken out and the whole thoroughly cleaned. It is impossible to write well with a dirty pen.

CHAPTER IV
ACQUIRING A FORMAL HAND: MODELS

Models

  The best training is found in the practice of an upright round-hand (p. 229). Having mastered such a writing, the penman can acquire any other hands — sloping or angular — with comparative ease (p. 246).

  The English Half-Uncial writing in <u>Plate VII</u> is an excellent model. Those who have sufficient time to spare for the careful study of this, or any other legible and beautiful round-hand, should obtain access to the MSS. in a museum, or procure good facsimiles (See Plates at end of Book, & p. 300).

  Those who have not sufficient time for a careful and thorough study of an early MS. will find it easier to begin with a simplified and modernised writing, such as Script I. (Fig. 49).

abcdefghilm nnopqrrſstux

"Durham Book" hand (copy).

abcdefghijklm nopqrstuvxyz :

Modernized Half-Uncial (I.).

FIG. 49.

Before copying a hand, it is well to examine carefully the manuscript from which it is taken: observe its general appearance: note the character and mode of the ruling, and the sizes and relative proportions of page, text, margins, and ornaments.

With regard to the actual forms of the letters and the mode of their arrangement, such a method of analysis as the following will be found useful, as an aid to accuracy in copying, and definiteness in self-criticism.

A METHOD OF ANALYSIS		Example: Analysis of Script I. (as in Fig. 50)
1. THE WRITING: (Ruling)	General character Double or single lines, &c. (See pp. 304, 305):	*Modernized Half-Unical* *Double lines (See Figs. 59, 65)*
Letters	Round or angular: Upright or sloping: Coupled or separate:	*Round* *Upright* *Coupled*
2. THIN STROKES:	Horizontal or oblique (See Figs. 10, 9):	*Horizontal*
3. THICK STROKES:	Heavy, medium, or light (See Fig. 183):	*Medium*
4. "HEADS" & "FEET":	Character (See Fig. 145):	*Solid, triangular, &c.*
5. STEMS (ascending & descending)	Short, medium, or long (see Fig. 183):	*Medium*
6. SPACING (Letters, Words, Lines):	Close or wide (See Fig. 154):	*Fairly close (See Figs. 54, 55)*
7. ARRANGEMENT:	In mass (of equal lines), or in column (of unequal lines) (See Fig. 154)	*In mass of equal lines (See Fig. 66)*
8. MEASUREMENTS (& proportions see pp. 324, 327):	Width of thick stroke (see p. 83): Height of a and d (See pp. 82, 84): Writing lines, distance apart (See p. 82):	*l = about $3/32$" wide* *o = about $3/8$" high* *d = about $11/16$" high*
9. COMPONENT PARTS:	Number and forms (See Fig. 51, 57, p. 47):	*a has 3 strokes* *b has 3 strokes* *c has 2 strokes* *And so on (See Fig. 51)*

abcdefg
hijklmn
opqrstu
vwxyz&
?:df,wyz

Modern. Half-Uncial. I. — MCM IV

FIG. 50.

toinx

+ normal position ("Straight pen").   m. & n.

cLceĩm

x = "Slanted pen".   v. & w.

orsuvz

&bdhkl

(g. s. & y. tail strokes may be carried up)

fgjpqy

coupling strokes "feet" bows   t.   x.
UP

FIG. 51.

Notes On Construction — Script I

The pen generally is held so as to give approximately horizontal thin strokes (See p. 30), but in making v (w, y) and x, parts of z, &c., it is "slanted." In Figs. 51 and 57 these forms are marked with a small diagonal cross x.

Most of the strokes begin as down-strokes, but at the end of a down-stroke, when the ink is flowing freely, the stroke may be continued in an upward direction (as in coupling-strokes, &c., the feet of letters, the thin stroke of x, and, if preferred, in making the last stroke of g, s, and y).

While the ink is still wet in a down-stroke, the nib may be replaced on it and be pushed upward and outward to form the round arch in b, h, m, n, p, and r. This stroke, reversed, is also used for the top of t.

The making of these UP-strokes is shown diagrammatically in Fig. 51.

Note. — The forms **+oin**x in Fig. 51 contain all the principal strokes in this alphabet, and are therefore useful for early practice.

Coupling The Letters

The letters are joined together by means of their coupling-strokes, which for this purpose may be slightly drawn out, and forward, from the naturally round forms of the letters (See c, e, &c., Fig. 52 & Fig. 59).

The coupling-strokes are finishing strokes — and as such are akin to serifs (p. 179) — growing out of or added to such stems as need "finishing."

Coupling enables one to write faster and with more freedom, the concluding or "coupling" stroke not being slowed down, but written with a dash, which is covered by the first stroke of the succeeding letter. It keeps the individual words more distinct, and therefore permits closer spacing of the text. Coupling is for convenience and legibility, and where it tends to interfere with legibility, we must be careful. The freer and more cursive the hand, the greater is the tendency to join and run letters together, as in ordinary writing.

It is preferable to couple letters below, if possible. Couplings above are sometimes apt to confuse the reading; for example, the cross-bar of t (though the most natural coupling for the scribe to use — See petatis—Plate

VII.) should generally be made to pass over or fall short of the succeeding letter (See Fig. 52).

> I. a c d e h i k l m n u (t. see ?)
> (I.) join below ⎤ to any
> II. f g r/q/........... join above ⎦ letter in front.
> *t or u
> III. f m n p r v w x y ? t { join above to any letter (not in class I.) behind.
> IV. b j o s w y z have no coupling-strokes.
>
> ? t usually joins below.*⎤ forward ⟩⟩⟩→
> may join above to ⎬ thus &
> any in Class III.⎦
>
> special
> fl
> ff
>
> Ex. tu, tw, tu ; tr, ty ;
> *right . rt . (doubtful) . permissible.
>
> COUPLING OF LETTERS
> for reference only :   ⎯naturally.
> Shewing how the letters of Script I. join most

FIG. 52.

Spacing: Letters, Words, & Lines

The letters of a word are fitted together so that there is a general effect of evenness. This evenness is only to be attained by practice: it is characteristic of rapid skilful writing, and cannot be produced satisfactorily by any system of measurement while the writer's hand is still slow and uncertain. It is worth noting, however, that the white interspaces vary slightly, while the actual distances between the letters vary considerably, according to whether the adjacent strokes curve (or slant) away or are perpendicular (Figs. 53, 152).

It is sufficient for the beginner to take care that two curved letters are made very near each other, and that two straight strokes are spaced well apart.

FIG. 53.

If the curves are too far apart there will be spots of light, and where several heavy stems are made too close together, "blots" of dark, marring the evenness of the page.

Words are kept as close as is compatible with legibility. The average space between two words is the width of the letter **o** (Fig. 54).

this and that

FIG. 54.

The Lines in massed writing (See p. 91) are kept as close together as is compatible with legibility. The usual distance apart of the writing-lines is about three times the height of the letter **o** (See also Fig. 148).

The descending strokes of the upper line must "clear" the ascending strokes of the lower line.

Interlocking of these strokes may be avoided by the experimental placing of **p** over **d** (Fig. 55).

FIG. 55.

Uncial Capitals: Script II.

These modernised Uncials (See Fig. 56, & p. 300) are intended to go with Script I, and their analysis and mode of construction are almost identical with those of Script I. (See pp. 72, 73).

Grouping: Uncials have no coupling-strokes: when several are used together, they are not joined, but evenly grouped, allowing as before for curves and (3) Models straight strokes (See p. 40).

Spacing: (a) When used with Script I., Uncials are written on the same lines, and have to follow the same spacing (in spite of their longer stems).

(b) When Uncials are used by themselves, their spacing may be wider (p. 297).

Note. — The height of Uncial **o** is about equal to the height of the Half-Uncial **d**.

ABCDE
FGHIJK
LMNO
PQRST
&UVXYZ
MCMIV. Uncials. II

FIG. 56.

Numerals & Punctuation Marks (See Fig. 57)

These are best made with a "slanted" pen (Fig. 9).

When writing "Arabic numerals," 1 and 0 may be made on the line, 2468 ascending, and 3579 descending.

FIG. 57.

Of Copying Mss. Generally

When copying a MS., it is best to choose a complete page — or part of a page — to be copied in facsimile.

Two or three lines are copied to begin with; then the composition of the individual letters and words is studied by means of a large pen; and finally, the whole page is copied in facsimile. (Of practising, See pp. 48, 49).

Make a general examination and analysis as suggested at p. 36. Accurate measurements will be found helpful.

Take the heights of the **o** and the **d**, and the distance apart of the writing-lines with dividers.

The width of the thick stroke is best found by making experimental thick strokes — the full width of the pen nib — on a scrap of paper: cut the paper in half across the thick strokes, and place the cut edge on the thickest strokes in the original MS., you will then find whether the pen nib should be cut wider or narrower.

The direction of the thickest strokes is approximately at right angles to the direction of the thin strokes; which commonly approaches the horizontal in early round hands, and is oblique in other hands (See Figs. 9 and 10). The positions both of these strokes in the model, and of your pen, determine the angle of the nib. Therefore, cut the nib across at such an angle to the shaft of the pen that, when you hold the pen naturally, the direction of the thin strokes which it makes on the writing paper will coincide with the direction of the thin strokes in the model; but

(a) The way in which the shaft is held,
(b) The angle at which the nib is cut,
(c) The position of the writing paper,

may all be slightly varied, so that the direction of the thin strokes can be followed exactly (See p. 30).

The writing paper is cut and ruled exactly in accordance with the model; and the heights of the letters and the widths of the thick strokes in the copy agree as nearly as possible with those in the original. It is therefore a good test for accuracy — when a few lines of writing have been copied — to measure and compare their lengths. If they correspond with their originals, it goes far to prove the copy a good one.

Before copying more of the page, the construction of the letters should be carefully studied. The number and the forms of pen-strokes in each letter are found by examination — with a magnifying glass if necessary — and by the experimental putting together of strokes, to form a similar letter. For this plan to write individual letters and words exactly two, three, or four times their height in the model: both the pen nib and the individual letters are made correspondingly two, three, or four times as wide as in the original.

It is particularly important, in copying, to preserve accurately the proportion of the thick stroke to the height and width of a letter (See p. 247). These are conveniently measured by the pen nib itself, or by the estimated width of the thick stroke; thus, in the writing shown in Fig. 50, the width of the **o** is approximately five, and the height approximately four, times the width of the thick stroke.

Not only must the copier ascertain what the forms are like and what are their proportions, but he must try to find out how they were made. This is of the greatest importance, for the manner of making a letter, or even a single stroke, affects its form and character with a definite tendency (See p. 333 & Fig. 172). And this becomes more marked the faster the writing. An apparently right form may yet be wrongly — if slowly — made; but in rapid writing, a wrong manner of handling the pen will inevitably produce wrong forms. As the real virtue of penmanship is attained only when we can write quickly, it is well worth training the hand from the beginning in the proper manner.

Patient and careful examination should be made of the changing pen-strokes, and of the mode in which they join — to form letters — and begin and end — to form "heads "and "feet." This, accompanied by practical experiments in cutting and handling the pen, will bring out details of the utmost technical value. A certain amount of legitimate "faking" (p. 246), play of the pen, and sleight of hand (p. 311), may be found, but, in the main, the regular, natural, thick and thin strokes of the pen, and the orderly arrangement of the writing, give to a manuscript its beauty and character.

Then having cut the nib rightly, you may, in a sense, let the pen do the writing, while you merely follow the strokes of the model, and you will, in course of time, have the pleasure of seeing the same beautiful writing — in the very manner of the ancient scribes — growing under your own hand.

CHAPTER V
ACQUIRING A FORMAL HAND: PRACTICE

Practice—Scripts I & II

In acquiring a formal writing, the penman should have two paper books constantly in hand: one for the study of the forms of letters, the other for both the letters and their arrangement. The first should contain large and very carefully made writing — with perhaps only one word to the line; the second should have smaller and quicker writing, neatly arranged on the pages, with four or five words to the line. (See MS. Books, Chap. VI.)

A broad nib is used in preference to a narrow one, so that the characteristics of true pen-work are brought out and the faults made clear. A fine, light handwriting is often very pretty, but it is certain to mislead the novice in penmanship (See p. 247).

Having acquired a formal hand the penman may modify and alter it, taking care that the changes are compatible, and that they do not impair its legibility or beauty. Such letters as are obsolete he replaces by legible forms akin to them in feeling, and, the style of the selected type becoming very naturally and almost unconsciously modified by personal use, he at length attains an appropriate and modern Formal-Handwriting. The process of "forming" a hand requires time and practice: it resembles the passage of "Copy-book" into "Running" hand, familiar to us all (See p. 246).

SCRIPTS I. & II.

Having cut the nib of a reed or large quill to the exact width required for the thick stroke, copy the component strokes of the letter **α** (Script I.), and immediately make the complete letter: go through the whole alphabet in this way several times (Fig. 58). Next join the letters together (See p. 73) to form words — writing always between ruled lines (Fig. 59 & p. 329).

FIG. 58.

Script II. is similarly practised: the letters are grouped (p. 46) to form words (Fig. 60).

coupling

FIG. 59.

GROUPING

FIG. 60.

Next make a neat page of large writing, and, if possible, write such a page every day. The more definite and methodical practice is, the better. "Practising" *anyhow* on scraps of paper, does more harm than good.

Arranging & Ruling A Single Sheet

The size of an inscription is commonly settled before the arrangement of the text is planned out, being determined by considerations of its future position and office, or by custom and use (See pp. 60-63 & 269).

> TO the rational animal the same act is according to nature and according to reason

FIG. 61.

The proportions of the writing, spacing, and margins will likewise properly settle themselves (See pp. 198, 63, 269), but where the size of the sheet only is fixed, we have, broadly speaking, to decide between "large" writing with "small" margins (Fig. 61), and "small" writing with "large" margins (Fig. 62).

> TO the rational animal the same act is according to nature and according to reason. M. Antoninus.

FIG. 62.

Generally, a compromise is arrived at and the proportions are more evenly balanced (Fig. 63).

> TO the rational animal the same act is according to nature and according to reason

FIG. 63.

Ruling (See also pp. 192, 60). — The mode of ruling marginal lines and writing lines is shown in Fig. 65. The ruling should be light, but firm and accurate. A fine pen, or hard pencil, or a blunt point may be used. Where the writing lines are double (as for round hands, p. 229), it is best to have a double ruling point (See Fig. 77). Two hard pencils firmly lashed together make a convenient tool for large work: the distance between the points is easily adjusted by means of a small wedge.

et dimitte nobis debita nostra

3½ inches

2⅔ inches

These 5. words take about 10 sq. inches: therefore the complete (50) words of text wd take abt. 100. sq." (say a space 8½"× 11½". v. fig.)

FIG. 64.

Problem I. (A Sheet Of Prose)

To write out the Pater noster (50 words) in a formal round-hand (arranged in "mass" of equal lines) on a sheet of "foolscap" (i.e. 17 inches high and 13½ inches wide).

If the size of the writing be considered of the first importance, a few words are written out in a script chosen to suit the subject, the space, &c., and these are measured to find the area which the whole text so written would occupy (Fig. 64). The size of the script is then modified, if necessary, to suit the available area.

Frequently it is desirable first to determine the sizes of the margins. These depend on various considerations of the position and office of the MS., but more particularly on the size of the sheet and the character of its future environment[14] (See p. 269).

The top and side margins may be of equal width — or the top may be a little less (See a, Fig. 70). Ample space should be allowed for the foot margin, which is generally about twice the width of the top, but may vary in different cases, according as the text falls short of or encroaches upon it (See pp. 270, 263). For a plain foolscap sheet: sides (each) 2½ inches, top (approx.) 2 inches, and foot (approx.) 4 inches, may be taken as suitable margins (Fig. 65).

The width of the sheet (13½ inches) less the two side margins (2½ inches each) gives the length of the writing lines (13½ - 5 = 8½ inches). One or two such lines are written experimentally in a suitable script (say, $5/16$ inch), and the average number of words per line (four) is found.

The number of words in the complete text (fifty) will determine the number of lines: an extra line or so may be allowed for safety ($50/4$ = 12 ½ say, thirteen). The spacing of these is calculated —

$5/16$ in. writing requires about $7/8$ in. (close) spacing (p. 42):
Thirteen lines at $7/8$ in. gives 11 $5/8$ in. = depth of text:
11 $5/8$ in. from 17 in. leaves 5 $5/8$ in.[15] for head and foot margins

---

[14] For example, a framed sheet does not require such wide margins as a similar sheet unframed.

[15] Really about 6 inches, because the top line of writing will not occupy its full $7/8$ inch, the unused part of which adds to the top margin (See Fig. 65).

— and if the space is not sufficient, the writing is made a little smaller. If, on the other hand, the marginal depth left over were excessive, the writing might be made a little larger in order to fill up the space.

A sheet 17 inches high & 13½ inches wide (f'cap.) Ruled with thirteen (double) lines – 5/16″ gauge – distance between WRITING-LINES = 7/8 inch : v. ↕ : Side margins, 2½″ (each): Foot margin, 4 inches : Top margin approx. 2 in. (2½″ to 1st WRITING-LINE).

FIG. 65.

Pater noster, qui es in
coelis: sanctificetur nomē
tuum. Adveniat regnum
tuum. Fiat voluntas tua,
sicut in coelo et in terra. ✝
Panem nostrum quotidi-
anum da nobis hodie ✝
Et dimitte nobis debita
nostra, sicut et nos dimittimus debitoribus nostris
Et ne nos inducas in ten-
tationem. Sed libera nos
a malo. A M E N

FIG. 66.

Problem II. (A Sheet Of Poetry)

To write out "He that is down, needs fear no fall" in a formal round-hand on a sheet of foolscap (i.e. 17 inches high x 13½ inches wide).

Here there are three verses of four lines each: these with two space lines, left between the verses, give a total of fourteen lines (Fig. 67).

A poem has a given number of lines of various lengths, and only very strong reason or necessity can justify our altering its proper form (e.g. by breaking up the lines) in order to make a mass of equal lines. Such theoretical margins as are possible in the treatment of prose can therefore seldom be observed in writing out a poem, and, unless the height or the width of the sheet can be altered, there is apt to be an excess of margin in one or the other direction. When such excess margin is obviously unavoidable, no objection can be made to its appearance. Poetry may conveniently be treated as "fine writing" (See p. 196).

If the size of the writing be considered of the first importance, several of the longer lines (e.g. the first and the eleventh in the poem given) are written on a piece of paper in the size of writing preferred (say, ¼ inch). By laying this paper on the given sheet, it is seen whether such lines would allow of sufficient side margins. (If they would not, the writing may be made smaller.)

The height of the writing (¼ inch) must allow of the full number of lines (fourteen) being properly spaced on the sheet (17 inches) with sufficient head and foot margins. This is calculated —

¼ in. writing requires approximately ¾ in. spacing (p. 42):
Fourteen lines at ¾ in. gives 10½ in. = depth of text:
10½ in. from 17 in. leaves 6½ in. for head and foot margins

— and if the space were not sufficient, the lines might be made a little closer, or the writing a little smaller (or, if necessary, the blank lines might be left out between the verses: p. 79).

THE SIZES OF THE MARGINS — It will be seen that the above method is primarily for settling a length of line which will allow of sufficient side margins. The process can be reversed; if necessary, the side margins are made of a given width, thus determining the exact length of the line, the size of writing which this line allows being found experimentally.

Note. — The extra-long lines may slightly encroach on the right-hand margin: the effect of this is balanced by the falling short of other lines.

> He that is down, needs fear no fall;
> He that is low, no pride:
> He that is humble, ever shall
> Have God to be his guide.
>
> I am content with what I have,
> Little be it or much: I crave,
> And, Lord, contentment still I
> Because thou savest such.
>
> Fulness to such a burden is,
> That go on pilgrimage:
> Here little, and hereafter bliss,
> Is best from age to age

FIG. 67.

Spacing & Planning Manuscript

In penmanship great nicety of spacing and arrangement is possible. The ascending and descending strokes may be shortened or drawn out, the spaces between letters and words may be slightly increased or decreased, the lines may be written near or far apart, and the letters may be written with a broader or narrower nib.

Elaborate spacing and planning, however, should not be attempted at first, and straightforward, undesigned work is often the best. The student is apt to waste time writing out an elaborate draft in order to ascertain how to space the matter. This is a mistake, because if written well, it is a waste of good writing on a mere draft; if written ill, it is bad practice. The briefer experiments and calculations are, the better, though the simplest problem always requires for its solution a calculation or process of guess and trial (such as suggested in the preceding pages). Practice will make people very good guessers, and the best work of all is done when the worker guesses rightly, and follows his guesses with the actual work, itself the trial and proof of accuracy.

CHAPTER VI
MANUSCRIPT BOOKS[16]

MS. Books: Tools & Materials

The making of manuscript book, based on a study of the early MSS., offers the best training to the scribe and illuminator in writing, lettering, rubricating, gilding, illuminating initials and borders, and miniature painting, and is the best means of mastering the foundations of Book Typography and Decoration.

Materials, &c. for MS. Books: Paper (See pp. 17, 63, 68, 241); Vellum and Parchment and Pounce (See pp. 68, 115, 122-4) — Cut a small sheet the size of a page of the book, and clip the long edge between two flat pieces of wood (holding it as it would be if bound). If the page will bend over and stay down by its own weight, it is thin enough (R) Fig. 68; if it stands up (W), it is too stiff.

FIG. 68.

CUTTING SHEETS — A frame or template (the size of the sheet desired) is used by parchment makers. It is useful for cutting out the sheets for a common size of parchment book. They are cut on the end-grain of wood, or on card or glass.

FOLDING — A Folder, as used by bookbinders (or a bone paper-knife), is useful, and also a Set or T-Square for testing right angles, &c. The fold and the top edge of each book-sheet are commonly squared by proper folding.

---

[16] MS. Books are further considered in Chap. XVI.

RULING, &c. (See p. 264). — For marking distances of lines, a carefully prepared paper[17] scale or pattern and an awl (p. 67), or a "star-wheel" — having regular intervals between the spikes — may be used. Or the ruling — of the writing lines — may be simplified by using a stout card frame (internally the size of the text-column) with strips glued across it: for a common size of book this might be made in stout tin or other metal. The lines are commonly ruled with a ruling stylus (See Figs. 72, 77), or a sort of "rake" may be made to rule six lines at once.

Writing, Colouring, Gilding, Binding (Chaps. II., X., IX., XVI.).

Methods & Proportions

Having to make a manuscript book for a specific purpose, the scribe formulates in his mind a general plan of the work, and decides approximately the respective sizes of page and of writing which seem most suitable.

He endeavours to fashion the book in accord with its use, and therefore allows the (most suitable) material, the subject-matter and the office of the book, and the way in which it will be read and handled, to determine as far as is possible the proportions of its parts, and its treatment as a whole.

Its material may be vellum, parchment, or paper, on which a variety of pens, brushes, and other tools, with inks, colours, and metal foils, may be employed. Its office may be "useful" or "ornamental"; its contents may be long or short, weighty or light, and of greater or less worth; it may be for public or for private use; and the book may be intended to be placed on a lectern, to be held in the hand, or to be carried in a coat pocket.

In following out such natural indications, the practised craftsman relies greatly on his working methods, preferring a direct mode of treatment to one which is too ingenious or subtle. In deciding a doubtful point, a common-sense of proportion is a sufficient guide, and one may generally assume that great works are best "writ large," and that large letters look best on an ample page, and vice versa.

---

[17] The direct use of a thick wood or metal scale may lead to inaccuracy.

The main proportions which have to be considered are interdependent, and follow one another in their natural order (See p. 190), thus —

1. The size and shape of the book.
2. The widths of the margins.
3. The size of the writing, &c.

And the methodical scribe makes his books of certain definite and regular sizes, each size having corresponding and regular proportions of margins and writing. Though these may greatly depend on individual taste and experience, it is suggested that — like all good designs — they should be allowed as far as possible to settle and arrange themselves.

The Size & Shape Of The Book

A book is thought of by the scribe chiefly as an open book, and the width and height of its pages are chosen with a view to its convenient shape and pleasant appearance when open. The most economical sizes into which a suitable sheet of paper can be folded (or a skin of parchment can be cut) may commonly be allowed to decide these proportions.

When a printer is about to print a book, he chooses a sheet of paper which will fold into a suitable shape and size. If the sheet be folded once to form two leaves, the book is called a folio (Fig. 69); folded again to form a "section "of four leaves — a quarto (4to); or folded a third time to form a section of eight leaves — an octavo (8vo).[18] The book is made up of a number of sections sewn on to strings or tapes (See p. 267).

The penman will find that, besides saving time and labour, it conduces to good work if he keep to certain regular sizes for "large," "medium," and "small "books: and, if the ordinary sheets of paper which he uses will fold in convenient folio, quarto, and octavo sizes, it is well that he make these his standards for paper books.

Paper being made in sheets of various dimensions, by folding a large or a small sheet, a "large" or "small" folio — 4to, 8vo — can be obtained.

---

[18] The two, four, eight (or more) pages are printed on both sides of the sheet before it is folded. Two or more sheets are generally folded and put together to form a folio "section."

FIG. 69.

It may be noted that the length and the width of sheets of paper[19] are very commonly about as 9 is to 7. And therefore, when the sheet is folded for folio or octavo, the proportions are roughly about 7:4½, which are very good proportions for a page of a book. It is obvious that a narrow ("upright")book is easier to handle and more pleasant in appearance (when open) than an album or "oblong" shape of book (b and c, Fig. 70).

---

[19] Such as Foolscap (17" x 13½"), Crown (20" x 15"), Demy (22½" x 17½"), Royal (25" x 20"), &c.

64

Single Sheet (a.)   *"Upright" shape of Book (b.)*
Inter proportions of WIDE MARGINS *&c.*

"Oblong" shape of Book (c.): double columns: see also fig. 202.

FIG. 70.

The Widths Of The Margins

 Margins are necessary in order to isolate and frame a text: thus, they contribute to its legibility and beauty. It is better that they be wide rather than narrow (See p. 65, & Note, p. 198); but excessively wide margins are often neither convenient nor pleasing (See p. 159).

 The "page" or column of text should be in such proportion to the page of the book, and be placed on it in such a way as to leave adequate margins on every side. A narrow column of text is generally best, for short lines are easiest to write and to read, and do not tire the hand, or the eye, in passing from one line to the next. For this reason, the text is often divided into two or more columns when the page is wide, or the writing is very small in comparison.

 The exact proportion of margin to text in a given page depends on circumstances, and is largely a matter of taste (ex. Fig. 71 & note 2, b, p. 190). But just as it is advantageous generally to keep to certain sizes of pages,

65

it is well to keep to certain — corresponding — sizes of margins for regular use.

Inner margin ⅜ inch.

Top margin approximately ⅞ inch (*measured to the top of the writing on the first line—see also fig. 65*).

length of Writing-line 2⅞"

CAPS.&c

Side margin 1¼ inch.

163

FIG. 71.—Diagram showing the ruling of a (*Recto*) page 4¾ inches × 7¼ inches as for a manuscript book (allowing five or six words to the *Writing-line*). There are fifteen Writing-lines, the *Line-space* being 1/6 inch.
The proportions of large CAPITALS, shown above, are set by the Line-space (*footnote*, p. 163).
The Foot margin is 1¼ inch.

66

The proportions of the margins to each other follow a sort of tradition (See Fig. 70), the foot margin (4) usually being twice as wide as that at the top (2), the side margins generally greater than the top and less than the foot. The two pages of an opening may be viewed as one sheet having two columns of text; and the two inner margins, which combine to form an interspace, are therefore made narrow (about 1½ each), so that together they are about equal to one side margin (Fig. 70). These proportions (1½ : 2 : 3 : 4) approximate to the proportions common in early MSS.

Sufficient and proportional margins add greatly to the usefulness and beauty of a book. That the writers and illuminators used them when books were read and valued in a way we can scarcely realise now, shows that such things are not, as some might suppose, a matter of affectation. Besides the natural fitness of the common proportions commends them: a deep foot margin is a foundation to the whole, and gives a spare piece for the reader to hold,[20] and wide side margins rest the eyes and keep the text from "running off the page" at the end of each line; and (the two) narrow inner margins combine to separate the pages sufficiently, but not too far, so that they form two "columns" together, framed by the outer margins of the open book.

When books are meant to be bound, from $1/16$ inch to $1/8$ inch extra margin should be allowed all-round the page for the cutting down and binding. The binding is apt to encroach on the inner margins, especially in vellum books, which do not open fully; in order, therefore, that the inner margins may keep their proper width, an extra width of $1/8$ to $1/4$ inch (according to the stiffness of the material) is allowed.

The Size Of The Writing, &C.

The shape, size, and margins of the page (already settled) together determine the length of the writing-line (See Fig. 71); and the size of the writing should be such as will allow a reasonable number of words to that line.[21]

Eight or nine words to the line is a common proportion in ordinary printed books, and may be taken by the scribe as his ordinary maximum. Lines having very many words are difficult to read.

---

[20] In Oriental books, which are sometimes held by their top margins, the top is deepest.

[21] If the average number of words be previously fixed — as in a poem (See p. 95) — that will practically determine the size of the writing.

On the other hand, lines of only two or three words each are generally tiresome, though they may be allowed in special cases of fine writing (See p. 195), where it is less necessary to economise space or time, and the effect of an even mass is not desired. But in any case, where there is an attempt to make the right-hand edge of the text approximately even, at least four or five words to the line are necessary; the scribe may therefore take four words per line as his ordinary minimum.

We may say generally, then, that an ordinary manuscript book should contain between four and eight words (or between 25 and 50 letter-spaces) to the line.

The exact size of the writing allowed in a given case may be found by a process of guess and trial, but this is seldom necessary for the practical scribe who uses regular sizes for regular occasions.

THE LINE SPACING — The size of the letter determines approximately the distance apart of the writing-lines (See pp. 42, 249). Much depends on whether the ascending and descending letters are long or short (See Fig. 154).

The number of writing-lines to the page equals the number of times that the line-space is contained in the text-column (i.e. the height of the page less the top and foot margins) — allowing for the top line not requiring a full space (See Fig. 71). Any fractional space left over may be added to the foot margin, or, if nearly equal to one line-space, a little may be taken from the margins to complete it.

The Large Capitals are commonly one, two, or more of the line-spaces in height (Fig. 71, & p. 84).

Ruling

Having folded and cut the large sheet of paper into small (book) sheets of the size determined on, take one of these as a pattern and rule it throughout as if it were to be used in the book. The ruling stylus has a blunt point, which indents the paper, but does not scratch it. A stout pin bent to a claw shape and held in a piece of wood does very well (Fig. 72).

FIG. 72.

Under the writing paper there should be a "pad" of ordinary paper (or blotting paper).

The marginal lines are ruled from head to foot of each leaf (a, Fig. 73). Besides being a guide for the writing, they give an appearance of straightness and strength to the written page.[22]

The writing lines are ruled across, between the marginal lines, their places having been indicated by equidistant dots (b, Fig. 73).

(a.) (b.)

FIG. 73.

A dozen or more of the small sheets of the book are piled together on a board with their top edges exactly coinciding, and the pattern sheet is accurately placed on the top of the pile. The pile of sheets may be fixed by a narrow piece of wood placed across and screwed down (Fig. 74). (See Addenda, p. 14.)

The writing line dots are pricked through all the sheets by means of a fine awl or needle set in a wooden handle (Fig. 75).

FIG. 74.

---

[22] They are often ruled double (See p. 343), and sometimes the top and foot lines are ruled from edge to edge of the sheet.

69

The writing lines are ruled as in Fig. 76 (sometimes across the narrow inner margins).

FIG. 75.

FIG. 76.

For double writing lines a double-ruling stylus may be made of two pins fixed in a wooden handle at the exact width of the writing gauge (Fig. 77).

FIG. 77.

MS. Books General Remarks

SECTIONS (p. 102). — A section, or "gathering" commonly consists of four book-sheets, folded in half into eight leaves (i.e. sixteen pages), but three or even two sheets are sufficient when they are extra thick, and five or six may be used when extra thin. Parchment sheets should have their smooth sides so placed together that each "opening" of the book has both its pages rough or both smooth and the pages are pounced after they are ruled (See p. 122).

Before the writing is begun the pages of the section are numbered on the inner marginal line, about ½ inch or so below the footline. This will prevent mistakes.

FLY-LEAVES — One or more leaves of the first and last sections in a book are left blank (besides the extra sheet or section (p. 266) which is used in the binding — attached to the cover). A book of any size or importance ought to have at least three fly-leaves at the beginning, and three or four at the end. These extra leaves protect the manuscript, and, in a sense, constitute margins for the whole body of the text. They may also be used to make thin books thicker, for the sake of the binding. At the end of Service books, or other books likely to be of permanent interest, additional fly-leaves should be provided for notes and annotations (See pp. 265, 266).

ROUGH OR SMOOTH EDGES — The rough "Deckle" edges of hand-made paper are inconvenient in a book of any thickness, and should be trimmed off after folding, though they may be left in the case of very thin books. The deckle edge should not occur at the top of the page, as it would there be a trap for dust, and because it is important that the tops of pages should all be level. The top edge or head of a book is often cut and gilt in order to keep out the dust — this is called "Library gilt." It is more suitable, however, that all the edges be gilt.

The Top Margins throughout the book are kept quite level. Any irregularity at the top of a page catches the eye at once, while slight differences at the side, or considerable differences at the foot, may occur without spoiling the appearance of the margins. All measurements for marginal and writing lines, &c., are therefore made from the in fold of the book-sheet and from the top edge, which is cut at right angles to the fold.

REGULAR WRITING — In writing one page it is a good plan to have its fellow page, or a similarly written one, fixed on the desk beside it as a pattern. This will save the beginner from a very common error — writing larger or smaller (which of course spoils the look of the pages).

INITIAL PAGE — The text of a book commonly begins on a recto, or right hand, page (See p. 280).

CHAPTER VII
VERSAL LETTERS & COLOURED CAPITALS

Development Of Versals

The earliest books consisted of a number of lines & of continuous writing in capital letters. There were seldom any divisions of the text — into para graphs, chapters, or the like — or even of one word from another; nor were important words distinguished by larger initials. The first division of paragraphs was made by a slight break in the text and a mark; later, the first letter of the first complete line of the new paragraph was placed in the margin and written larger. When "small-letters" were evolved, capitals ceased to be used for the body of the text, and became distinguishing letters for headings and important words.

The capitals written at the beginnings of books, chapters, and paragraphs grew larger and more ornamental, and at length were made in colour and decorated with pen flourishes. Such letters, used to mark the beginnings of verses, paragraphs, &c., were called "Versals."[23]

In modern printing and ordinary writing, the first line of a paragraph is generally indented (a, Fig. 78), but the earlier method of employing a special mark or letter (b or c) is more effective, and it might very well be used,

FIG. 78.

---

[23] Though Versals may generally be regarded as paragraph marking letters, it is convenient to apply the term to the Versal type of letter — e.g. "a heading in Versal letters" (See Fig. 91).

73

even in modern printed books, for fine editions. Affording a legitimate opening for illumination and book-ornament, it was (and is) the natural method for the penman, who, starting with these useful capitals, by flourishing them — in their own colour, or by dotting, outlining, or ornamenting them, with a contrasting colour (See Fig. 79, from an old MS.), evolved the Illuminated Initial.

Types of Versal Letters (examples: Plates IX., X., XI., XII., and Figs. 1, 78 to 94, 150, 161, 165, 166, 189). — The earlier Versals had very simple and beautiful pen shapes, and are the best models for the modern penman to follow. After the fourteenth century they were often fattened and vulgarised and overdone with ornament. In this way they not only lost their typical forms: but their "essential forms" — as letters derived from the Roman Alphabet — became much disguised and confounded (See Fig. 128).

FIG. 79
(13th century).

General Analysis Of Versals

1. THE LETTERS: (Pen-made), Built-up, Ornamental (coloured), "Gothic" Capitals (Round and Square forms).
2. HORIZONTALS—
    STRAIGHT: Medium — commonly the width of the nib.
    CURVED: Thin — the thin stroke of the pen.
3. PERPENDICULARS: Built-up, slightly curved in on either side.
4. SERIFS: Long, thin, slightly curved.
5. LONG STEMS: Various (See p. 76, & Figs. 84, 90).
6. SPACING—
    Letters & Words: Various (See Figs. 89, 92, 166).
    Lines: Usually one or more of the line-spaces apart (See pp. 81, 84).
7. ARRANGEMENT: Singly: set in text or margin, or part in both (Fig. 86).
    Grouped: after large initials (Fig. 92).
    In Lines: wide or close, often one word to the line (Fig. 89).
8. MEASUREMENTS: Stem -width; commonly two or three widths-of-nib across thinnest part (Fig. 165).
    O height: commonly one, two, or more of the line-spaces.
9. COMPONENT PARTS: A has approx. 10 strokes & filling.
    B has approx. 8 strokes & filling.
    C has approx. 7 strokes & filling.
    and so on (See Fig. 81).

Notes On Construction Of Versals (See Figs. 80, 81, 85, 165)

    Versal Letters are properly built-up (p. 220) with true pen-strokes (b, Fig. 81). Drawn or painted, they acquire a different character (p. 221). Their office being to mark important parts of the text, they are generally distinguished by colour and freedom of form — tending to curves and flourishes.

    The pen has an extra-long slit (½ inch to ¾ inch), and the writing-board may be lowered (See Fig. 46, b) to permit of the thick, liquid colour running out freely. The nib is of the ordinary shape (but not too oblique), and generally rather less in width than the nib used for the accompanying text (a, Fig. 81).

AABBCCD
DEEFGGH
hIJKLM
MMNOPP
QQQRR
SSTCTU
UWWXYYZ

"VERSAL" LETTERS 1904. † MSS.
freely copied from XI·XII·and XIII Cent!
J K W W Y y are made to match +
For facsimiles see plates IX, X, XI, & XII

FIG. 80.

The outlining strokes are quickly written and immediately filled in, each letter being loaded well with the colour, which thereafter dries evenly, with a slightly raised "flat" surface. The liquid colour should be fairly thick (See colour, p. 123).

76

FIG. 81.

"Gothic lettering" is a term used for "Black-letter" and related types, as distinguished from "Roman" types. "Gothic" capitals tend to roundness, the small-letters to angularity, but in each the abrupt change from thick to thin strokes, and the resulting contrast of stroke, are characteristics — the result of pen work.[24] In Versals this contrast is marked; the ends of the thinner

---

[24] In "Roman" letters the thicks and thins are not necessarily strongly marked, though their pen-forms have often a natural "Gothic" tendency.

strokes spread (See Addenda, p. 14, & cross-bar of A, Fig. 71), and the heavy parts are crossed by thin serifs. Versals may retain their pen character and yet approach the "Roman Letter" (p. 222), or be changed into the ornate "Lombardic" (Fig. 1). They are capable of great variety, and the "round" or "square" D, E, H, M, and W Capitals may be used at pleasure.

The Stems curve in slightly on either side. When they are very tall the mid part may be quite straight, imperceptibly curving out towards the ends (b, Fig. 82). This gives an effect of curvature throughout the length, while keeping the letter graceful and straight. The head of a stem (especially of an ascender) should be slightly wider than the foot (Fig. 83). This applies generally to every sort of built-up capitals.

The stem width may be nearly the same in Versals of different heights (a, Fig. 84): generally the letters tend to become more slender in proportion as the letters grow taller (b). Very large Versals (or initials) are often made with a hollow stem to avoid a heavy appearance (L, Fig. 84).

FIG. 82.

FIG. 83.

FIG. 84.

The Serifs are long and slightly curved in ornamental forms (Fig. 79): shorter, and nearly straight in stiffer forms (Fig. 166). In many cases the serifs appear to have been written first, the stems being added between them (f, Fig. 81) — in old MSS. the stems often show ragged ends crossing the serifs. Sometimes the serif appears to have been added to

78

the stem in two pieces, half on either side springing from the corners of the stem (g). The safest way seems to be the complete finishing stroke added to, and forming sharp angles with, the stem (h).

ARMS OR BRANCHES — Width of nib at start, and built-up at free end. (Pen horizontal, Figs. 81, 165).

The Bows or Curves of Versals (and of built-up letters generally) are begun with the inside stroke — a rather flat curve: and finished with the outer stroke — a pronounced curve (a, Fig. 85). This preserves the continuity of the interior curve, together with the clean contrast of the thick and thin strokes (See inside shapes, p. 187). The normal form may be flattened or curved a little (b), but exaggeration in either direction produces a degraded form. Part round letters, as D, P, and Q, may be begun with a complete inner oval, or a nearly completed O (to which the stem is added); this preserves their interior symmetry (c).

flat curve

Construction of "bows" (a.)

normal *flat* *curved* (b.)

(Complete) A way of making
← Another
method (c.)
D
P, q
&

FIG. 85.

The beauty and quality of Versal letters depends very much on their freedom; touching-up or trimming after they are made is apt to spoil them; and when good letters are made with a free hand, minute roughnesses, which are due to their quick construction, may be regarded as shewing a good rather than a bad form of careless workmanship (See (c) Fig. 164).

Spacing & Arrangement Of Versals

(Allowing for the special treatment of Versals called for by the extreme freedom and elasticity of their pen forms, the following remarks apply generally to the spacing and arrangement of coloured capitals in written pages)

Versals set in the text
ESPECIALLY when versals are large : say three Line-spaces or more in height
a.

Versal set partly in text. Paragraphs beginning with tailed letters, such as A O F h J K L P &c. are conveniently treated in this manner
b.

Versals in margin. Often used when the versals are small: Suitable for comparatively small or numerous capitals
c.

FIG. 86.

Versals accompanying Small Text are generally dropped below the writing-line, so that their tops are level with the tops of the small letters (Fig. 86).

SIZES OF VERSALS — Letters which are of the same importance — i.e. serve the same purpose — are usually of like size and form throughout; and the more important a letter, the more it tends to be elaborated and decorated (See Figs. 90, 92).

SPECIAL WORDS IN TEXT MARKED BY VERSALS — Where coloured capitals are used throughout the text (Fig. 92), the colours are usually varied (pp. 89, 130).

LINE BEGINNINGS MARKED BY VERSALS — Where every line on a page begins with a coloured capital, the majority of the forms are kept rather plain (See (5) p. 89). They may be effectively treated as a band of simple or variegated colour (p. 89). This is a common treatment for a list of names or a poem; sometimes, especially if there are many lines, simple-written capitals (p. 225) may be used instead of Versals.

Verses or Paragraphs may be marked by Versals set in the text (a) or part in margin, part in text (b) or wholly in the margin (c, Fig. 86). The marginal capital is the simplest, and it has the advantage of leaving the page of text entire; it may, however, sometimes be desirable to break the continuity by an inset capital, especially in cases of closely written text, or of stanzas not spaced apart (See p. 91).

The first word of a paragraph, which is begun with a Versal, is often completed in simple-written capitals of the same colour as the text (a, Fig. 86).

VARIOUS WAYS OF MARKING PARAGRAPHS — (a) The ⁋ ¶ paragraph marks, preferably coloured, may be used instead of (or even with) Versals (comp. Fig. 95); (b) by one word or line (or several words or lines) of simple-written (or built-up) capitals in black or colour (See Fig. 93); (c) by some suitable ornament (See Fig. 87); (d) in many cases it is well to have spaces between the paragraphs or verses (See p. 91).

Line-Finishings at the ends of Verses, &c. (pp. 145, 351), may be made with the Versal pens and colours.

the end of one paragraph.
THE NEXT PARAGRAPH
*may be marked by a line
of written capitals in black
or colour (on or below line)(a.)*

*Or: a band of suitable
(usually pen-made) ornament may be interposed(b.)*

FIG. 87.

To mark Chapters (or even Books), extra-large Versals (Fig. 88) may be used, in lieu of more elaborate initials. Smaller Versals may be grouped round about, beside or inside initials (p. 148 & Fig. 92).

BEGINNINGS of books are marked by an initial letter. A large versal — three or more line-spaces high — is quite effective & simple.

FIG. 88.

HEADINGS AND PAGES IN CAPITALS (See also pp. 84, 87) — Each line of capitals is generally kept uniform throughout its length,[25] though different lines vary in size and colour (See Fig. 89). If it be possible it is well

---

[25] The mediaeval scribes often made the first line of a chapter or book in uniform capitals (excepting the initial letter). The succeeding line generally was smaller, and of a different colour and type — even when a divided word was carried over into it. and to let the heading or page contain the complete initial phrase or sentence (See Fig. 91).

82

to keep the individual word entire and to let the heading or page contain the complete initial phrase or sentence (See Fig. 91).

Generally, the greater the number of capitals the plainer their forms are kept, and the closer their spacing. It is best to keep to the regular method of spacing the lines of Versals one of the writing-line spaces [or more) apart — though in special cases the Versals may be independent of the writing-lines.

SPACING OUT — Coloured letters and ornaments are usually put in after the plain MS. has been written. A very little practice enables the scribe accurately to guess the amount of space which he should leave for the Versals, &c., whether it is designed to have several lines of them, or a single letter only on the page. A few pencil marks may be used to settle a doubtful point, but an elaborate sketching or setting out in pencil spoils the freedom of the work.

CHAPTER VIII
BLACK & RED

Rubricating

"Red, either in the form of a pigment or fluid ink, is of very ancient and common use. It is seen on the early Egyptian papyri; and it appears in the earliest extant vellum MSS., either in titles or the first lines of columns or chapters. The Greek term was μελάνιον κόκκινον; Latin minium[26], rubrica."— (Thompson's "G. & L. Palaeography," p. 17.)

Rubricating, or the adding of Red, or other coloured, letters, line-finishings, or signs, to a MS. or Book, in which the main body of the text is already completed in black, constitutes in itself a very useful and effective form of decoration. It is, moreover, a connecting link between plain writing and illumination proper; and we may safely assume that the artists who made the beautiful illuminations of the Middle Ages were trained as scribes and rubricators.

Initial Pages Or Title Pages

Fig. 89 represents an Initial Rage in Red Capitals. (The same arrangement may of course be used with a variety of colours and with gold: See Note (4) below). Such a page is, as it were, an "illumination" to all the pages, following it in black text.

Title Pages came into fashion after printing was introduced. Early MSS. commonly began with the opening words written in large, decorated capitals, the title sometimes being written quite small, near the top of the page: other details were commonly put in the colophon in early books (See p. 95).

When the title is more important, in a literary sense, than the opening sentence, it may be well to follow the modern fashion. But when there is a finely worded opening sentence — perhaps the key-note to the rest of the text — while the title is merely for reference, it seems reasonable to

---

[26] Minium = red-lead, used in early times for "rubrics" and drawings, hence is derived the word "Miniature."

magnify and illuminate the actual beginning of the book rather than the mere name of it (See p. 280).

IN
Evangelium Secundum Joannem

**PRIN-
CIPIO
ERAT
VERBUM**

FIG. 89.
I

Note (1). — In Fig. 89 the title — (JESU CHRISTI) Evangelium Secundum Joannem — is written in as a decoration of the initial word; the old form "IHV XPĪ" is used for "Jesu Christi" (these letters, it will be noticed, are here employed to lighten the large capitals, See p. 148).

(2) Where IN is an initial word, to enforce narrow initial I, both letters may be magnified.

(3) The scale of the lettering corresponds with that of the ruled lines (these do not show in the figure): the letters and the interlinear spaces are each one line high; the initial word is four lines high. Such a mode of spacing is very simple and effective, and will save the rubricator much unnecessary trouble and fruitless planning (See footnote, p. 159).

(4) *Other Colour Schemes.* — All Burnished Gold (or with Title in red); or IN gold, with smaller capitals Red (or in Blue and Red lines alternately — or Blue, Red, Green, Red: See p. 128).

Prefaces & Notes In Colour

Fig. 90 represents a preface, or note, written in red.

It was a frequent practice in old MSS., where there were prefaces, or prologues, or notes — not actually part of the text — to keep these distinct by writing them in red. A somewhat similar usage still exists in modern typography, where such parts are sometimes distinguished by Italic type (See p. 241).

The distinction of a preface, "rubric," or note from the main body of the text makes a book more readable, and, as a page of red (or blue) writing is very pleasant and effective, we may certainly take advantage of such a reasonable excuse for introducing it. Entire books have been written in red, but this is a questionable mode, as too much red text would tire the eye.

Note (1). — The writing is founded on the tenth-century English hand given in Plate VIII.

(2) The flourishes on **s** and **e** fill gaps at the ends of the lines, and the spread out AMEN fills the last line.

(3) The Headline is in simple written capitals.

(4) The effect of colour contrast of the built-up **P**s with the simple writing: the solid **P**s (though really the same colour) appear to be a much deeper red than the writing, which is lightened by the intermingled white of the paper.

(5) *Other Colour Schemes.*— The Versal (PP) in burnished gold; the rest in red or blue.

FIG. 90.

Pages With Coloured Headings

Fig. 91 represents the first page of a chapter (or a book) with a Heading in red capitals.

It is convenient in practice clearly to distinguish between the two modes of beginning —

(a) with an illuminated Initial-Page (See Fig. 89), or,

(b) with an illuminated Heading (See Fig. 91).

WHO HATH BELIEVED OUR REPORT

and to whom hath the arm of the Lord been revealed? For he grew up before him as a tender plant, & as a root out of a dry ground: he hath no form nor comeliness; & when we see him, there is no beauty that we should desire him. He was despised, & rejected of men; a man of sor=rows, & acquainted with grief: & as one from whom men hide their face he was despised, & we esteemed him not.

FIG. 91.

The former may be treated as though it were a decoration to the whole book. The latter is intended more particularly to decorate its own page.

The Heading should therefore be proportionate to the body of the text below it. About one-third Heading and two-thirds text make a good proportion. A "Heading "occupying half, or more than half, of the page is apt to look disproportionate, and it would be preferable to this to have a complete, or nearly complete,[27] Page of coloured capitals.

Note (1). — The full effect of black and red is obtained by an arrangement of the two colours in marked contrast.

(2) The lines are used as a scale for the Heading, the red capitals and interspaces each being one line high. If a Heading so spaced appear too close to the first line of black writing, another line space may be left.

(3) The round Es are used to fill out the second line, and the square, narrow E to relieve the crowded third line.

(4) Other Colour Schemes. — The entire heading, or the letters W, H, B, O, R, in burnished gold; or the whole variegated (See p. 127).

Page Or Column Heading & Initial

Fig. 92 represents the first page of a book or chapter in two columns, beginning with a rather ornate Heading, in which the Initial is made the principal feature, and having coloured Versals and line-finishings throughout the text.

It is more difficult to get a good effect in this way than by means of a marked colour contrast (See p. 97), or variegated colour, and gold (See Note 7).

Note (1). — The lines bounding the text would naturally be indented, or pale (not black as in the block), and ruled from head to foot of the page (See Note (2) on the next figure).

(2) The red ornamental line-finishings (See p. 145) would be more effective if variegated.

---

[27] An illuminated Page will allow of a few lines of black text at the foot (an arrangement very common in the elaborate Initial Pages of the fifteenth century), but these should be quite subordinate to the "Illumination."

FIG. 92.

(3) The Versals in the text are made about a line high, but are dropped below the line (p. 79).

(4) The Versals in the Heading are made one line high, with one-line spacing — between O and D increased to two lines (partly filled by a flourish from the D), in order to fit the U, O, and D in evenly beside the Initial.

(5) The Initial Q should project slightly up and out — beyond the bounding lines — to mark the top, left corner more strongly (See footnote, p. 150).

(6) All the rubricating on this page is done with the same pen (See pp. 145, 156).

(7) Other Colour Schemes. "QUOD FUIT AB INITIO," the filigree ornament and the VV in burnished gold (or the Q and VV in gold), the rest of the Versals and line-finishings in Red and Blue, or Red and Green, or Red, Blue, and Green (See pp. 128, 130).

Versals In Column Or Marginal Bands

Fig. 93 represents two columns of black text, consisting of short verses, &c, which are marked by coloured capitals — forming bands of colour — in the margins.

Note (1). — The coloured capitals in the figure are made rather larger than usual, to enforce the effect of the two lines of red and mark their contrast with the columns of black text. In practice, however, they would be better and more distinct if rather smaller.

(2) The lines bounding the text would naturally be faint, or grooved (p. 264); but, ruled from head to foot of the page, they would be sufficiently apparent to add materially to the general effect of orderly arrangement. (Lines are printed here to show clearly the way the two columns are ruled and to suggest this effect, though the process block necessarily gives a false impression in making them appear too short and too heavy).

(3) Extra width between the columns (and also in the margin) may be allowed for the coloured capitals (compare Fig. 92).

(4) Words in simple written capitals are used to mark slight divisions, or changes of sense, in the text.

(5) A stiff Versal of a rather "Roman" type is used, partly because of the number of the capitals (See p. 81).

(6) *Other Colour Schemes.* — The larger capitals might be in burnished gold, the rest in red (or in red, blue, and green); or all might be in red, blue, and green.

Surely there is a mine for SILVER
And a place for gold which they refine.
Iron is taken out of the earth,
And brass is molten out of the stone
Man setteth an end to darkness,
And searcheth out to the furthest bound
The stones of thick darkness and of the shadow of death.
HE BREAKETH open a shaft away from where men sojourn;
They are forgotten of the foot that passeth by;
They hang afar from men, they swing to and fro.

As for the EARTH, out of it cometh bread:
And underneath it is turned up as it were by fire.
The stones thereof are the place of sapphires,
And it hath dust of gold.
THAT PATH NO BIRD OF PREY KNOWETH,
Neither hath the falcon's eye seen it:
The proud beasts have not trodden it
Nor hath the fierce lion passed thereby.
hE PUTTETH FORTH his hand upon the flinty rock;
HE OVERTURNETH the mountains by the roots.
hE CUTTETH out

FIG. 93.

Stanzas Or Verses Marked By Versals

Fig. 94 represents a poem in two verses which are distinguished by interspaces and by coloured capitals — a brief introductory line also being in colour. (It is supposed that the poem occurs in a book — mainly in prose — written in Roman small-letters.)

It is generally best to distinguish the verses of poems by one-line interspaces. When this is done, coloured initials are not so necessary, and their value become chiefly decorative (See p. 79).

Note (1). — The writing is founded on "Italic"(See Plate XXI.), and (it is supposed that) it would be used here wherever the songs occurred; firstly, to distinguish them from the rest of the text, and secondly, to keep the lines of the poem entire — Italics occupying less room than ordinary, round Small-Letters (See p. 241).

(2) The story opens with the first line, which may in this case be regarded either as a Title or as a prefatory note in red.

(3) The two red capitals are made of a rather "Roman" type to match the Italic (and the small Roman text of the book). The difference in height made between the W and the S is intended to balance the difference in width, and to give them an appearance of equal weight. This may be permitted where there are only a few capitals: where there are many, their heights are generally kept more uniform.

(4) Another Colour Scheme. — W and S would look better in burnished gold.

'Tis of Aucassin and Nicolete.

WHO would list to the good lay?
Gladness of the captive grey?
Tis how two young lovers met,
Aucassin and Nicolete,
Of the pains the Lover bore
And the sorrows he outwore,
For the goodness and the grace,
Of his Love, so fair of face.

SWEET the song, the story sweet,
There is no man hearkens it,
No man living 'neath the sun,
So outwearied, so foredone,
Sick and woful, worn and sad,
But is healed, but is glad
Tis so sweet.

So say they, speak they, tell they the Tale:

FIG. 94.

Music With Red Staves

Fig. 95 is a reproduction, in facsimile, showing quarter of a page of a folio Service Book (probably French, early sixteenth century). The page consists of two columns of ten staves each, and is headed ℭ *In vigi (lia), natiuitatis dnī*. The book is printed on vellum in red and black; the columns of music have faint red bounding lines ruled by hand (not shown in the figure).

The red stave is very effective, and it was commonly used in early MSS. and printed books. There appears to be some doubt, however, as to its practical value, and I have been advised that it is not so legible as the black line stave, and also that, in Church Service Books (See p. 265), in order to make an absolutely clear distinction, red should be reserved entirely for the rubrics.

The "plain-song" chant, with its four-line stave, has a simpler and finer appearance than the more modern and elaborate five-lined stave and tailed notes. The latter, however, may yet be treated very effectively.

Note (1) — The mark ℭ and the capitals 𝔖, 𝔅, and 𝔇, were blotted — it can scarcely be called "painted" — with yellow. Yellow or red were often used in this way to mark the small black capitals in printed books (p. 359, & comp. p. 228). It is a questionable method. (These blots have been removed from the figure — except, by an oversight, in the case of 𝔖).

(2) Other Colour Schemes. — (a) The title, or (b) the text and the notes, might be in burnished gold (the other parts in either case remaining in red and black).

☾In vigi.natiu

autem genuit salmon. Sal-

mon autem genuit booz

de ra ab. Booz autem ge-

nuit obeth ex ruth.

Obeth autem genuit

FIG. 95.

Tail-Pieces, Colophons, &c.

Fig. 96 represents a coloured Tail-piece or decorative finish at the end of a book (or chapter).

The Colophon (See p. 84 & Figs. 13, 191), generally-distinguished from the text by a smaller or different hand, and — especially in early printed books — by colour or other decorative treatment, occurs at the end of a book, where it is the traditional right of the penman and the printer to add a statement or a symbolical device. The Name (of craftsman and assistants), Time, and Place are commonly stated — preferably quite simply — e.g. "This book, written out by me, A.B., in LONDON, was finished on the 31st day of DECEMBER 1900." Any reasonable matter of interest concerning the text, the materials, methods, lettering, or ornament, and an account of the number of leaves and their size, &c., may be added. But the craftsman, properly and modestly keeping his name off the title-page, is at liberty to exercise his right, marking the end of, and signing his work in any way he chooses — even in a speech or a sentiment — provided the form of the colophon be unobtrusive and its language natural. Printer's devices or book-marks, consisting of symbols, monograms, &c. (p. 278), were likewise used.

The opportunity generally provided by the final
margin, and the natural wish to close the book
with a fitting ornament, also led to the use of colour
or capitals in the concluding lines; and sometimes
the "tail" of the text was given a triangular form,
the lines becoming shorter and shorter
till they ended in a single
word, or even one
letter.

But I have not finished the five acts, but only three of them"—— Thou sayest well, but in life the three acts are the whole drama; for what shall be a complete drama is determined by him who was once the cause of its composition, and now of its dissolution: but thou art the cause of neither

Depart then satisfied, for he also who releases thee is satisfied.

FIG. 96.

Rubricating: General Remarks

CONTRAST OF RED AND BLACK — The most effective arrangement of red lettering with black text involves a sharp contrast, and, as a rule, the concentration of the red in a line or mass (See Figs. 91, 93, and 96, where the red lettering is massed at the head, side, and foot of the black). Too many red capitals scattered through a page lose their effect, and appear as though they were brown-red rather than bright red (See pp. 89, 130). Printed title-pages, &c., may be seen with promiscuous lines of black and red, in which the fine effects obtainable by the use of bright colour is dispersed and lost; while the same, or even a less, amount of red, massed in one or two places in the page, would show to great advantage.

NOTES IN RED IN MARGINS — Red lettering, and particularly small red writing, may be used freely in the margins: being much lighter than black, it appears there as a marginal decoration, not interfering with the regular look of the page. Indeed, red may be used more freely, and I think its decorative effect is greater, in the form of rubrics, than in any other simple form of ornament (See Red in Church Service Books (pp. 93, 265) and Red substituted for Italics (p. 241).

PARAGRAPH AND OTHER MARKS — Various symbols, numerals, and marks, such as ☞ ¶ ℭ ✸ † ‡ § ✠ U ℣ ℟, Addenda, p. 14, may be made in red.

RED LINES — Lines made to divide, or outline, pages ("rules "or "rule borders ") should be sparingly used, and then rather in black than in red (See p. 279). If in red, particularly between lines of writing, these should be "ruled feint" with diluted colour.

RED FOR ORNAMENTS — Red may be used pretty freely with other colours (blue, green, and gold), but by itself more sparingly.

OTHER COLOURS — The foregoing remarks refer mainly to contrasts of black and red, but apply, to a certain extent, to black with any bright colour (or gold) (See "Other Colour Schemes "given above, and p. 180).

CHAPTER IX
LAYING & BURNISHING GOLD

Tools & Materials

These should be kept together in a convenient box, as it is important that the process should not be interrupted by a search for a missing tool.

TOOLS AND MATERIALS	SUMMARY OF PROCESS
HARD LEAD PENCIL	For drawing forms if necessary
POUNCE	For preparing surface: "pouncing"
"SIZE" OR RAISING PRE-PARATION	For raising and backing leaf
SMALL SAUCER	For mixing size in
NEEDLE SET IN HANDLE	For bursting bubbles, &c.
QUILL PEN	For "laying" the size
KNIFE	For trimming size, &c.
GOLD-LEAF	For gilding
SCISSORS	For cutting gold-leaf
BURNISHING-SLAB	For backing the parchment or paper while under pressure
BREATHING-TUBE	For damping size
RUBBING-PAPER	For pressing leaf on to size
CHALK OR SOFT LEAD PENCIL	For marking form on rubbing-paper
BURNISHER, TOOTH SHAPE	For (1) pressing down, and (2) burnishing gold-leaf.
FEATHER (Brush, &c.)	For dusting off the pounce
BRUSH	For brushing off waste leaf
(HARD INDIARUBBER)	(For removing gold from parchment.)
(POWDER GOLD & FINE BRUSH)	(For "mending" in certain cases)

Laying The Ground

DRAWING THE FORM — Elaborate letters or ornaments may be drawn with a hard pencil, which will leave slight indentations in the surface of the page when the marks of the lead have been removed with indiarubber. In the case of free lettering or old writing, however, the forms should be made directly with the pen (See pp. 101, 113).

PREPARING THE SURFACE: POUNCING — The surface is thoroughly cleaned and prepared with powdered pumice stone, or other suitable "pounce" (See pp. 167, 174). This being rubbed well into the actual part which is to take the size absorbs grease and slightly roughens[28] the surface. The surrounding parts are also pounced to prevent the gold-leaf from sticking to them later.

COMPOSITION OF THE GROUND OR SIZE — The chief substance in a "size" or raising preparation is generally some kind of earthy matter, to give it body. Other substances, having toughness and stickiness, are used to bind the earthy matter and prevent its breaking when the page is turned over or bent, and also to make the size adhere to the page and the gold-leaf stick to the size. Yellow or red colouring matter is often added. A preservative, such as oil of cloves — in a minute quantity — may be present: this will permit of the size being kept in a semi-liquid condition, in a closed jar.

The following recipe was given to me by Mr. G. Loumyer: —

"Chalk (Whiting).
Oxide of Iron — ½ grain.
Glue (Carpenters) — 4 grains.
Gum Arabic — 2 grains.
Water — 50 grains.

Melt the gum and the glue together in the water, then add the oxide of iron, and lastly put in enough chalk to make the whole a rather liquid paste. Apply to the parchment, which you have previously well rubbed with whitings and, when dry, apply the gold-leaf with alcohol."

MIXING THE SIZE WITH WATER — A little of the size, taken from the jar (See above), is put in the saucer with a few drops of water to soak for an hour or two. It is then rubbed down with a finger-tip, care being taken to mix it very thoroughly and to avoid making bubbles. The right consistency is judged by experience — it should be thick rather than thin.

It is essential that all the ingredients be present in their right proportions, and the mixture should be stirred every now and then.

---

[28] The surface of horny or greasy parchment may be slightly roughened with a pen-knife till little hairs are raised which will hold the size, care being taken that this roughening does not extend beyond the actual parts which are to be covered with size. (Oxgall: See footnote, p. 175.)

Otherwise the earthy matter settles down, and the sticky parts, remaining in solution above, are liable to be used up. What is left in the saucer after use is apt to be deficient in its sticky parts, and it is best thrown away. Take out of the jar only what is required at the time, and mix a fresh lot the next time.

Bubbles, formed in the mixture, may be burst by a needle, or by adding a minute drop of oil of cloves.

METHODS OF LAYING THE SIZE — The parchment or paper is laid flat on a table; if on a slope, the size would run down and lie unevenly. A quill pen with a finely cut nib and an extra-long slit (about $5/8$ inch) is used for laying the size. It is filled pretty full by means of a quill or a brush; if by the latter, special care must be taken to avoid bubbles.

Experiments should be made in various methods.

I. Perhaps the best way of laying the size, so that it may set properly and that the burnish may retain its brilliance, is to put on a thin coat with a pen — in the direct manner in which coloured Versals are made (q.v.) — and afterwards add two or three thin coats, allowing each coat to dry thoroughly. This requires considerable patience and skill, as it takes a long time, and there is a danger, in adding several coats, of spoiling the form by going over the edges.

II. The simplest method for ordinary gold letters is to make them with one extra thick coat[29] of size, exactly like coloured Versals — first a natural pen outline, and then the filling in (See Fig. 81). This requires some practice to do well, as the thicker size is more difficult to manage than the colour.[30] Very narrow parts — such as the thin strokes — are apt to be deficient in size, and therefore, while they are still wet, the pen — held nearly vertical with the nib in contact with the surface of the size — is moved slowly along it until the stroke has received sufficient size and is properly filled out.

III. A method that may be found more convenient for heavy forms, is to hold the pen across the form to be gilded (which has previously been marked on the parchment) with its nib resting on the further outline (a, Fig.

---

[29] As this is usually allowed to dry for twenty-four hours, make sure, before laying the size, that you will be able to lay the gold-leaf on it at or near the same time on the next day.

[30] Should a drop fall on the page it can be removed quickly with the knife, but it is safer to allow it to dry and then to pick it off carefully. Size which has flowed beyond the bounds of the form may be trimmed away when it has set

97). The nib being moved along that line, by contact with the parchment restrains the size from passing beyond it, while allowing it to flow out freely behind and below (a, 2). The opposite side is similarly treated, and, if the form be narrow, the size as it flows out blends with that already laid (b). The

FIG. 97.

ends of the form are finished in like manner (c).

The angle of the pen with the parchment is less for a wider form (b, Fig. 98).

angle of pen (a.) for narrow form   angle of pen for wide form (b.)

FIG. 98.

As a general rule the size should stand pretty high when wet; it shrinks in drying, and, if it forms too thin a coat, it will neither hold the gold-leaf fast nor burnish well. While the size is still wet it is easy to raise it to any height desired by running more size into the form in the manner described above. It is well, however, not to raise the size too high, as burnished gold too much raised looks out of place on a page and has a heavy and vulgar appearance (p. 129). Very high raising also does not dry so well, and when dry it is more liable to chip.

The work of laying the size should be carried out as quickly as possible. If one part of the form is left any appreciable time before the remaining parts are sized, the first part will begin to settle and dry, and the different layings will not blend or lie evenly. Though the size is thick and awkward to use at first, a little skill will coax it quickly and evenly out of the pen, and it will all blend and dry with an even surface.

When it is sized, put the work away to dry in a drawer or safe place where it cannot be smudged or get dusty.

DRYING THE SIZE — The average time allowed is twenty-four hours, but it varies with the weather and the temperature; damp weather may make a longer time necessary, and dry weather or heat will shorten the time. The thickness of the raising affects the time very much; a very thin coat will dry in an hour or two, while an extra thick coat may take several days. Size not dry enough is too sticky to burnish; if too dry, it is so absorbent that it sucks up all the moisture which is breathed on it. To ensure the gold-leaf's sticking thoroughly, it is safer on the whole to gild the size while it is still slightly damp, and delay the burnishing till it is drier.

The time to allow and the right condition of the size for gilding can only be accurately judged by experience.

Laying The Gold-Leaf

Note. — In illuminated MSS., in order to avoid risk of injury to the gold it may be laid last of all (See pp. 117-18). The inexperienced illuminator, however, may find it better to follow the easier method of finishing the gold before applying the colours.

The process of gold-laying must be carried out steadily and quickly; all the necessary tools, &c., should be ready to hand (See p. 98).

THE GOLD-LEAF — This is sold in books of twenty-five leaves. The ordinary leaf, about 3¼ inches square, consisting of gold and alloy, is said to be beaten out to less than $\frac{1}{200{,}000}$ inch in thickness. As gold sticks readily to gold, especially when very thin and liable to wrinkle and fold over, or to paper, red & bole or ochre is scattered between the leaves of the ordinary book. This powder will come off on the work and give it an ugly colour, when burnishing, unless it is dusted off very carefully.

It is better to get gold "double" (or "quadruple") the ordinary thickness, specially prepared for fine work such as illuminating, quite pure, and put up in white books (without bole).

CUTTING THE LEAF — With the scissors, which must be quite clean and sharp (or else the gold will stick to them and tear), cut a whole or half leaf of gold, together with the paper leaf on which it lies, out of the book.

FIG. 99.

The gold is cut on one paper (Fig. 99) (not between papers, for then it would stick and tear), and the cut edges of the paper and the gold stick together slightly. If the edge of the gold is anywhere loose and apt to flap about, it and the corresponding paper edge can be nicked together with the scissors (Fig. 100). The gold-leaf being lightly held to the paper in this way is easily handled.

A piece of gold, about $1/8$ inch larger all round than the form to be gilded, is cut from the leaf in the manner described above (a, b, Fig. 100). Except in the case of a very large form, it is not worth trying to save gold by cutting it out in the same shape. Square, oblong, and triangular shaped pieces are suitable for ordinary use; these are laid in a convenient place — the edge of a book cover will do very well (Fig. 101) — ready to be picked up at the right moment.

FIG. 100.

The burnishing slab (a flat piece of vulcanite, celluloid, or metal) is placed under the page to give it a hard, firm back, which will make the pushing and rubbing of the burnisher effective.

FIG. 101.

108

PREPARING THE SIZE — If the size has dried rough, it may be lightly scraped with the pen-knife — a form should not require trimming, though if its edges have accidental roughnesses, these may be trimmed a little with the pen-knife.

DAMPING THE SIZE — The breathing tube is about ½ inch (or less) in diameter, and 6 inches or more in length; it may be made of paper or cane. One end of the tube being lightly held between the lips, the other is moved about over the size, which is gently breathed upon (Fig. 102). The breath condensing on the surface of the size, moistens it and renders it sticky. The amount of moistening required depends on the condition of the size.

Care has to be taken that the breath does not condense in the tube and drop on to the work.

leaf placed on the size immediately after breathing

FIG. 102.

LAYING THE GOLD-LEAF — Immediately that the size has been sufficiently breathed upon, the piece of paper with gold-leaf adhering (held ready in the right hand) is placed upon it, gold-leaf downwards, care being taken to place it steadily down, and not drag it across the size (Fig. 103).

FIG. 103.

THE RUBBING PAPER — a convenient piece of thin but tough paper (held ready in the left hand) — is immediately laid above the gold-leaf paper, and is then rubbed over firmly with the finger-tip, in order at once to attach the leaf to the size (Fig. 104). It is then quickly rubbed with the soft pencil or chalk till the raised form underneath is indicated on the surface of the paper (Fig. 105).

The burnisher is shewn here - held in the right hand - ready for the next operation — See Figs. 106. & 107.

FIG. 104.

These two operations may be combined by having a little blue chalk either on the fingertip or on the upper surface of the rubbing paper.

Round the outline of this form the point of the burnisher[31] is worked, pressing the gold-leaf firmly — through both the papers — against the size, in the angle formed by the size and the surface of the parchment (Fig. 106).

FIG. 105.

---

[31] A finer metal or ivory point may also be used.

(a.) Pressing the gold leaf into the angle formed by the size & parchment.

(b.) Enlarged diagram of above
- burnisher.
- rubbing-paper.
- g.l. book paper.
- gold leaf.
- parchment &c. (bearing size.)
- burnishing slab.

FIG. 106.

The fore part of the burnisher is then passed rapidly all over the rubbing paper with a firm pressure (Fig. 107).

The rubbing paper and the other paper are picked off, and an experienced eye can usually tell if the gold is sticking properly by a peculiar, smooth appearance which it then has.

Note: The rubbing-paper is held steadily by the left hand and not allowed to shift during the time that the gold-leaf is being pressed on to the size. See figs. 106. & 104.

FIG. 107.

Several Letters or Forms which are close together may be gilded simultaneously — with one piece of gold-leaf — as if they were one complex form. This saves time, but if too many forms are gilded together, some of them are liable to be less thoroughly and effectually treated.

SMALL SCATTERED FORMS (DOTS, &c.) — For these the gold-leaf may be cut into a sufficient number of little pieces, which are allowed to fall (gold side downwards) on a sheet placed to receive them.

They are picked up separately by means of a needle stuck into their backing-paper.

ADDITIONAL COATS OF GOLD-LEAF — A second leaf of gold may be laid on immediately on the top of the first; this will ensure richness and facilitate burnishing. Additional leaves may be laid after burnishing, but, unless the first gilding is absolutely clean, there is a risk of the second leaf peeling off when re-burnished.

Burnishing The Gold

THE BURNISHER — A tooth-shaped agate burnisher (Fig. 108) is commonly used.

The point is used for pushing the leaf into angles and for burnishing angles (a).

The fore-part for general burnishing (b).

The bend for cross-burnishing and for angles (c).

The side for very gentle and light burnishing (d).

The burnisher is kept scrupulously clean, and to ensure this it is frequently rubbed on a cloth.

DUSTING OFF THE POUNCE — The edge of the parchment may be tapped smartly on the desk to

FIG. 108.

shake off the pounce, and a feather or a soft handkerchief may be used, care being taken not to brush the pounce over the gold.

BRUSHING OFF WASTE LEAF — The superfluous gold round the edge of the gilded form may be lightly brushed off with the tip of the brush. This may be done after or before the burnishing — preferably after (See p. 170).

Any gold which may have stuck to the surrounding parchment, in spite of the pouncing, may be removed with the knife or with the hard indiarubber point, great care being taken not to touch the gilded size.

BURNISHING THE GOLD — The gold-leaf may be burnished immediately after laying when the size is very dry, but it is safer to wait for a quarter of an hour — or longer, if the size is at all damp (See Drying, p. 151).

The slab is again put under the work, and the burnishing is begun very gently and cautiously: should the burnisher stick in the very least, it is instantly stopped (or else the gold will be scratched off), examined, and cleaned.

The first strokes of the burnisher are generally carried all over the work, very lightly and with a Laying & circular movement (Fig. 109), till the gold begins to feel smooth, and the matt surface gives place to a dull polish.

FIG. 109.   FIG. 110.

As the gold gets smoother a little more pressure is used, and the burnisher is moved in straight lines in every direction across the gold (Fig. 110). At this point the gold should have a peculiar and agreeable feeling of smoothness under the burnisher, an unmistakable sign that all is going well.

A rapid light polish with the bend of the burnisher across a gold stem will give a very good finish (c, Fig. 108).

Properly burnished gold in a right light is at first as bright as a mirror, and in some lights may look quite dark by reason of its smoothness. A piece of white paper may be held at such an angle that the white light from it is reflected by the gold; this will show the quality of the burnish, and also show up any brown spots which the leaf may have failed to cover. It is helpful, moreover, during the actual process of burnishing to have a reflecting paper folded and standing beside the work (Fig. 111).

FIG. III.

At first the size under the burnished gold is not thoroughly hardened, and great care should be taken of it (not to breathe on nor finger the gold in any way, nor allow it to lie about and get dusty). It is best to put it away safely in a drawer for a week or two.

After a week or fortnight, when the size has set a little more, it may be very gently re-burnished, and this may be done again at the end of another fortnight. This final burnishing, when the size is nearly hard, will give it a very lasting polish. It is well, however, to take every care of burnished gold, and to secure it from risk of damage as soon as may be. Illuminated miniatures were often protected by a piece of silk between the leaves — and this should be done now, in the case of fine work. That a bound volume protects the burnished gold within it is proved by the large number of MSS. in which the gold, laid and burnished 500 years ago, is in perfect and brilliant preservation.

Remedying Faults In Gilding

To lay and burnish gold satisfactorily requires considerable experience. Careful practice with a good "size" will overcome the chief difficulties: these, and their probable causes, are here summarised: —

To make the Size stick to the Surface	Probable Causes of Size not sticking to Parchment or Paper	
Clean and pounce thoroughly: roughen if necessary (pp. 100, 115)	Dirty, Greasy, Horny, or Non-porous	Surface
Procure or make a proper composition, mix thoroughly always, and stir frequently If is at fault, add — a. Sticky matter b. Toughening matter (pp. 101, 114, and Appendix).	Size not sticky enough Size not tough when in use (and crumbling off)	Due to faulty composition, or mixing

To make the Gold-leaf stick to the Size	Probable Causes of Gold-leaf not sticking to Size	
Breathe on thoroughly and avoid delay in laying the gold (p. 103) Do not allow size to dry too long (p. 103)	Size not damped enough	Due to insufficient breathing on, or too absorbent nature or condition of, size
More, and more careful, rubbing and pressure (p. 106)	Not sufficient rubbing and pressing on of gold.	
(See above.)	Size not sticky enough	
Raise the size sufficiently (p.102). If not enough when dry, roughen surface and add another coat.	Not enough size, particularly in thin lines and edges	
Try re-gilding (p. 107), or, if spots persist, scrape them gently and try again: failing that, gently scrape off all the gold and try white of egg (dilute), or a slight re-sizing (as above). If the spots are very small and there is not time to spare for re-gilding, they may be touched with powder gold and dilute white of egg, and burnished when dry.	The gold may refuse to stick in spots with no apparent reason, but probably from one or other of the above causes. Or the size may have been touched accidentally and have become greasy or dirty.	

To make the Gold-leaf smooth and bright	Probable causes of Gold-leaf's not burnishing properly	
a, b.)Allow longer time (p. 103). c.) Remove size and re-size with proper composition. Sometimes this difficulty may be overcome by using several coats of gold-leaf (p. 107).	Size too sticky	Due to: a) Damp weather b)Insufficient time allowed for drying c) Too much sticky matter in size
Scrape smooth with sharp knife. (Sometimes the size itself is burnished before the gold-leaf is laid.)	Size rough surfaced	
Clean burnisher frequently	Burnisher becoming dirty	

Both paper and parchment when much wet with size are apt to cockle. Generally, it is not possible, or desirable (See p. 122), to guard against this by first stretching the material, but the size may be used with less water, so that it will dry sooner. In cases where there is a gold background it may often be divided into small parts (to be sized at different times) by the pattern (See p. 134). For large unbroken patches of gold several thin coats may be put on, one after the other.

Some sizes have a tendency to crack: this is difficult to guard against. But if the cracks are very minute — such as may be seen in many instances in the best early MSS. — they do not constitute a serious blemish.

Burnished gold is often damaged by careless handling or insufficient protection.

Gold Writing

The page (having been ruled as for ordinary writing) is thoroughly pounced all over.

The pen has an extra-long slit, and the size is made a little more fluid than usual to allow of its flowing freely and making true pen-strokes (p. 28).

The desk is lowered (Fig. 46, b), or flat, so that the size may flow freely.

The nib sometimes makes only a wet downstroke on the parchment, but by lightly pushing the pen up again, the stroke will be filled by the size which flows out from under the nib. Simple pen-strokes in small writing hold but little, and so ought to be filled as full of size as possible (pp. 102, 129). They will be found to dry much more quickly than larger forms, and may be gilded Laying & within a few hours of writing. Half-a-dozen or Burnishing more letters are gilded together (See p. 106).

Other Methods & Recipes For Gilding

Gold-leaf may be cut with a "gilder's knife" on a "gilder's cushion" and picked up with a "gilder's tip."

Water, white of egg, or alcohol may be used to make the gold-leaf adhere to the size.

"Transfer gold-leaf" is convenient, but the greasiness of the transfer paper is apt to dim the gilding.

Gold-leaf is made in many shades, from "red" (gold + copper) to "green" (gold + silver); though these may be used very effectively, they are liable to tarnish, and it is best to begin with pure gold (See pp. 103, 117).

Silver-leaf oxidises and turns black; platinum (a good substitute) costs about 2s. 6d., and aluminium (not so good) about 6d. per book.

"Gold Ink" has been made with powdered gold: its effect is inferior to raised and burnished writing.

The following is from "The Book of the Art of Cennino Cennini" (written about the beginning of the fifteenth Century): Translated by Christiana J. Herringham, 1899: —

"Chap. 157. — How you must do miniature-painting and put gold on parchment.

"First, if you would paint miniatures you must draw with a leaden style figures, foliage, letters, or whatever you please, on parchment, that is to say, in books: then with a pen you must make the delicate permanent outline of what you have designed. Then you must have Burnishing a paint that is a sort of gesso, called asiso, and it is made in this manner; namely, a little gesso sottile [See chap. 116, below], and a little biacca [whitelead], never more of this than equals a third part of the gesso; then take a little candy, less than the biacca; grind these ingredients very finely with clear water, collect them together, and let them dry without sun. When you wish to use some to put on gold, cut off a piece as large as you have need of, and temper it with the white of an egg, well beaten, as I have taught you. [The froth is allowed to stand for one night to clear itself.] Temper this mixture with it; let it dry; then take your gold, and either breathing on it or not, as you please, you can put it on; and the gold being laid on, take the tooth or burnishing-stone and burnish it, but hold under the parchment a firm tablet of good wood, very smooth. And you must know that you may write letters with a pen and this asiso, or lay a ground of it, or whatever you please — it is most excellent. But before you lay the gold on it, See whether it is needful to scrape or level it with the point of a knife, or clean it in any way, for your brush sometimes puts more on in one place than in another. Always beware of this."

"Chap. 116. — How to prepare gesso sottile (slaked plaster of Paris) for grounding panels.

"You must now prepare a plaster for fine grounds, called gesso sottile. This is made from the same plaster [plaster of Paris] as the last, but it must be well purified (pur-gata), and kept moist in a large tub for at least a month; renew

the water every day until it almost rots, and is completely slaked, and all fiery heat goes out of it, and it becomes as soft as silk. Throw away the water, make it into cakes, and let it dry; and this gesso is sold by the druggists to our painters. It is used for grounding, for gilding, for working in relief, and other fine works."

Appendix: On Gilding (by Graily Hewitt)

Success with raised gilding can only be expected when practice has rendered attention to the details of the process automatic and there is no need to pause and think. Even then the results must be somewhat uncertain and experimental. For our own preparations of size are usually unsatisfactory, and the ingredients of the best we can buy are unknown to us. And our vellum is certainly not of the quality we find in the old books. Someone is badly wanted to investigate the chemistry of the one and an appropriate preparation of the other. But we can take as much care as our time allows, passing nothing as "good enough" which we have not well examined, and bringing to the business all the patience and deftness available.

Vellum is too stiff, or too dry, or too greasy. When stiff, it is too thick for books: when dry, too apt to crack or cockle; when too greasy, exasperating. And yet the soft and rather greasy sort can be rendered more agreeable than the rest with labour. It should be rubbed by the flat of the hand with powdered pumice (or even fine sand- paper on the rough side) and French chalk, especially on its split (or rougher) side, until it is serviceable. A few trials will teach how long to give to this. Five minutes for one side of a lamb's skin would not be too much. It can then be beaten with a silk handkerchief, but not rubbed with this until the size has been laid. It may be rubbed cleaner between the laying of the size and the gilding. Especially must those parts of pages be thoroughly rubbed clean which in the book, when made up, will lie upon and be pressed against gold letters on the page opposite; or the pumice left behind will scratch them. On the other hand, if the vellum has not been thoroughly pumiced on both pages, the greasiness in it will dim the gold in time, both from above and below; or even make the size flake off altogether. The size is often blamed for faults of the vellum and its want of preparation.

Again size, or "raising preparation," is too sticky or too dry. If the former, the gold will not burnish well; if the latter, it will burnish, but will not stick at the edges, and will crack sooner or later. And though the essential quality of gilding is brightness, one may be content to fail of this rather than have letters ragged in outline or broken on the surface.

The size in use should be just liquid enough to flow evenly from the pen. More water makes it dry too brittle, and tends to cockle the vellum also; less tends to blobbiness and unevenness. Even when it is put on fairly an uncomfortable groove is apt to form as it dries down the centre of letters: but this can be either filled up as soon as the first layer is dryish, or the sides of the groove can be scraped (when the letter is quite dry) down to the level of the groove itself with a sharp knife. The knife must be sharp. As this scraping does not affect the extreme edges the power of the size there to hold the leaf is not impaired by it; and certainly a well-scraped surface is extremely even and pleasant to gild. If the surface, however, be burnished and not scraped before laying the leaf, it will not hold the size well, and remains lumpy also where lumps were there originally; while scraping gets rid of these. During use the size should be kept thoroughly mixed; and a small sable brush serves well for this purpose, as soon as it can be used so carefully as not to cause bubbles.

To know the exact time to allow between laying and gilding one had need to be a meteorologist, so much "depends on the weather." Very dry and very wet weather are equally unkind. Generally an interval of about twenty-four hours is right; but it is better to gild too soon than too late, provided one can be content, on testing the naked surface of the gilded letter with a burnisher, and noting that the glitter is reluctant to come, to leave the burnishing for a while, and only lay the leaf, pressing it well home to the outline of the letters. The burnishing can then be done in a few more hours. But if the size be too dry, the difficulty will be to make the leaf stick to it at all. In this case the leaf adhering can be scraped off, the size scraped down further, and another thin coat added and gilded after a shorter interval. If the letter be so fouled that such repairs are difficult, it should be entirely scraped away and the size relaid altogether. In doing this care is needed that the vellum be not injured round the letter.

The best gold-leaf for ordinary work costs about 3s. for twenty-five pages. More expensive leaf, being thicker, does not stick so well to the edges: cheaper is too thin to burnish well. Two kinds may be used together with good results, the finer leaf being put on next the size, and the thicker at once on to the top of that. The letter is then pressed and outlined as usual through paper, and the thin leaf will be found of considerable assistance towards the making of a clean-cut edge. Generally, however, the piling on of several leaves is inadvisable, as bits are liable to flake away as the letter goes on drying, leaving dim specks where they have been. Yet if, after the outlining through the paper, the leaf is seen to be very dull or speckled with the colour of the size, this means that the size has been partly pressed through the leaf; and another laid immediately will have enough to stick to, and will burnish well. The best result comes of one moderately thick leaf laid and burnished at the right time as quickly as possible. Thicker leaves need only be used for large surfaces, where the edge can be scraped even and clean, or where a black outline is to be added.

As soon as the leaf is laid, and from that point onward, the breath must be kept from the letter with a shield (of cardboard or tin) held in the left hand or otherwise. Inattention to this is responsible for many failures. Not only should the actual letters under operation be so protected, but where a quantity are sized ready for gilding on the page these should be protected also, as well as any parts already finished; for breath not only moistens but warms, and on warm size moisture condenses less easily. If the work to be done presently is so warmed, it will be found more difficult to deal with when its time comes. The first work done in the day is often the best, and for this reason, that the size for it is cool; but in gilding this portion one almost necessarily warms that to be done later. Two pages, where possible, should therefore be gilded alternately, one cooling while a portion of the other is gilded. Or thin plates of metal, or even cardboard, may be placed about as shields to protect all surfaces not under actual operation.

Superfluous gold is best removed by dusting lightly with an old and very clean and dry silk handkerchief. Indiarubber will certainly remove gold from the vellum, but it will as certainly dim any part of the gilding it touches. If the vellum was properly pounced to start with the silk will easily remove all the leaf unstuck, except little odds and ends, and these are safeliest taken away with the point of a knife.

As the pressure of burnishing helps the leaf to stick, it is best to wait till the letter has been burnished before this dusting. Such spots as are visible ungilded may be afterwards treated with a slight breath and transfer gold-leaf, or gold dust, may be painted on them. In the latter case the spots must be most carefully burnished, if burnished at all, or their surroundings will be scratched.

When a gold letter is to be set on a coloured background, or in the neighbourhood of colour, it is best put on after the colour; as may be observed was the method occasionally with the old books. If the gold is put on first, it will certainly be dimmed by warmth and breath during the colouring. On the other hand, if it is put on lazy, great care must be taken that the gold-leaf shall not stick to the coloured portions. Where possible, a stencil pattern of the parts to be gilded should be cut out of paper. This is easily made from a pencil rubbing taken after the size is laid, the raised pattern being of course cut out carefully a trifle larger than the outline so obtained. The paper is then laid over all the work, and the sized portions showing through the cuttings can be gilded without injury to the colour.

All gilded work should be retained, if possible, for a week or more, and then re-burnished. And in burnishing generally the burnisher should not be used, even when the size is hard, with any great force or pressure at first. For the size in drying sets as if moulded, and this mould cannot be squeezed about or actually crushed without being loosened or cracked. Throughout the whole process a gentle and vigilant alacrity is required. Success will come easily if it means to come. It cannot be forced to come.

The binder of a book with gilding in it should be warned to press the sheets as little as possible, and to use all his care in handling it, so as to keep moisture, warmth, and fingering from the gold. The folding of the sheets, when left to him, should also be done rather differently from usual, for all gilded pages need to be kept as flat as possible. None of the sizes in use seem capable of resisting bending of their surfaces without crimping or cracking. Where there is much gilding, the book will be the better for being sewn with a zigzag[32] through the sections, as this helps to "guard" the gilded work.

---

[32] Vide D. Cockerell, "Bookbinding and the Care of Books," p. 81.

CHAPTER X
THE USE OF GOLD & COLOURS IN INITIAL LETTERS & SIMPLE ILLUMINATION

Tools & Materials For Simple Illumination

TOOLS, &c., FOR GILDING — See Chapter IX. (pp. 98-9).

IVORY TRACING POINT — This is useful for various purposes, and for indenting patterns in burnished gold (See p. 134).

BRUSHES — Red Sables are very good. A separate brush should be kept for each colour — or at least one brush each for Reds, Blues, Greens, White, and gold "paint" — and it is convenient to have a medium and a fine brush for each.

PENS FOR COLOUR — Quill pens are used: "Turkey" or "Goose." The latter is softer, and is sometimes preferred for colour work. For very fine work (real) Crow Quills may be tried. A separate pen should be used for each colour.

COLOURED INKS — Brown ink (tempered with black if desired) may be used for fine outlines: if the outlined forms are to be coloured afterwards, it is convenient if the ink be waterproof.

Coloured inks seldom have as good a colour as the best paint colours (See Colours for Penwork, p. 123).

COLOURS — (p. 124). MATT GOLD (See p. 129)

PAINT-BOX — The little chests of drawers, sold by stationers for 2s. 6d., make very convenient "paint-boxes": pens, &c., may be kept in one drawer; gilding, tools, &c., in another; and colours and brushes in another.

PAPER (See pp. 17, 59, 63).— PARCHMENT, VELLUM, & POUNCE (*See below*).

Parchment, "Vellum," & Pounce
(See also Appendix on Gilding, p. 115 and pp. 59, 273)

The name "Vellum" (strictly applicable only to calf-skin) is generally given to any moderately good skin prepared for writing or printing on. All the modern skins are apt to be too stiff and horny: chemical action (substituted for patient handling), followed by liberal sizing and "dressing," is perhaps responsible. The old skins have much more life and character, and are commonly much softer. Their surface is generally very smooth — not necessarily glazed — often with a delicate velvety nap, which forms a perfect writing surface.

Parchment (sheepskin), as supplied by law-stationers, though rather hard, still retains the character of a skin, and is in every way preferable to the Vellum[33] which is specially prepared for illuminators. A piece of parchment about 26 inches by 22 inches costs about 2s. 6d. Lambskin is still better.

"Roman Vellum "is a fine quality of sheep or "lamb" skin, made in imitation of the Vellum used in the Vatican.

The surface of a modern skin may be greatly improved by "pouncing," but there seems to be a danger of its becoming rough or porous.

POUNCE — Fine powdered pumice (as supplied by Illumination drysalters) is very good. It is rubbed on with the hand (p. 115), or with a pad or a piece of rag. Law-stationers use a pounce in which the main constituents are chalk (or "whiting") and powdered resin. The latter, when used before gilding, is apt to make the gold-leaf stick to the surrounding parchment. (Before Writing, See Note 7, p. 276.)

Chalk, "Whiting," "French Chalk," and Powdered Cuttlefish Bone might be used as substitutes for pumice, or as ingredients in preparing a pounce. Sandarach (a resin) rubbed on an erasure appears to prevent ink spreading when the surface is written over.

A skin of parchment has a smooth (whiter) side — the original flesh side — and a rougher, yellower side — the original hair side. The penman will find the smooth side preferable for writing on (though, of course, both sides must be used in a book: See p. 68). This side is more easily damaged, and erasures have to be very carefully made with a sharp knife, or by gentle rubbing with indiarubber.

On the rough side, erasures cause little or no damage to the surface. A piece of rubber — or a paper stump — dipped in pounce may be used. It is better — as it is more straightforward — to avoid erasures if possible, and to correct mistakes frankly, as in ordinary writing (See p. 265).

---

[33] The very costly, specially prepared calf-skin is too highly "finished," and has much the appearance of superior cardboard. It is stiff and shiny, and its surface is objectionable to work on.

For ordinary purposes parchment should be cut to the size desired, and be held on the desk by the tape, guard, &c. (See p. 16). It is generally a mistake to pin it down, or to damp and stretch it on the drawing-board (See p. 273).

Parchment is stained a fine purple with "Brazil-wood": this may be obtained from a "store chemist." Three teacups full of Brazil-wood are stewed in about two pints of water, with two teaspoonfuls of alum (which acts as a mordant). The colour of this liquid is brownish-red, and to make it purple, carbonate of potash is added (very carefully, or it will become too blue). The liquid is poured into a tray, and the parchment skin is placed in it for half a day or a couple of days. The colour dries lighter, so it should be prepared rather dark, and diluted if necessary: strips of parchment should be used to test it; they are taken out and dried at the fire.

The parchment skin is stretched on a frame, the edges being caught up over little buttons or pegs, and tied at these points with string. It is allowed to dry slowly.

Colours

POWDER COLOURS are the purest: they may be mixed with gum arabic and water. Yolk of egg and water is sometimes used as a medium (or white of egg) (See pp. 114, 126). It is more convenient for the beginner to use prepared colours, which are ready and dependable.

CAKE COLOURS rank next to powder colours for purity: they seem to need tempering with a little gum or honey or glycerine (or egg — see above) for use on ordinary parchment.[34]

PAN COLOURS are very safe for ordinary use.

TUBE COLOURS sometimes seem to have too much glycerine; they are, however, very convenient for preparing mixed colours in any quantity, because of their semi-fluid condition, and because the amount of each colour in the mixture may be judged with considerable accuracy by the length which is squeezed out of the tube (p. 125).

COLOURS FOR PEN WORK, &c. — For simple letters or decoration it is well to use a pure

---

[34] OXGALL may be used for a greasy surface; painted on it, or mixed with the colour. plain with water, they are apt to flake off when dry.

RED — neither crimson nor orange tinged:
BLUE — neither greenish nor purplish:
GREEN — neither bluish nor "mossy"

A little "body colour" is generally used with blues and greens to keep them "flat"(p. 74). These colours should be mixed as required, and be diluted to the right consistency with water (See p. 74). Colour which has been mixed and in use for some time — especially if it has been allowed to dry — is best thrown away (See mixing size, p. 101).

If there is much rubricating to be done, a quantity of each colour sufficient to last several days may be mixed, and kept in a covered pot. A little pomatum pot is convenient — the smaller the better, as it keeps the colour together, and does not allow it to dry so quickly.

The filling-brush (a rough brush kept for filling the pen) may rest in the pot (See Fig. 112), being given a stir round every time it is used to prevent the settling of the heavy parts of the colour. A drop of water is added occasionally as the liquid evaporates and becomes too thick.[35]

TINTS FEW AND CONSTANT — Red, Blue, and Green (and perhaps purple) with Gold, White, and Black, are sufficient for everything but the most advanced type of Illumination. And it is in every way desirable that, until he has become a Master Limner, the Writer and Illuminator should strictly limit the number of his colours (See p. 154).

The paint pot, or saucer, may conveniently stand inside a larger vessel. A small tin, with the seam opened and the bottom melted off in a gas flame, will do.

FIG. 112.

It is one of the "secrets" of good "design" to use a limited number of elements — forms or colours or materials — and to produce variety by skilful and charming manipulation of these.

It is well to follow the early Illuminators in this also: that these few colours be kept constant. When you have chosen a Red, a Blue, and a Green — as pure and bright as you can make them — keep those particular tints as fixed colours to be used for ordinary purposes. For special purposes (pp. 128, 142) paler tints may be made by adding white, and varied tints may be mixed,

---

[35] And the nib is cleaned out now and then (with the filling brush), or wiped, to prevent the colour clogging it (See p. 70).

but even when your work has advanced so that you require a more complex "palette," you should stick to the principle of constant tints and modes of treatment for regular occasions: this is the secret of method.

RED — Vermilion is prepared in three forms: "Vermilion," "Scarlet Vermilion," and "Orange Vermilion." For ordinary use "Scarlet Vermilion" is the best (it may be tempered with a minute quantity of white). "Vermilion" is not quite so bright, and tends more to crimson, but, mixed with "Orange Vermilion" it gives the "scarlet" form. The pan colour is generally most convenient.

Where scarlet is in juxtaposition with gold, their effect may be harmonised by having a large proportion of blue in the neighbourhood: sometimes a more crimson colour than vermilion may be used.

Chinese Vermilion is a fine colour, but difficult to obtain; it is even said that the genuine pigment is reserved exclusively for the Chinese Emperor (whose edicts are written with "The Vermilion Pencil").

GREEN — Verdigris is a very fine colour, closely resembling, and possibly the same pigment as, the green in early MSS., but I believe that it has not been rendered permanent in modern use.

Green Oxide of Chromium (transparent) (or "Veridian") is a very good permanent green. It is rather a thin colour, and requires body, which may be given with lemon yellow, or with white and yellow ochre; being a rather bluish green, it is the better for a little yellow. This (mixed) green is most conveniently prepared from tube colours.

BLUE — Ultramarine Ash (whole tube about 4s.) is a very beautiful colour. It is rather pale and transparent (and a little "slimy" to work) when used alone. A mixture (preferably made with tube colours) consisting of Ultramarine Ash and Chinese White and (a very little) Prussian Blue makes an extremely fine, pure blue. A similar mixture with cobalt as a base makes a very good blue.

Ultramarine or Powdered Lapis Lazuli (unfortunately known as "Genuine Ultramarine"[36]) is a fine colour; it may have a slightly purplish tint and need tempering with green to make a pure blue (whole cake about 18s.).

---

[36] "French Ultramarine'" is an artificial compound, and a poor colour.

The Blue in common use in early MSS. (before Ultramarine came into use) has a fine, pure colour, and considerable body: it is more raised than any other colour; it is often seen to be full of little sparkles, as though there were powdered glass in it. It is supposed to have been prepared from a copper ore.

The following note on this blue has been given to me by Mr. C.M. Firth: —

"The blue is Native Carbonate of Copper finely powdered and tempered with white of egg (Vermilion is tempered with the Yolk)."

"The ore is of two kinds, a crystalline of a medium hardness found in France at Chessy, and hence called Chessylite, and a soft earthy kind which is obtained in Hungary, and largely now from Australia. The latter is from its ease of manipulation the best for paint making. It should be ground dry till it is no longer gritty and is of a sky blue (pale) colour."

"The Blue in MSS. was liable to wash off, but the oil in the Yolk prevented a similar result with the Vermilion. The Blue is identical with the Azzuro della magna (for d'allemaigne) of the Middle Ages. The frequently advanced hypothesis that the blue was due to a glass is based on the accounts of (I.) The Vestorian blue copper 'frit' for enamels probably; (II.) on the accounts in sixteenth century of the Manufacture of Smalt, which owes its colour to a glass tinted with Cobalt. This Azzuro is the oldest known Western blue, and was probably employed on Egyptian walls, where it has gone green, as also in Italian Frescoes."

"The Green tint of the chemical change in the Copper is seen in initials in books too much exposed to the damp. These exhibit a bright green tint in places where the colour was thinly applied." It appears that Yolk, besides being unsuited in colour for tempering this blue, changes it to a greenish colour (the effect of the oil, which forms about 30 percent, of Yolk of Egg).

WHITE — The tube Chinese White[37] is the most convenient to use when tempering colours.

"White Line or Hair Finishing"(See p. 129). Various tools have been recommended for this. A sable pencil with the outer hairs cut away, "the

---

[37] For white lining, &c. — if in constant use — the Chinese White in bottle is said to be the best; a little Spirits of Wine should be poured into it, to keep it moist and make it work better. It should be stirred well, and a sufficient quantity for immediate use is taken out and mixed in a small saucer. The bottle is kept tightly corked

smallest brush" made, and even a fine steel pen. I am inclined to believe that some of the early Illuminators used a fine quill — such as a crow quill, or a goose quill scraped thin and sharply pointed.

PURPLE is seldom used in simple pen-work, lettering, &c, but largely and with very fine effect in complex illumination. A reddish-purple is to be preferred. A good colour can be made from the purple stain described on p. 124, or from Ruby madder and a little Rose madder, with a very little Ultramarine.

Simple Colour Effects

SIMPLE "RUBRICATION" (See p. 82) — Red letters were most commonly contrasted with blue (the "warmest" and "coldest" colours),[38] in

Red cap.	in columns of Versal letters (see Fig. 93)	**RED**	in lines of Caps. (see Fig. 89)
Blue cap.		**BLUE**	
Red cap.		**RED**	
Green cap.		**GREEN**	
&c.		&c.	

some MSS. with green alone, but more commonly the three colours were used together, the alterations being generally—

REPETITION AND LIMITATION OF SIMPLE COLOURS (AND FORMS) — The uniform treatment of a MS. necessitates that no colour (or form) in it should be quite singular, or even isolated if it can possibly be repeated. If, for example, there be a Red capital on the "Verso" page, the "opening" is improved by some Red — a capital, a rubric, or even a line-finishing — on the "Recto" page. Very often the one piece of colour is very small, and, as it were, an echo of the other (compare Line-finishings and Initials, pp. 145, 135). While it is not always possible or desirable so to treat both pages of an opening, yet, in the book taken as a whole, every colour used should be repeated as often as there is a reasonable opportunity. And, therefore, where the opportunities for colour in a book are few and far between, it is well to limit the "colours" used to two, or even one.

This necessity for repetition applies to simple rather than to complex "Illuminated" Forms — e.g. a book need not have more than one Illuminated

---

[38] And single forms were often parti-coloured, as III., IV., Blue, with red serifs, or vice versa (See also pp. 208, 216).

Initial — but within such complex forms themselves repetition is recognised as one of the first principles of "decorative design" (See p. 154).

PROPORTIONS OF COLOURS — In Harmonious Illumination, Blue very commonly is the predominating colour; but no exact proportions can be laid down, for the combined colour effect depends so much on the arrangement of the colours.

EFFECTS OF NEIGHBOURING COLOURS[39] — When blue and red are in juxtaposition, the blue appears bluer and greener; the red appears brighter and more scarlet. With Red and Green, the Red appears more crimson, and the green, greener and bluer. A greenish blue will appear plain blue beside a pure green; a blue with a purplish tinge will appear more purple. Experiments might profitably be made with simple arrangements of Red, Blue, Green, Black, White, and Gold in combinations of two or more.

TEMPERING COLOURS WITH WHITE — Forms such as flower petals, &c., may be painted in Blue or Red, paled with White, and then be shaded with the pure colour; this gives considerable richness, and the effect may be heightened by very careful white line work (*q.v.*). Green leaves, &c., may be made very pale and then touched with Yellow — this gives a brilliant effect.

BLACK OUTLINES — The effect of these is to make a bright colour appear brighter and richer, to define, and, to a certain extent, harmonise, neighbouring colours and shapes, and to keep the design flat (See p. 186).

For one or more of these reasons, all The Use of coloured forms — patterns, charges, &c. — in a compound colour scheme have an outline — strong or delicate, according to the strength or delicacy of the work (See pp. 131, 132, 142, 159, 113).

WHITE LINING — A black outline is often separated from the colour by a fine white line (See Fig. 129). White lines also are used to harmonise colours, one or more commonly being painted (or "penned") upon the colours. This tends to make the colours appear paler and lighter — brightening them if they are dark. Care must be taken not to overdo the white

---

[39] In "white light" three rays (known as the "Primary Colour-Sensations") have been distinguished — Red, Green, and Blue; any two of these are complementary to the remaining colour, and appear to be induced optically in its neighbourhood. (Yellow light is combined of Red and Green rays, and this may partly explain the particular fitness of Blue and Gold Illumination.)

lining, or it will make the colours chalky and cold. White is also used in groups of dots, and in fine patterns on backgrounds (See pp. 152, 352).

Gold is even more effective than white or black for harmonising colours. It is commonly Burnished in bars or frames (See p. 366), and in spots (pp. 366, 131), or in large masses (p. 134). Matt Gold (See below).

Matt Gold

Matt gold, or gold "paint" — the pure gold powder with white of egg is best — is generally painted upon colour. It was much used in old miniatures for "hatching" and lighting landscapes, houses, costumes, &c.; and stars, rays of light, and outlines of clouds were painted in delicate gold lines upon the blue of the skies. Such gold lining has a very mellowing and pleasant effect upon colour, but it can easily be overdone. Matt gold may be used besides, for letters, ornament, and patterns painted upon colour. Such forms have either no outline, or a very faint one: their effect depends upon their lightness, and they are not made to appear solid.

FIG. 113.

A very pretty effect may be obtained in a small and not very formal manuscript by painting into the spaces left for the capitals little squares of red and blue, and painting upon these the letters and ornament — all in gold powder — very freely and quickly. The kind of treatment is rather crudely suggested by Fig. 113. The pleasant appearance of the pages — as though they were scattered over with tiny squares of cloth of gold and red and blue — is produced with comparative ease, while the use of leaf gold might entail an expenditure of more time and pains than the book was worth. In the finest class of manuscripts, however, these matt gold letters would be somewhat informal and out of place.

Burnished Gold

Gold is always raised and burnished as bright as possible, unless there is a special reason for using matt gold.

The height to which it is raised varies, according to the effect desired, from a considerable thickness to the thinnest possible coat of "size." Extremely thin and extremely thick raising are both objectionable (See p. 102): roughly speaking, a suitable height for any ordinary purpose is between $1/100$ and $1/32$ of an inch.

The surface, in the case of large forms, is generally made as smooth and perfect as possible, so that, as Cennino Cennini says, the burnished gold "will appear almost dark from its own brightness"; and its brightness is only seen when the light falls on it at a particular angle. The gilding of a manuscript, however, is slightly flexible, and a large gilded surface is likely to be bent, so that some part of it is sure to catch the light.

Small surfaces highly burnished very often do not show the effect of, or "tell" as, gold, unless they catch the light by accident. It is well, therefore, where the forms are small to have several on the page, so that one or another will always shine out and explain the rest. And while the proper craftsman tries always to get the best finish which he reasonably can, the natural, slight unevennesses or varying planes of small gilded forms may be of advantage to the whole effect. The pleasant effect of such natural variations may be seen in thirteenth-century Initials, where numbers of little gold pieces are fitted into the backgrounds, and their changing surfaces cause the whole to be lit up with little sparkles of light. A parallel to this may be found in the hand-tooling of a book-cover, which sparkles with gold, because the binder could not press in each piece of gold-leaf absolutely level. On the other hand, the "deadness" of a machine-stamped cover is largely due to the dead level of its gilding.

BLACK AND GOLD — One of the finest effects in calligraphy can be obtained by the simple contrast of gold capitals with black writing (See p. 226).

While, as in the case of black and red, the strongest effects are obtained by a marked contrast, gold may yet be very effectively used for small capitals throughout the black text. It does not lose or blend its brilliance with the black of the writing as colour is apt to do, but lights up and illuminates the page. For this reason, gold will "help out" and make agreeable a black and colour effect which, by itself, would have been a failure (See p. 89).

Burnished Gold Forms & Outlines

Plain gold letters, symbols, and other detached forms, not having backgrounds, are usually not outlined. An outline cheapens their effect, making them darker and heavier, and, if the line be at all thick, concealing the true form of the letter, and giving it a clumsy appearance. It is an instructive experiment to make a gold (or plain white) letter with a thick outline (a, Fig. 114), and then paint a background round it. The effect is quite altered, and greatly improved (b, Fig. 114). The outline no longer tells as the outer line of the form, but partakes more of the nature of the background, in which it cuts out, as one might say, a little niche for the letter to rest in.

a.   *b.*

FIG. 114.

Gold-leaf forms on coloured backgrounds are outlined — generally in black — in order that letter and background may together form a flat design, stable and at rest in the page.

The distinction between the use of gold "paint" and the treatment of a leaf gold form should be carefully observed: the matt gold powder lies upon colour, and may appear to blend with it (p. 129); the bright gold-leaf constitutes a distinct form, which either lies upon the surface of a page, or is, as it were, set in a background.

GOLD (LEAF) FLORAL ORNAMENT, &c. — If the stalk and leaves are both gold: they are commonly not outlined, unless on a background.

If there be a thin stalk in black or colour with gold leaves: the leaves are outlined with the stalk-colour (they were commonly furred: c, Fig. 115).

If there be a thick coloured stalk with gold leaves: both stalk and leaves commonly have a black outline, the "leaves" often being treated as spots of gold (below).

Gold Spots or Dots are usually outlined and furred with black (Fig. 115). The effect produced is of a bright gold form on a grey background.

A simple "leaf" or detached spot of gold has a formless look, much as a small blot of colour or ink would have. The black outline and the grey background

FIG. 115.

135

effect seem in this case to give form and interest to the spot; at least they give it a place to rest in — a nest to hold the small golden egg. Even a stalk and tendril (d, Fig. 115) has the same effect of giving intention and meaning to what might otherwise be a mere blot.

When several spots of gold (or colour) are arranged in a simple design, together they constitute a simple form which does not require a background. Thus, the line-finishing ∴ (a, Fig. 126) has a formal and intentional arrangement in itself, and therefore need not be outlined.

Background Capitals

Background Capitals or Initials frequently employ burnished gold, either for the letters or the ground. All the parts (including "solid" patterns) are generally outlined in black, or dark colour.

The commonest colours for grounds are Reds and Blues. The grounds are frequently countercharged, or made one colour inside and another outside the initial (p. 133). Sometimes little or no gold is used, and many fine white lines are employed to separate and harmonise the colours of the Initial and the ground. It is well, however, for the beginner to keep the letter and the ground distinct, by observing the Herald's maxim, and using "Metal on colour, or colour on metal."

The forms of the letters vary from those of ordinary capitals in being thicker in proportion to their height, and frequently in having no serifs. A very thin line or serif is apt to be lost in the background.

A very good form of background initial may be made out of the ROMAN CAPITAL (a, Fig. 116) by thickening all its parts: in place of the serifs, curving out and shaping the ends of the stems (b, d) to a sort of "blunderbuss" pattern (g).

Applying The Background

FIG. 116.

It is well first to make the letter,[40] and then to apply the background to it (as though it were a sort of mosaic). The background is packed tightly

FIG. 117.

---

[40] In the case of a burnished gold letter, the gilding may be deferred until the adjacent coloured parts are finished (See p. 170).

137

round the letter, and the letter occupies the background, so that they appear to be in the same plane (a, Fig. 117)

Such "flatness" is secured even more certainly and effectively by using two colours (e.g. red and blue) in the background — one inside and one outside the letter (See Plate XII.).

The curves of the gold letter may with advantage slightly project, and so break the hard, square out- line of the background.

The letter should not have the appearance of being "stuck on," as it is apt to if the background is large and empty, or if the ornament passes behind the letter (b, Fig. 117).

In the case of letters with projecting stems or tails: the tail may be outside the background (a, Fig. 118), or the background may be prolonged on one or both sides of the tail (b and c), or the whole "field" may be enlarged to take in the complete letter (d).

There is no limit to the variety of shapes which backgrounds may take — symmetrical or asymmetrical, regular or irregular — provided they fit the initial or the ornament (which may itself partially, or entirely, bound them), are properly balanced (See Plate XII., and p. 339), and take their right place on the page.

FIG. 118.

Ornament Of Backgrounds

The ornament, as a rule, covers the background evenly, and is closely packed or fitted into its place.

Gold grounds are generally plain, sometimes bearing patterns in dots. These are indented in the surface by means of a point (p. 121) which is not too sharp. It presses the gold-leaf into tiny pits, but does not pierce it. Gold grounds may be broken up into small parts by coloured chequers (p. 154) or floral patterns.

Coloured grounds are, as a rule, more or less evenly-covered with some form of decoration in thin white or matt gold lines, or in "solid" patterns in various colours (See pp.142, 151). A simple and pretty diaper pattern may be made by diagonal lines of matt gold, cutting up the colour into small "lozenges," each alternate lozenge having a fleur-de-lis or little cross, or other simple ornament (Fig. 119).

A bolder design, in a broad white or coloured line, may be, as it were, woven through counterfeited slits in the letter (Fig. 120). This helps to preserve the general flatness of the letter, background, and ornament, and gives additional interest.

The mimic slits are made by black lines drawn on the burnished gold of the letter. Where the stem of the ornament comes over the gold, the size is cut away with a pen-knife; the part hollowed out is painted with white to cover any blemishes, and then painted with the stem colour, and outlined.

A plain or pale stem may have a faint or brown outline, and be "shaded" at the sides (with greys, browns, or yellows) to give an effect of solidity; a stem that is painted in strong colour (e.g. red or blue) may have a central white line painted upon it.

Simple Diaper Background in Shell Gold on COLOUR.

FIG. 119.

Note that where the initials have backgrounds, the line-finishings are commonly made with backgrounds to match, though their treatment is naturally much simpler (See Plates XV., XVII.).

FIG. 120.

CHAPTER XI
A THEORY OF ILLUMINATION

Illumination

It is convenient to give a wide meaning to the word when we speak of an "illuminated manuscript," for the scribe works with a very free hand, and when he wishes to decorate his pages he can write the words themselves in red, green, or blue, as easily as he could have written them in black.

He can take a clean pen and a new colour and initial and "flourish" any part of the work to his heart's content. He may acquire the art of laying and burnishing gold, and no possible brilliance of effect is denied him — within the limits of his skill as an illuminator (See also pp. 225-226).

A limited number of specially prepared printed books can likewise be illuminated. But the greater the number of copies, the less labour may be spent on each one, and the more their illumination tends to be simple "rubrication" — adding coloured capitals, flourishes, and the like (See p. 82). And, if a large edition is to be decorated, the printer must be content to use black, or black and red, in woodcut or "process" work (See pp. 280, 282).

Illumination proper may be defined as the decoration by hand, in bright gold or colours, of writing or printing.

There are three broad types of illumination, which for want of better terms I distinguish as "Barbaric" (or colour- work), "Filigree" (or pen- work), and "Natural" (or limner's). These types run naturally one into another, and they may be blended or combined in every possible way, but it is convenient to consider them and the distinctive treatments which they involve separately.

"Barbaric, Or Colour-Work, Illumination"
(See also pp. 143, 148, 149, 154-56, 329, 344, 345)

This is mainly a colour treatment in which forms seem to be regarded chiefly as vehicles for colour. Its effect appeals to the senses, rather than to the imagination; and such interest as the forms have lies greatly in their skilful disposal or intricate arrangement. Sometimes in their fantasy — where organic forms are introduced — as the "great fish" in the act of swallowing Jonah (in order to make the T of ET), Plate XII. This type of illumination appears to have reached its climax of barbaric splendour in the twelfth and thirteenth centuries.

Though its revival nowadays might seem a little out of keeping with the more sedate and grown-up point of view of modern life, we cannot doubt that it is still lawful to decorate our work with the brilliance and splendour of gold and colours. Whether it is expedient or not depends upon how it is done: to justify our work, it must succeed; it must be bright and splendid, and really gladden our eyes. And we must really take pleasure in the making of it, for if we do not, we can hardly expect that it will give pleasure to others.

SIMPLE AND COMPLEX FORMS — Between simple forms — which are in a sense permanent — and complex forms — which are always changing — it is necessary to make a careful distinction.

An equilateral triangle drawn by "Euclid" and one drawn by a modern Senior Wrangler are, or ought to be, practically the same thing. If the ancients made an ornamental band of geometrical forms, that is no bar to us: we also are at liberty to make decorative bands of circles, lozenges, or triangles.

The ancient Romans made a capital A — its essential form (See Fig. 142) two strokes sloped together and joined by a cross-bar (very like the A of "Pons Asinorum"), it could hardly be simpler —they used chisels and pens, which gave it its more characteristic and finished form. If we use chisels and pens properly, we shall get a similar result — not absolutely the same — for no two chisels or two hands can be quite the same — but closely resembling it and belonging to our own time as much as to any other.

The essential form of the "Roman" A is a purely abstract form, the common property of every rational age and country,[41] and its characterisation is mainly the product of tools and materials not peculiar to the ancient Romans.

But when there is any real complexity of form and arrangement, or sentiment, we may reasonably suppose that it is peculiar to its time, and that the life and virtue of it cannot be restored.

It was common enough in the Middle Ages to make an initial A of two dragons firmly locked together by claws and teeth. Such forms fitted the humour of the time, and were part of the then natural "scheme of things."

---

[41] It has even been supposed that we might make the inhabitants of Mars aware of the existence of rational Terrestrials, by exhibiting a vast illumination — in lamp-light — consisting of a somewhat similar form — the first Proposition in Euclid.

But we should beware of using such antique fantasies and "organisms"; for medieval humour, together with its fauna and flora, belong to the past. And our own work is only honest when made in our own humour, time, and place.

There are, however, an infinite variety of simple abstract forms and symbols, such as circles, crosses, squares, lozenges, triangles, and a number of Alphabets, such as Square and Round Capitals,

Small Letters — upright and sloping — which — weeded of archaisms — we may use freely. And all these forms can be diversified by the tools with which they are made, and the manner in which the tools are used, and be glorified by the addition of bright colours and silver and gold.

Very effective "designs" can be made with "chequers" and diaper patterns, and with the very letters themselves. And I have little doubt that an excellent modern style of illumination is quite feasible, in which the greatest possible rich- ness of colour effect is achieved together with extreme simplicity of form.

"Filigree, Or Pen-Work, Illumination"
(See also pp. 145-149, 156-58, 351, 359-60; Figs. 79, 92, 125-26, 150, 188-89; Plates XL, XIIL, XIV., XVII.)

This is a type of illumination which can safely be attempted by one who, having learnt to write, is desirous of illuminating his writing; for it is the direct outcome of penmanship (See p. 137), and consists mainly of pen flourishes, or semi-formal lines and shapes which can be made with a pen, suitably applied to the part to be decorated. Its effect may be very charming and restful: no colour standing out as in a positive colour scheme, no individual form catching the eye; but the whole having a richness of simple detail and smooth colouring more or less intricate and agreeably bewildering.

It may be compared to the tooling of a book-cover, both in the method of producing it, and in its effect. A book-binder has a number of stamps which bear the simplest forms and symbols, such as little circles and "leaves" and stars and curved lines, and with these simple elements he builds up a pleasant "design," which he tools, usually in gold-leaf, upon the cover.

The scribe can vary the forms which his pen produces, and the colours which he gives them, with a freedom that the set form and the method of using the binder's tools do not allow. But the skilled penman will find that his pen (or, at any rate, his penmanship) largely determines the forms of his freest nourishes and strokes, and that the semi-formal nature of such ornament demands a certain simplicity and repetition of form and colour, which do not unduly tax his skill as a craftsman.

Suppose, for example, that the scribe wishes to illuminate the border of a page of writing. He may choose a limited number of simple, pen-made forms for the elements of his design ; say, a circle, a "leaf," and a "tendril," and a few curved flourishes and strokes (Fig. 121), and with these cover the allotted space evenly and agreeably.

FIG. 121.

The ornament being treated as though it were a sort of floral growth, requires a starting point or "root." The initial letter is the natural origin of the border ornament, the stalk of which generally springs from the side or from one of the extremities of the letter. The main stem and branches are first made with a very free pen, forming a skeleton pattern (Fig. 122).

Note. — The numbers in the diagram indicate the order in which the strokes were made. The main stem (111) sweeps over and occupies most of the ground; the secondary stem (222) occupies the remainder; the main branches (333 , &c.) make the occupation secure.

Next the minor branches are added to cover the space evenly, and then the flowers, fruit, and buds — made up of combinations of the "leaves," circles, &c. — are more or less evenly disposed in the spaces formed by the

FIG. 122.

146

large, round curves at the ends of the branches (Fig. 123).

The "leaves" are placed all over, wherever there is convenient room for them (just as the leaves of a real plant are). Then the stalks of the leaves are added, and, lastly, the interspaces are filled with "tendrils," which greatly contribute to the pleasant intricacy of the design (Fig. 124).

FIG. 123.

FIG. 124.

COLOUR SCHEMES — The safest treatment of such a "design "is in black and gold (See p. 131). The leaves, which are kept rather flat, may be outlined after gilding. The flowers, &c., may be made up in red and blue (tempered with white: See p. 128). This is the colour treatment of the example, Plate XVII.

If the leaves are green, the stem and outline may be more delicately drawn in pale or grey-brown ink, and the green may be a delicate pale olive or grey-green. (A strong, black stem with bright green leaves is apt to look crude and hard.) In such a delicate green plant border, delicate blue and red flowers, and one or two rather flat gold "berries" (single, or in threes) may be placed.

A very effective colour decoration of a much simpler type may be made in red and green (or blue) pen-work — using the pen and the colours with which the Versal letters and line-finishings are made. A red flourished stem with red leaves or tendrils, and green berries (or leaves), or a green stem with green leaves and red berries.

A floral pattern may also be made in plain burnished gold — both stem and leaves — not outlined (p. 131 & Plate XXII.).

A more complex decoration resembling the "floral filigree" has a "solid" stem in light or dark colour on a dark or light ground (or on a gold ground), as suggested in the rough diagram, Fig. 120.

The examples of Italian fifteenth-century work in Plates XVIII. and XIX. show a related type of illumination, known as the "white vine pattern." Very carefully and beautifully drawn, it strongly suggests natural form.

"Natural, Or Limner's,[42] Illumination"
(See also pp. 152, 157-59, 227, 346-48, 357-58, 376; Figs. 131a-141; Plates XV., XVI., XXIII.)

This, the finest type of illumination, has very great possibilities: and it is to be hoped that some craftsmen, who have the necessary skill, will find an opening for their work in this direction.

Plate XV. is a thirteenth-century example of the transition from the "barbaric" to the "natural." The dragon-tailed initial with its wonderful

---

[42] Note. — Limning strictly means Illuminating, but has come to imply drawing and painting, especially of portraits and miniatures. Here, all its senses are intended.

scroll-work and "ivy-leaf" being the perfection of barbaric form, carrying brilliant colour and serving to support and frame the delicate and beautiful drawing which it contains.[43] But in the drawing itself the skill of a fine illuminator combines with the fancy of a cunning draughtsman to satisfy an aesthetic taste and appeal to the imagination.

Plate XVI. shows a rare, and singularly beautiful, treatment of an Italian fourteenth-century MS. decorated with plant and insect forms (p. 358).

Plate XXIII. (modern) show a border of wild roses and climbing plants: the colour treatment in the original is very brilliant (See p. 376).

The "natural" type depends very much on the beauty and interest of its form; and a draughtsman before he had become an illuminator, might be content to decorate MSS. and printed books with pen drawings only faintly coloured or tinted; but when he had mastered the limitations which the craft would impose on his drawing for pure and bright colour, there is no degree of brilliance, even unto "barbaric splendour," which he might not lay upon his trained and delicate forms.

---

[43] The modern illuminator, having no tradition for making such scroll-work, would find that natural or organic forms — as of trees or plants (See p. 159) — would serve the same end and have more "sweet reasonableness" in modern eyes. Excellent scroll-work, moreover, might be formed out of ornamental Capitals — if sufficient excuse could be found for introducing them: a large flourished L, for example, could be made exactly on the same lines as the pendant and scroll in Plate XV. Narrow gold rods also may be used in a border to support a floral growth, or as frames if necessary (compare rules, p. 279).

CHAPTER XII
THE DEVELOPMENT OF ILLUMINATION

The Development Of Illumination[44]

An art or craft is so largely dependent on the tools and materials which are used by the craftsman, that we may reasonably say that it begins with the tools and materials, through which it has been produced. Now, "illumination" can be traced back step by step to simple penmanship. And its true development is most graphically sketched by Ruskin ("Lectures on Art," No. V.) when he says —

"The pen . . . is not only the great instrument for the finest sketching, but its right use is the foundation of the art of illumination . . . Perfect illumination is only writing made lovely; . . . But to make writing itself beautiful — to make the sweep of the pen lovely — is the true art of illumination;" **And also that those who have acquired** *"a habit of deliberate, legible and lovely penmanship in their daily use of the pen, . . . may next discipline their hands into the control of lines of any length, and, finally, add the beauty of colour and form to the flowing of these perfect lines."*

Line-Finishings

Line-finishings are used to preserve the evenness of the text when lines of writing fall short. When the space left is small, or occurs in the middle of a sentence, a quick stroke of the pen — often a continuation of the last letter, or springing from it — is sufficient (Fig. 125); but where there are many and long gaps (as, for example, in a psalter at the ends of the verses), they may be filled in with dots (See Plate VIII.) or flourishes (a, b, c, Fig. 126) either made in black with the script pen, or with another pen, in colour or gold.

Line-finishings commonly echo the treatment of the initials (See p. 128). In twelfth-century MSS. long delicate flourishes are commonly found, in red, blue, or green — matching the colours of the Versals, and probably made with the same pen. The latter being rather finer than the text pen keeps these flourishes from appearing too prominent (See e, f, Fig. 126).

---

[44] The steps in the development sketched very briefly in this chapter, refer both to the past history of the art of illumination and to its possible revival (See Author's preface, p. 16).

Line-finishings :
Pen-flourishing :
of Terminal strokes

e e f g e
e t s n
m v y
k r r r r
E F L L
T Z ✠ R

spread .... out ;
sometimes
h J 1
IN ornamental LETTERING,

FIG. 125.

Such work should be simple and characteristic pen-work, showing the thicks and thins and crisp curves, the result of the position of the pen, which is usually "slanted" (See p. 8).

Bands of pen-made "geometrical" patterns — used with rather close writing — may be very simple and direct, though appearing pleasantly elaborate (See Figs. 87 and (g) 126, Plate XIV., and p. 154).

FIG. 126.

Initial Letters

(See also pp. 15, 69-72, 80, 89, 128, 132-137, 135-41, 150-54, and the Collotype Plates)

The development of Illumination proper was — and still is — bound up with the growth and decoration of the Initial Letter.

The first step in this development is the mastery of the pen-made Versal letter, and the right treatment of simple coloured capitals (See chapters VII., VIII., and X.). The next step is their elaboration.

The simplest ornamental treatment is found in the flourishing of a terminal of the initial letter (Fig. 150), or the arrangement of the remaining letters of the word inside or beside it. Pen flourishes may consist of the simplest curved and zigzag strokes (sometimes springing from the actual letter: See p. 185), ending with a "twirl" of the pen in a loop or a "bud" (Figs. 150, 79); or they may strike out a sort of formal floral pattern, filling or surrounding the initial (Fig. 92), and such a pattern in its turn may spring from the letter into the margin, and grow into a complete "illuminated border" (See p. 140).

HOLLOW LETTERS — A large capital is often made hollow, primarily with a view to lightening its appearance, which might be rather heavy if the letter were made solid (p. 76). The hollow — which is commonly left plain (i.e. the colour of the paper or parchment) — may be a mere line, straight or curved or zigzag (Fig. 189), or a pattern, or lettering (Fig. 89). Sometimes it is made large and filled in with a contrasting colour, leaving a white line, however, between the two colours. And sometimes half the letter is made in one colour, and the other half (on the opposite side of the hollow centre) is made in a contrasting colour. A "hollow" letter (especially if very large) may be strengthened and improved by a filling of colour or ornament. (Addenda, p. 14.)

"WOVEN" FORMS — A simple form of ornament (related to "Basket work") which effectually strengthens the construction of a hollow letter —

without impairing its lightness — consists in a crossing and "weaving" or knotting of its actual parts (Fig. 127).

The elaborated Ɛ (in Fig. 127) is from a 10th or 11th century MS. (Brit. Museum, Egerton, 608). The Initial and its inwoven ornament cut up the background into a number of distinct parts (distinctly coloured). Note also that the entire background is contained by the Initial.

The "knot" (Fig. 127), or a basket-work ornament, is sometimes used as an arbitrary starting-point for a filigree border (See p. 359) where an initial is lacking.

FIG. 127.

VARIETY IN INITIALS — The sizes and styles of the initials which are used for the same purpose throughout the book vary very slightly or not at all. Generally, the more important the division which the initial marks, the larger the initial and the more ornate (p. 226). A slight complexity in the opening letter or word of a book does not seriously interfere with the readableness of the book as a whole. The general rule is followed that the greater the number of (decorative) forms the plainer they are kept (See p. 81), and if a book contained an "initial" on every page, it would be both an artistic and a working economy (if there were many pages) to make the majority of them rather plain.

But however simple the treatment of the initials may be, there is still room for considerable variety of form or ornament or type — as "round" or "square" letters (See Fig. 80, and especially Plate XI.). Such variety is found in the best work; it adds a liveliness and charm which are quite lacking where there is unnecessary or mechanical repetition.

"LOMBARDIC" VERSUS ROMAN CAPITALS — The round, fat letters which are known as "Lombardic" (See Fig. 1, and Plates XV., XVII.) have been generally used for "illuminated initials" in Northern Europe since the thirteenth century. But — though they are capable of very beautiful treatment — they are rather doubtful models for us to follow. The fact that such letters will always pack neatly into a square niche or background — though an obvious convenience — is not an unmixed advantage. And the majority of examples show a debased type of Letters — often so unlike their originals, and so like one another, as to be scarcely readable. For the sake of readableness the stems should be made longer (Fig. 128). The more slender

Diagram showing the tendency to confusion between "Lombard-ic" forms of this type, & also a severe type in which the letters are more distinct: their characteristics being more marked.

FIG. 128.

"Roman" type of initial, commonly used in Italy (Plate XVIII.), is in every way a more legible letter.

The Roman Alphabet still remains the finest model, and it is better that fine lettering should be almost too slender and delicate, than that it should be at all heavy or clumsy.

Borders & Backgrounds

The illuminated border was originally an extension or branching out of the initial decoration. It commonly occupied the greater part of the left-hand margin, and from thence it extended into the head[45] or foot margin (or into both), or completely surrounded the text, and even the eight margins of

---

[45] Where it is possible it is desirable to mark the top left-hand corner of the "'page" (and also the lower corner) by a branch, flourish, bud. or flower (See Plates XIX., XXII.). A top left-hand corner appearing vacant or rounded off is apt to weaken the whole effect (See p. 89).

a complete opening are sometimes covered with illumination. In late and modern usage, the border is frequently separated from the initial, constituting an Illumination "framing border."[46]

FIG. 129.

Note. — This diagram suggests a simple treatment of an initial word in colours and gold. The graphic method employed by heralds for indicating these — by lines and dots — is here discarded for the stronger contrasts of black, white, and "grey."

The letters contained inside the initial P are kept distinct — (1) crimson ("grey" in diagram) being used solely for the patches of ground adjoining the (gold) letters, and for filling the hollow part of the (gold) P, the whole word stands out in crimson and gold; (2) the floral pattern is also in gold, but it does not cover or hide any part of the word. The remaining ground is green inside and blue outside the P. The dots ∴ ∴ are in red on the green ground, in cream with a red centre dot on the blue.

The gold throughout is outlined black, and the blue ground has a black outline, separated from it by a "white line."

In some MSS. there are two side-borders on a page, one springing from the Initials on the left, the other sending branches into the gaps on the

---

[46] Framing borders, or borders which surround the text, may be allowed nearly to fill the entire marginal space.

right (See Plates XVII., XVI.). In some cases, the two pages of an opening are balanced by a side-border in each of the wide side margins (p. 428).

Backgrounds of Initials (See pp. 132-138, 344-46) and borders are treated very similarly. It may be noted that, where a solid-stem pattern cuts up the ground into small pieces, these are often painted in different colours — commonly red, and green, and blue (See pp. 149, 352). And the groups of dots (Fig. 129) — in white or other colours — may fill the interstices of a background, putting the finishing touch to the even covering and pleasant intricacy of the decoration (comp. p. 141). Or little flowers and leaves may be used instead — growing from a thin (white) stem which appears to twine throughout the main pattern — just as the smaller plants in a hedge creep and twine among the larger stems. There is no better model in nature for the illuminator than a country hedgerow.

CHAPTER XIII
"DESIGN" IN ILLUMINATION

"Design"

Perhaps the nearest right definition of "design" is "contrivance" — applied to the actual doing of the work, rather than to the work when done: "decoration" (when that is the sense intended) is a safer word,[47] because it implies "of something ." And generally, that "something" lies at the root of the matter. For example: "illuminated initials" and "illuminated borders," so called, are really illuminating: they are properly a decoration of manuscript or print.

To consider a "piece-of-decoration" as a thing existing apart from that which it decorates, as something drawn or copied, and, so to speak, stuck on to the finished work, is as unnatural as it would be to contemplate the flame-of-a-candle as a thing apart from the candle.

The finest decoration is really part of the work itself, and may be described as the finishing touches given directly to the work by the tools which are properly employed on it.

The illuminator has, as a rule, to decorate a given manuscript with pen or brush work — it may be with the simplest pen flourishes, or with the most elaborate figure "design." How to make that illumination part of the work, he can learn only by patient practice and by careful handling of his tools.

Elementary Patterns In Decoration

Nearly all simple Decoration consists of a comparatively limited number of elements — simple forms and pure colours — which are built up into more complex forms to occupy an allotted space. A primitive type of such built-up decoration is seen in the dotted patterns, which are found in every age — in the remains of the most ancient art, and in the shell decorations which children make on the sands at the present day. Examples of dotted "backgrounds" in the "Durham Book" are shown in Fig. 130 (a and

---

[47] "Design" has been associated so much with bad cleverness in the artist, or clever badness in the natural man, that if we use the word in a good sense it is apt to be misunderstood. Decoration is derived from decus, decor = comeliness or grace.

b). Chequers and Diapers — in which two or more elements are employed — are related patterns.[48] (See also Addenda , p. 14 and Fig. 191a.)

A simple way of filling a band (or long narrow space) is to run a zigzag line along it (c). This may be treated either as a line or wavy stem, which may send out buds, leaves, or flowers into the spaces (g), or as two series of triangles which may be "countercharged" (f).[49] A second zigzag, cutting the first, would produce two series of triangles and a central row of lozenges (d). And it is not a very great step from this to the "twist" where the two lines pass over and under, the lines being made "solid" in white or gold on a coloured background (e, Fig. 130). The main difference appears to be that while the one is of the nature of an abstract form, the other suggests a concrete form, such as might be made with twisted cords or rods.

These primitive patterns never become antiquated; they are still the root forms of "design," and the pleasant even covering of a given space by simple elements — which is their métier — accounts for much of the unconscious pleasure which we take in good bricklaying or sewing or writing, and in a thousand things, where "many littles make a mickle."

For their decorative possibilities in Illumination we can experiment in the most delightful way — framing our writing with bands of countercharged triangles in burnished gold, and blue and white, or with golden zigzags on a blue ground, or chequering backgrounds with scarlet and blue, and trying a hundred and one other ways (p. 139). Such patterns have been made the most of in Heraldry, an art which in itself would form foundation for a splendid and complete scheme of Illumination.

---

[48] Chequers in colours and gold were largely used in the fourteenth-century MSS. for backgrounds in miniatures. There is an example of very beautiful heraldic diapering (in enamel) on the shield of William de Valence, Earl of Pembroke, in Westminster Abbey (A.D. 1296). On p. 258 of this book there is a diagram of a very fine shield bearing a diapered chequer.

[49] If the triangles were countercharged in colour and colour — e.g. red and blue — the zigzag would be made white, black, or gold, to separate and harmonise the colours (See pp. 128-29).

Fig. 130.

Scale & Scope Of Decoration

PENMANSHIP — Many of the most beautiful MSS. were made in pen-work throughout.[50] And it is well that the penman should stick to his pen as much as is possible. Not only does it train his hand to make pen ornaments, the forms of which are in keeping with the writing, but it helps to keep the decoration proportionate in every way. It is an excellent plan for the beginner to use the writing-pen for plain black capitals or flourishes, and to make all other decoration with similar or slightly finer pens than the one used for the writing. Again, the direct use of the pen will prevent much mischievous "sketching." Sketching is right in its proper place, and, where you know exactly what you wish to do, it is useful to sketch in lightly the main parts of a complex "design" so that each part may receive a fair portion of the available space. But do not spoil your MS. by experimental penciling in trying to find out what you want to do. Experiments are best made roughly with a pen or brush on a piece of paper laid on the available space in the MS., or by colouring a piece of paper and cutting it out to the pattern desired and laying it on. Such means are also used to settle small doubts which may arise in the actual illuminating — as to whether — and where — some form or some colour should be placed on the page.

FILIGREE, FLORAL, & OTHER DECORATION — The acquired skill of the penman leads very naturally to a pen flourishing and decoration of his work, and this again to many different types of filigree decoration more or less resembling floral growths (See Figs. 125, 126; pp. 139-142; Plates XI., XVII.).

Now all right decoration in a sense arranges itself, and we may compare the right action of the "designer's" mind to that necessary vibration or "directive" motion which permeates the universe and, being communicated to the elements, enables the various particles to fall into their right places: as when iron filings are shaken near a magnet they arrange themselves in the natural curves of the magnetic field, or as a cello bow, drawn over the edge of a sand-sprinkled plate, gathers the sand into beautiful "musical patterns."

---

[50] A most beautiful twelfth-century MS., known as the "Golden Psalter," has many gold (decorated) Initials, Red, Blue, and Green (plain) Versals and Line-Finishings, every part being pen-made throughout the book.

And to most natural growths, whether of plants or ornament, this principle of self-arrangement seems common, that they spread out evenly and occupy to the greatest extent possible their allotted space. Branches and leaves most naturally grow away from the stem and from each other, and oppose elbows and points in every direction. In this way the growth fits its place, looking secure and at rest — while in disconnected parallels, or branches following their stem, there is often insecurity and unrest.[51] (See also Addenda, p. 15.)

For example: a circular space is filled more decoratively by a cross (a, Fig. 131) than by a contained circle; a square is better filled by a "lozenge" or a circle (b and c) than by a smaller square set square and parallel (compare the diapering of the chequers in Fig. 191a). A circular or square space might be filled on this principle with a filigree arrangement such as is suggested by (d, Fig. 131). Note. — In the case of two curves in the ornament touching (either internally or externally) they may be linked at this point by a (gold) band or circle or lozenge (e, Fig. 131, See also Plate XVII.).

FIG. 131.

Miniatures and Drawing. — In drawing and painting, the difficulty which is apt to beset the illuminator is how to strike a balance between "Naturalism" and "Conventionalism," so called. While the only criterion is good taste, we may be guided by certain general principles.

To limit the number of elements in a "design" — whether of form or colour — is nearly always an advantage (pp. 177, 181, 198). And the

---

[51] In a spiral the stem, following itself, may be tied by an interlacing spiral, or the turns of the spiral may be held at rest by the interlocking of the leaves (See G, Plate XXII.).

miniaturist, while depicting the nature of a plant, usually limits the number of its branches and leaves and shades of colour. Every part of a "design" should be drawn clearly and distinctly, and in proportion to the whole. The miniaturist, therefore, usually draws in careful outline every branch and leaf making the whole proportional with the MS. which it decorates.

In fact, the qualities of good illumination are the same as the qualities of good writing — Simplicity, Distinctiveness, Proportion, &c. (See p. 175). And the "convention" (here literally a coming together) required is only such as will make the drawing and colouring of the illumination and the form and colour of the writing go well together.

Note. — Figs. 135 to 141 (woodcuts — with part of the text — from a Herbal printed at Venice in 1571 [p. 283-4]) and Figs. 132, 133, and 134a (wood engravings by T. Bewick, printed 1791) are suggested as examples of drawing — of plants and animals — suitable for book-decoration (See also Figs. 134b, c, d, Plates XV., XVI., XXIII., and notes on "limner's illumination," p. 143).

Of "Designing" Manuscripts Generally

Cultivate the simplest and most direct methods, and make "rules of thumb"[52] for work-a-day use, to carry you successfully through all routine or ordinary difficulties, so that your hand will be trained and your mind free and ready to deal with the harder problems when they arise.

Use a limited number of pure, bright colours, and keep your work clean, neat, and definite.

Go straight ahead, trusting to workman-like methods, and not calculating overmuch. Do the work in a regular order, settling, first, the general scheme, the size of the book, the writing, and the margins: then when you are ready —

1. Prepare the sheets (See pp. 60, 68, 115)
2. Write the text—Leaving spaces for decoration
3. Write in —
    (a) The coloured writing
    (b) The coloured capitals
    (c) The line-finishings
4. Illuminate—
    (a) The Initials
    (b) Line-finishings
    (c) The borders

} Following a regular order in the various processes involved

5. Bind the book (p. 266), or have it bound, in order to make a real and finished piece of work.

---

[52] As an example of a good "rule of thumb," use the ruled lines of a manuscript as a scale for other measurements and proportions, leaving one, two, three, or more of the line-spaces for capitals, ornaments, &c.: you have this scale — as it were, a "ready reckoner" — present on every page, and following it enables you more easily to make the decoration agree and harmonise with the written text and with the book as a whole (See p. 84 & Figs. 89, 91, 71).

Practise an artistic economy of time and space: usually the quicker you write the MS. the better it is. Allow sufficient margins to make the book readable and handsome, but not so wide as to make it appear fanciful. Allow sufficient ornament, not overloading the book with it. Let the ornament be of a type suited to the book and to the subject — not too painstaking or elaborate in an ordinary MS.; not too hasty and slight in an important work.

Endeavour to strike a balance between what may be called "practical" and "ornamental" considerations: an illuminated MS. is not meant to be entirely "practical," but it is a greater failure if made entirely "ornamental." Let the text be readable in every sense, and let the ornament beautify it: there should be give and take, as it were, and that most desirable quality — "sweet reasonableness."

HISTORY OF QUADRUPEDS.

THE SPRINGER.

The *White-Antelope*, which is fuppofed to be the fame with the *Pygarg*, mentioned in the book of Numbers, is an inhabitant of the Cape of Good Hope, where it is called the *Spring-bok;* and is to be feen in herds of feveral thoufands, covering the plains as far as the eye can reach. Sparrman fays, that, having fhot at a large herd of them, they formed a line, and immediately made a circular movement, as if to furround him; but afterwards flew off in different directions.

The height of this beautiful creature is two feet and a

FIG. 132.

HISTORY OF QUADRUPEDS.

THE CHEVROTAIN AND MEMINNA.

The Chevrotain, or little Guinea Deer, is the smallest of all the Antelope kind, the least of all cloven-footed quadrupeds, and, we may add, the most beautiful. Its fore legs, at the smallest part, are not much thicker than a tobacco-pipe; it is not more than seven inches in height, and about twelve from the point of the nose to the insertion of the tail; its ears are broad; and its horns, which are straight, and scarcely two inches long, are black and shining as jet; the colour of the hair is a reddish-brown; in some a beautiful yellow, very short and glossy.

These elegant little creatures are natives of Senegal and the hottest parts of Africa; they are likewise found in India, and in many of the islands adjoining to that vast continent.

Fig. 133.

FIG. 134.—*Part of Fig. 133. Enlarged twice linear.*

"The intricacies of a natural scene (Fig. 134a — after Bewick) may be simplified when rendered in such a simple medium as the pen drawings of a MS. (comp. Fig. 134 b). Figs. 134 c & d are old examples of strong, simple drawing. Students should practise themselves by translating Figs. 132, 133 into fine, Quill-pen drawings."— (N. R.)

FIG. 134 c.

(This and Fig. 134 d are copies from a thirteenth century MS. in the possession of Mr. Yates-Thompson.)

FIG. 134 a.

ARVNDO, Græcis, Κάλαμος.] Arabibus, *Casab.*]
manis, *Roebr.*] Hispanis, *Canas*:] Gallis, *Cann*
ARVNDO.

Domes
Aqu
nien
Aru
bant

Satiua,
lis se
ad d
dinē
ac fit
com
la ge
mose
te. F,
lij I
vbiq
ta ci
illi e
bero
geni
quo
ctæq

Domes
rum
noso
quat
ueni

FIG. 135.—THE REED.

ASPARAGVS SYLVESTRIS.

Fig. 136.—Asparagus.

1.] Hispanis, *Lenteyas*.] Gallis, *Lentille*.

LENS.

FIG. 137.—THE LENTIL.

VITIS vinifera, Græcis, Αμπελος οινοφόρος.] Italis, bibus, *Harin Karin, seu Karm.*] Germanis, Vuein
VITIS VINIFERA.

Vitiun
adeò
ris, tɔ
libu
rusti
nê si
earu
stinɛ

Q
Folia
Idei

Folia δ
res
tion
horr
succ
exci
uida
dem
capi
velɔ
cress
lit,
pras
nat.
illit
max
sis sp
vnct
nes
& sa
litui
tis, ɪ
luxa
& cɩ
allin
ceto
scer
fem
dici
iest

FIG. 138.—THE VINE.

FIG. 139.—THE CARNATION.

PÆONIA FOEMINA.

FIG. 140.—THE PEONY.

PERSICA.

A.
o reperiuntur
enim rubent,
algent, aliis vi-
ili, alia sangui-
, alia duracina
niore fint pul-
n diducantur.
ia nuciperſica,
um faciem re-
itur. Sunt etiã
\ygdalam dul-
\ amygdala ap

A.
ſt foliis Amyg
ililibus, quem-
ius, quamuis
urpuraſcentes
nateries fragi-
tilles, nec alte
t fit, quod hæc
cat, & cadat.

S.
\ in Italia, ſed
ma prouenit.

TES.
cêtem habent
1. Alioqui ſa-
medicamen-
o eius, nempe
ſicum, humi-
r temperie

S.
cohibent, ſed
. Decoctum e
qi fluxiones ſi
unt, & quæ ſa-
¶ Flores re-
a ſolum aluũ
uones quoq;
srum aquam
ſque ægrotantium incommodo. Lacryma arboris datur ex plantaginis,
ad ſanguinis reiectiones. tuſſientibus verò, & anheloſis ex Tuſſilaginis
nento rfacit quoq; ad raucedinem, & arteriæ impedimenta. Datur calcu-
hæc, aut limonum, duarum drachmarum pondere. Recentia folia illi-

FIG. 141.—THE PEACH.

PART II
LETTERING

CHAPTER XIV
GOOD LETTERING SOME METHODS OF CONSTRUCTION & ARRANGEMENT

Good Models

If lettering is to be rightly constructed and arranged, the study of good models is essential. Some of the writing and lettering in the old MSS., and the letters used on various old tombstones and brasses, weeded of archaisms, will be found almost perfect models. Yet to select one of these from the many which are "more or less" good, requires much discrimination.

It is suggested below that the essential virtues of good lettering are readableness, beauty, and character. If, then, we can discover some of the underlying qualities which make for these, our choice will at least be better considered, and instead of forming our "style" on the first type of letter that pleases, we shall found our work on a good model, full of possibilities of development.

METHODS OF THE ROMAN CAPITAL (Chap. XV.) — The ancestor of all our letters is in undisputed possession of the first place: but it is open to comparatively few to make a practical study of its monumental forms by means of cutting inscriptions in stone with a chisel.

The Pen-formed letters are more easily practised, and the mastery of the pen acquired in the practice of a root form — such as the half-uncial — is the key to the majority of alphabets (which are pen developed) and to those principles underlying the right construction and arrangement of lettering, which it is our business to discover.

Doubtless a "school" of lettering might be founded on any fine type, and a beautiful alphabet or fine hand might be founded on any fine inscription: but the practical student of penmanship may be sure of acquiring a knowledge of lettering which would be useful to any craftsman concerned with letters, be he printer, book-illustrator, engraver, or even inscription carver.

The Qualities Of Good Lettering

The first general virtue of lettering is readableness, the second, fitness for a given Use. And the rational basis of the following summary is the assumption that such fitness is comprised in beauty and character, and that a given piece of lettering having readableness, beauty, and character has the essential virtues of good lettering.

The qualities on which these virtues seem chiefly to depend, and their special significations in the case of plain writing, may be set forth as follows: —

THE QUALITIES OF GOOD WRITING
READABLENESS

RIGHT FORM

1. Simplicity: As having no unnecessary parts (and as being simply arranged: See 6)
2. Distinctiveness: As having the distinguishing characteristics of each letter strongly marked (and the words distinctly arranged: See 6).
3. Proportion: As having no part of a letter wrongly exaggerated or dwarfed (and as the lettering being proportionally arranged: See 6).

BEAUTY

4. Beauty of Form: As having beautiful shapes and constructions, so that each letter is an individual and living whole (not a mere collection of parts) fitted for the position, office, and material of the object bearing the inscription.
5. Beauty of Uniformity: As the assimilation of the corresponding parts — "bodies," "limbs," "heads"— and as the "family likeness" of the different letters, so that they go well together.

RIGHT ARRANGEMENT

6. Beauty of Arrangement: As having a general fitness in the placing, connecting, and spacing of letters, words, and lines, in the disposal of the lettering in the given space, and in the proportioning of every part of the lettering and its margins.

CHARACTER

RIGHT EXPRESSION

7. Essential qualities of (Hand and Pen) work: As being genuine calligraphy, the direct outcome of a rightly made and rightly handled. (See p. 209.)
8. Freedom: As having skilled and unaffected boldness. (See pp. 79, 250, 246, 283-84.)
9. Personality: As having the characteristics which distinguish one person's hand from another's. (See also pp. 209, 246.)

This summary, while not presuming to define the Virtues, or achieve Beauty by a formula, does indicate some guiding principles for the letter-maker, and does suggest a definite meaning which may be given to the terms "Right Form," "Right Arrangement," and "Right Expression," in a particular craft.

It is true that "Readableness" and "Character" are comprised in Beauty, in the widest sense; but it is useful here to distinguish them: Readableness as the only sound basis for a practical theory of lettering, and Character as the product of a particular hand & tool at work in a particular craft.

The above table, therefore, may be used as a test of the qualities of any piece of lettering — whether Manuscript, Printing, or Engraving — provided that the significations of those qualities on which "Character" depends be modified and adapted to each particular instance. It is however a test for general qualities only — such as may help us in choosing a model: for as to its particular virtue each work stands alone — judged by its merits — in spite of all rules.

Simplicity
(As having no unnecessary parts)

ESSENTIAL FORMS AND THEIR CHARACTERISATION — The "Essential Forms" may be defined briefly as the necessary parts (See p. 206). They constitute the skeleton or structural plan of an alphabet; and One of the finest things the letter-craftsman can do, is to make the Essential Forms of letters beautiful in themselves, giving them the character and finish which come naturally from a rightly handled tool.

If we take the "Roman" types — the letters with which we are most familiar — and draw them in single pencil strokes (as a child does when it "learns its letters"), we get a rough representation of their Essential Forms (See diagram, Fig. 142).

Such letters might be scratched with a point in wax or clay, and if so used in practice would give rise to fresh and characteristic developments,[53] but if we take a "square cut" pen which will give a thin horizontal stroke and a thick vertical stroke (Figs. 10 and 40), it will give us the "straight-pen" or simple written, essential forms of these letters (Fig. 143).

---

[53] In fact, our "small-letters" are the formalised result of the rapidly scratched Square Capitals of the Roman era (p. 2 & Fig. 3).

ABCDEFGHIK
LMNOPQRST
VXYZ + JUW later forms

Square Capitals.

ðehmu + ntw late forms

Round Capitals.

aabcdefghiklm
nopqrstuvxyz {jw ш + 3

Small Letters.

A rough Diagram of the structural or "ESSENTIAL FORMS" of the three main types of Letters.

FIG. 142.

> ABCDEFGHI
> KLMNOPQRS
> TVXYZ & JUW
> Square Capitals. (pen forms).
>
> dehmunt
> Round Capitals. (v. Uncials).
>
> aabcdefghikl
> mnopqrst uvx
> yz&jwɯʒ Small Letters.
>
> A Diagram of the "ESSENTIAL FORMS"
> (of the three main types) AS   ┼
> produced by a "straight Pen"

FIG. 143.

These essential forms of straight-pen letters when compared with the plain line forms show a remarkable degree of interest, brought about by the introduction of the thin and thick strokes and gradated curves, characteristic of pen work.

Certain letters (A, K, M, N, V, W, X, Y, and k, v, w, x, y) in Fig. 143 being composed chiefly of oblique strokes, appear rather heavy. They are lightened by using a naturally "slanted" pen which produces thin as well as thick oblique strokes. And the verticals in M and N are made thin by further slanting the pen (Fig. 144).

> AKMNVW
> Oblique-stroke Letters — as
> X Y & S & kvwxys
> produced by a "Slanted Pen"
> from the "ESSENTIAL FORMS"

FIG. 144.

To our eyes, accustomed to a traditional finish, all these forms — in Figs. 143 and 144, but particularly the slanted pen forms — look incomplete and unfinished; and it is obvious that the thin strokes, at least, require marked terminals or serifs.

FINISHING-STROKES — The pen naturally produces a variety of finishing-strokes — "heads," "feet," serifs, &c. — each type of which strongly characterises the alphabet in which it is employed.

The main types (Fig. 145) are —

(a) Hooks or beaks,
(b) Straight (or curved) strokes, thick or thin according to the direction of the pen.
(c) Triangular "heads" (and "feet"), straight or slanted, and more or less curved and sharpened.
(d) Thin finishing-curves, horizontal or oblique.

To give uniformity to the various letters of an alphabet it is necessary to treat similar parts as consistently as possible throughout (See No. 5, p. 175). And the remarkable way in which "heads" impart a "family likeness" to letters closely resembles the same phenomenon among human beings (See pp. 247, 188).

FIG. 145.

Straight-pen forms of serifs & Square ends +

Slanted-pen forms of serifs & oblique ends ×

If we consider the four types of serif, as applicable to straight-pen writing, we find —

(a) Hooks or Beaks
(d) Thin Finishing-Curves
} Suitable for only certain parts of certain letters (and for informal writing)

(b) Straight (or Curved) THIN Strokes
} Informal or (Ornamental)

(c) Triangular "Heads"
} Formal and capable of imparting great elegance & finish

For a formal, straight-pen writing, therefore, we may assume that a form of triangular head is, on the whole, the most suitable, while some of the letters may be allowed to end naturally in finishing hooks and curves.

Heads are easily built up at the ends of thick fettering — strokes, but some practice is required to enable a penman to make them on the thin strokes properly and skillfully. On the thin horizontals they are made with an almost continuous movement of the point of the nib from the thin stroke itself (See (a) to (h) Fig 146) closely resembling the termination of some of the thin strokes in the Irish half-uncial (Plate VI.). On the thin oblique or vertical stems, a thin crossing stroke is first made, and then shaped with the pen point to meet the stem (See (i) and (k) Fig. 146).

horizontal (a.)   pen turns here (c.) on to left half-nib point (d.) which runs up
& curve (b.)

"head" (or Serif) filled in (e.)   Reverse head: Above action is reversed (f.)   Combined head: Actions combined (g.)

E. shewing three heads (h.)   Heads on obliques (i) and on vertical thins. (k.)   Heads on vertical thicks (l. m.)

FIG. 146.

We may write out the letters now with their suitable serifs, and we see that the Pen character and finish, given to the "Essential, or Skeleton, Forms" (Fig. 142) result in a very formal and highly finished alphabet (Fig. 147).

Slanted-pen characters and serifs (See Fig. 145)—

(a) Hooks or Beaks
(d) Thin Finishing-Curves
} Suitable for most of the letters, but tending to be informal

(b) Straight (or Curved) THICK Strokes
} Formal and strong

(c) Triangular "Heads"
} Formal and suitable for small-letters, and free capitals (See Fig. 168)

The alphabets (Fig. 148), produced from the skeleton forms (Fig. 142) by the slanted pen, while not having such a conscious air of finish as the straight- pen letters, are much easier to write, and have in a greater degree the virtues of strong,[54] legible, natural penmanship.

They are eminently suitable for general MS. work (See p. 230) when the beginner has mastered an early form of round-hand (See pp. 35, 229).

Distinctiveness
(As having the distinguishing characteristics of each letter strongly marked)

The "Characteristic Parts" are those parts which most particularly serve to distinguish one letter from another (Fig. 149). We should therefore, when constructing letters, give special attention to their preservation, and sometimes they may even be accentuated with advantage — always with an eye to the life-history, or evolution, of the letter in question, and allowing for the influence of the special tool with which it is to be made (See Proportion, below).

---

[54] Their greater strength may not at first be apparent in Fig. 148, as the nib used therefor is narrower, in proportion to the height of letter, than that used for Fig. 147 (See also Fig. 151).

ABCDEFG
HIJKLMN
OPQRST&
UVWXYZ
abcdefghij
klmnopqrs
tuvwxyz;ȝ:
Formal types of Letters 1904
produced chiefly by "Straight-PEN" +

FIG. 147.

ABCDEFG
HIJKLMN
OPQRST&
UVWXYZ

abcdefghij
klmnopqrs
tuvwxyz:ʒ:

"Slanted-Pen" characterization of Letters.

FIG. 148.

FIG. 149.

Proportion
(As having no part of a letter wrongly exaggerated or dwarfed — See pp. 205, 208-09)

The right proportioning of letters entails the preservation of their Essential Forms and their Characteristic Parts, and, provided these are not seriously interfered with, a certain amount of exaggeration (and dwarfing)[55] is allowable in special cases; particularly in ornamental writings, and Pen-flourished capitals or terminal letters (See Figs. 79 and 125).

---

[55] The exaggeration of one part may be said relatively to dwarf the other parts of a letter; but it is seldom advantageous, and often not permissible, to dwarf part of a letter absolutely.

Rational exaggeration usually amounts to the drawing out or flourishing of tails or free stems, or branches — very often to the magnifying of a characteristic part (See Fig. 150, & pp. 184, 252). It is a special form of decoration, and very effective if used discriminately.

FIG. 150.

Beauty Of Form

(As having beautiful shapes and constructions, so that each letter is an individual and living whole (not a mere collection of parts) fitted for the position, office, and material of the object bearing the inscription)

To choose or construct beautiful forms requires good taste, and that in its turn requires cultivation, which comes from, the observation of beautiful forms. Those who are not accustomed to seeing beautiful things are, in consequence, often uncertain whether they think a thing beautiful or not.

Some — perhaps all of us — have an intuition for what is beautiful; but most of us have to achieve beauty by taking pains.

At the least we are apt to be misled if we label abstract forms as essentially beautiful or essentially ugly — as by a mistaken recipe for beauty. For us as craftsmen "achieving beauty by taking pains," means acquiring skill in a special craft and adapting that skill to a special piece of work. And perhaps the surest way to learn, is to let our tools and materials teach us and, as it were, make beautiful shapes for us.

"Inside Shapes"— The beauty of a letter depends very much on its inside shape — i.e. the shape of the space enclosed by the letter form. As this is often overlooked, it may be briefly referred to. Frequently when it seems difficult to say what is wrong with a piece of bad lettering, a glance at the inside shapes will reveal the fault. In simple writing, if the pen be properly cut and properly held, these shapes will generally take care of themselves, and internal angles or asymmetrical lines which occur are characteristic of that particular form of penmanship, and not accidental (b, Fig. 151).

aon (a.) +
Inside shapes: round-ness & symmetry.
angles
I.S. tend to angular-ity & asymmetry. (b.) ×

FIG. 151.

In making Built-up letters — which have both outer and inner strokes — the inner strokes should generally be made first (See p. 78).

PLAIN AND ORNAMENTAL FORMS — Not only for the sake of readableness, but to promote a beautiful and dignified effect, the forms of letters are kept simple when the text is long. And, generally, the less frequent the type, the more ornamental may be its form (See pp. 81, 149, 226, 251).

Beauty Of Uniformity
(As the assimilation of the corresponding parts — "bodies," "limbs," "heads" — and as the "family likeness," of the different letters, so that they go well together)

Right uniformity makes for readableness and beauty, and is the result of good craftsmanship.

READABLENESS — Where the text letters are uniform, the reader is free to give his attention to the sense of the words, whereas the variations in an irregular or changing text are distracting.[56]

BEAUTY — The abstract beauty-of-uniformity may be said to lie in this, that the different letters, or individual elements, "go well together." The beautiful effect of uniform lettering is thus caused by the united forces, as it were, of all the letters.

GOOD CRAFTSMANSHIP — A pen, or other letter-making tool, being handled freely and regularly, the uniform movements of the tool in similar cases will produce uniform strokes, &c. (On the other hand, the interruption and loss of freedom to the writer who is irregular, or who forces an unnatural variety,[57] results in inferior work.)

---

[56] As when the construction of a part of some letter is peculiar (all the y or g tails, for example, catching the eye, and standing out on the page), or, as when promiscuous types are used, giving the impression of a confused crowd of letters.

[57] Variety. — There is a variety both readable and beautiful (See pp. 210, 369), but it is founded on uniformity (and sincerity).

Right Arrangement

BEAUTY OF ARRANGEMENT } (As having a general fitness in the placing, connecting, and spacing of letters, words, and lines, in the disposal of the lettering in the given space, and in the proportioning of every part of the lettering and its margins)

The particular fitness of a given inscription depends upon considerations of its particular office, position, material, &c. (See pp. 100, 351). For general use, however, the craftsman has certain regular modes of disposing and spacing the lettering, and proportioning the whole. And, as in constructing individual letters, so in treating lettering as a whole, he endeavours to give his work the qualities that make for readableness: viz. simplicity, distinctiveness, and proportion.

Simplicity in the Disposal of the Lettering. — For convenience of construction, reading, or handling, the simple, traditional arrangement of lettering is generally followed in dealing with flat surfaces (paper, vellum, &c.):[58] —

THE TEXT FORMING
A RECTANGAL CON-
SISTING OF A NUM-
BER OF EQUAL LINES

Good Distinctiveness in the Spacing of the Lettering necessitates sufficient interspaces: the following common spacing of Letters, Words, Lines, &c., may be modified to suit special circumstances.

- Letters, as a rule, are not equidistant, but their interspaces are approximately equal (a, Fig. 152).

- Words, commonly one letter-space apart (b and c).

---

[58] "Bands" and symmetrical or asymmetrical groups of lettering adapted to the available space are used — usually as ornament — upon friezes, furniture, chests, book covers, flagons, dishes, and the like (See Fig. 156 & p. 258). The special treatment of such things is a matter for the craftsman who makes them.

- Lines of Capitals, frequently half (d) or whole (e) letter-height apart. Lines of Small-Letters, commonly ascenders and descenders just clearing (f).
- Divisions of Text a clear line apart, or marked by a difference in colour or size (See Figs. 94, 96, 186, &c.)

Proportion in the Treatment of the Whole Inscription. — The spacing-proportions referred to above apply to lettering generally, but the proportions of an inscription as a whole involve the consideration of a special case. Example: —

The Proportions to be Considered in the Case of a Manuscript Book (See pp. 100-108, 341, &c.)	
(1) Size and shape of the Book and its page (proportion of width to height) (See p. 63).	(Set by custom, use of Book, size of material, &c.) (See Figs. 69, 70, and pp. 61, &c.).
(2) Width of Margins — Proportions — (a) to each other. (b) to size of page. (c) to the lettering.	(a) (Commonly about 1½:2:3:4) (See Fig. 70, and pp. 63-7). (b) (Frequently about, or more than, half the area of the page).
(3) Size of Writing — Proportion of height of letter to length of line.	(Set by page, and margin, and number of words in the line; usually more than four words to the line) (See pp. 65-6).
(4) Number of lines — Proportion of text to page.	(Set by page, margin, and height-of-letter, and modified by treatment of spacing) (See pp. 67, 195).
(5) Size of Large Capitals, Initials, &c.	(Set by Small-Letter; commonly one, two, three, or more of the writing - line - spaces high) (See footnote, p. 159).
6) Size of Decorative Divisions of the Text (marked by different treatment, colour, ornament, &c.).	(Set by page, &c.; usually such Division is relatively small or large — as a definite "heading," or a whole page) (See p. 87).

FIG. 152.
R

Setting Out, & Fitting In

RULING — The approximate sizes of margins and letters, and the number of lines of text, having been estimated, guiding lines are ruled on the surface (See p. 264) — a right and a left vertical marginal line, with the necessary number of horizontals between them. (In the case of a manuscript, these lines are ruled faintly (or grooved), and are left to form a feature of the page; for inscriptions on other materials than paper, parchment, &c., they are generally removed after setting-out.)

SETTING-OUT — An inscription of any size, or one requiring complex or very nice arrangement, is set-out in faint, sketchy outline of lead pencil or chalk. Simple writing is not set-out, but such slight calculation or planning as is necessary is carried out mentally, or on a scrap of paper. By practice the scribe, like the compositor, can fit his lettering to the given space with ease and accuracy. For writing and (to a large extent) printing, both combine setting-out and the act of "lettering" in one operation. And this shows how practice gives foreknowledge of the "mechanical" part of the work, leaving the mind free to take pleasure in its performance; and also how slight — if necessary at all — is the experimental setting-out of simple forms required by the practised workman.

DIVIDING MONOSYLLABLES — In simple writing — the beauty of which depends on freedom rather than on precision — I think that even such an awkward word as "through" should not be broken. If the space at the end of a line is insufficient, it should be left blank, or be filled in with a dash of the pen. But in the case of words in LARGE CAPITALS, especially in title-pages and the like, where spacing is more difficult, and smooth reading less essential, any word may be divided at any point if the necessity is sufficiently obvious. But (even when the division is syllabic) breaking words, as interfering with the ease of reading, may often be avoided with advantage, and divisions which give accidental words, especially when they are objectionable, as "TH-ROUGH," or "NEIGH-BOUR," should not be allowed. Among other ways of dealing with small spaces, without breaking words, are the following: —

ENDING WITH SMALLER LETTERS — The scribe is always at liberty to compress his writing slightly, provided he does not spoil its readableness or beauty. Occasionally, without harming either of these, a marked difference in size of letter may be allowed; one or more words, or a part of one, or a single letter, being made smaller (a, b, Fig. 153; See also Plate V.).

MONOGRAMMATIC FORMS, SEC. — In any kind of lettering, but more particularly in the case of capitals, where the given space is insufficient for the given capitals, monogrammatic forms resembling the ordinary diphthong Æ may be used; or the stem of one letter may be drawn out, above or below, and formed into another (c, Fig. 153).

LINKING — Letters which are large enough may be linked or looped together, or one letter may be set inside another, or free-stem letters may be drawn up above the line (d, Fig. 153).

TYING UP — One or more words at the end of a line of writing — particularly in poetry (See p. 55) — may be "tied up," i.e. be written above or below the line, with a pen stroke to connect them to it (Fig. 67).

Care must be taken that none of these methods lead to confusion in the reading. Their "Quaintness"— as it is sometimes called — is only pleasing when their contrivance is obviously made necessary.

AVOIDING
breaking *a.* words,
by writing smaller.
b.

MONOGRAMMATIC
TREATMEN:IF HE
SPACE DEMANDS IT *c.*

LOOPS:& *d.*
INSET LETTERS:& TALL:

FIG. 153.

"Massed Writing" & "Fine Writing"

We may distinguish two characteristic modes of treating an inscription, in which the treatment of the letter is bound up with the treatment of the spacing (Fig. 154).

"MASSED WRITING" (CLOSE SPACING) — The written or printed page is very commonly set close, or "massed," so that the letters support and enforce one another, their individual beauty being merged in and giving beauty to the whole. The closeness of the letters in each word keeps the words distinct, so that but little space is required between them,[59] and the lines of writing are made close together (ascending and descending stems being shortened, if necessary, for this purpose).

> And if I bestow all my goods to feed the poor, and if I give my body that I may glory, but have not love, it profit= eth me nothing.
>
> Love suffereth long, and is kind; love envieth not; love vaunteth not itself, is not puffed up,

FIG. 154.

---

[59] By closing up the letters and the words one may generally avoid "rivers," or accidental spaces straggling through the text. The presence of "rivers" is at once made evident by slanting the page and looking along its surface, across the lines. Note, that whether the lines be close or wide, the interspacing of the Small-Letters does not vary very much.

"FINE WRITING" (WIDE SPACING) — An inscription in "Fine Writing" may be spaced widely to display the finished beauty of the letters, or to give free play to the penman (or letter-craftsman). It consists generally of a number of distinct lines of Writing (or other lettering).

The two modes may be contrasted broadly, thus —

MASSED WRITING / Lines near together.	FINE WRITING / Lines spaced and separated.
Has an effect of richness, depending on tone of mass and close, even spacing.	Has an effect of elegance, depending on form of letters and distinct arrangement of lines.
Simple method (for ordinary use); saving of time and space, ∴ suited for long inscriptions or small spaces.	Refined method (for special use); lavish of space and time, ∴ suited for large spaces or short inscriptions.
Lines generally of equal length, or if some fall short, end-fillings may be used — gaps are avoided if possible.	Lines may be of unequal length, giving irregular, right-hand edge, as in poetry (See p. 196) — gaps allowed on either side.
Ascending and descending stems — medium or short: serifs simple, and not strongly marked.	Stems — medium or long: long stems often a marked feature, ending in carefully made heads and feet, or flourishes.
Suited for slanted-pen forms of "gothic" tendency, and heavy, black writing (example, "black letter").*	Suited for straight and slanted pen forms of "roman" tendency, and slender, light writing (example, "Italic").*
Requires generally contrasts of colour or weight (p. 251), and will bear more and heavier illumination (Line-fillings, Initials, Borders, &c.).	Allows variety in size of Letters (See pp. 226, 251): its typical treatment is as plain, fine lettering — better without heavy Borders, &c. (p. 226).

*NOTE-Both modes are suited for Roman Capitals and Small-Letters.

These two modes may not have been recognised by the ancient letter-craftsmen: their comparison here is intended chiefly as a stimulus to definite thought, not as a hard-and-fast division of two "styles"; for there may be any number of possible compromises between them. In practice, however, it will be found convenient to distinguish them as two modes of treating lines of writing which produce markedly different effects, the one, as it were, of COLOUR, the other of FORM.

Plates XI., XIII., XIV., XV., XVII. may be taken as examples of "Massed Writing," Plates IV., V., VI., VIL., IX., (XXI.) of "Fine Writing"; the other plates suggest compromises between the two.

Poetry (See p. 55), or any text consisting of, or which is conveniently broken up into unequal lines, may be treated as "Fine Writing." There is no objection to a straight left-hand edge with an irregular right-hand edge[60], where the cause of the irregularity is natural and obvious, and no fault of the scribe's. Such an arrangement, or rather, straightforward writing, of poetry is often the best by virtue of its freedom and simplicity (See p. 282).

In many cases, however, a more formal and finished treatment of an irregular line text is to be preferred (especially in inscriptions on stone, metal, &c.), and the most natural arrangement is then an approximately symmetrical one, inclining to "Fine Writing" in treatment. This is easily obtained in inscriptions which are previously set-out, but a good plan — certainly the best for MSS. — is to sort the lines of the text into longs and shorts (and sometimes medium lines), and to set-in or indent the short lines two, three, or more letters. The indentations on the left balance the accidental irregularities on the right (Fig. 154, and Plate IV.), and give an appearance of symmetry to the page (See Phrasing, p. 296).

Either mode of spacing (close or wide) may be carried to an unwise or ridiculous extreme. "Leading" the lines of type was much in vogue a hundred years ago, in what was then regarded as "high-class" printing. Too often the wide-spaced line and "grand" manner of the eighteenth-century printer was pretentious rather than effective: this was partly due to the degraded type which he used, but form, arrangement, and expression all tended to be artificial. Of late years a rich, closely massed page has again become fashionable. Doubtless there has been a reaction in this from the eighteenth century to an earlier and better manner, but the effect is sometimes overdone, and the real ease and comfort of the reader has been sacrificed to his rather imaginary aestheticism.

---

[60] The gaps on the right may be filled with line-finishings to preserve a "Massed" effect, but for many purposes this would be apt to look too ornamental (See pp. 145, 328).

By attaching supreme importance to readableness, the letter-craftsman gains at least a rational basis for his work, and is saved from the snares which lurk in all, even in the best, modes and fashions.

CONSIDER
WHENCE EACH THING
IS COME & OF WHAT
IT CONSISTS & INTO
WHAT IT CHANGES:

CONSIDER.
WHENCE EACH THING
IS COME & OF WHAT
IT CONSISTS & INTO
WHAT IT CHANGES.

CONSIDER
WHENCE EACH THING
IS COME & OF WHAT
IT CONSISTS & INTO
WHAT IT CHANGES

FIG. 155.

Even Spacing

In the spacing of a given inscription on a limited surface, where a comparatively large size of letter is required, what little space there is to spare should generally be distributed evenly and consistently (a, Fig. 155). Lavish expenditure of space on the margins would necessitate an undue crowding[61] of the lettering (b), and wide interspacing[62] would allow insufficient margins (c) — either arrangement suggesting inconsistency (but See p. 270).

Note. — A given margin looks larger the heavier the mass of the text[63] and smaller the lighter the mass of the text. And, therefore, if lettering be spread out, as in "Fine Writing," the margins should be extra-wide to have their true comparative value. The space available for a given inscription may in this way largely determine the arrangement of the lettering, comparatively small and large spaces suggesting respectively "Massed Writing" and "Fine Writing" (See p. 195).

THE LETTERS MAY BE KEPT VERY CLOSE, FORMING ORNAMENTAL BANDS, THO' THE LINES MAY BE WIDELY SPACED.

OR THE LETTERS MAY BE FAR APART & THE LINES CLOSE.

FIG. 156.

---

[61] In (b) Fig. 155, the letters have been unintentionally narrowed. The natural tendency to do this forms another objection to such undue crowding.

[62] In (c) the letters have been unintentionally widened.

[63] Experiment. — Cut out a piece of dark brown paper the exact size of the body of the text in an entire page of this Handbook, viz. $5^{1}/_{16}$ inches by 3 inches, and lay it on the text: the tone of the brown paper being much darker than that of the print makes the margins appear wider.

In certain decorative inscriptions, where letters are merely treated as decorative forms — readableness being a matter of little or no moment — the treatment of the spacing is adapted to a particular surface; and, for example: —

Theory & Practice

The above discussion of theories and "rules" for the construction and arrangement of good lettering is intended to suggest some useful methods — not to provoke excessive fitting or planning, but rather to avoid it. Straightforwardness is perhaps the greatest virtue in a craft, and whatever "rules" it may break through, it is refreshing and charming.

An excellent example for the scribe or inscription maker is the method of an early printer, who had only four or five sorts of type — say, "Small-Letters" and "Capitals" (Roman and Italic) and "Large Capitals," and who, without any elaborate "design," simply put his types into their proper places, and then pulled off his pleasant sheets of "commonplace" printing.

The scribe should choose the best and simplest forms and arrangements, and master them before going further; he should have a few definite types "at his fingertips," and, for everyday use, a matter-of-course way of putting them down on paper.

Ambiguity is one of the greatest faults in a craft. It comes often from vague ambitions. One may be inspired by good ambitions, but the immediate concern of the craftsman is to know what he is capable of doing at the present, and to do it.

Let the meaning of your work be obvious unless it is designed purely for your own amusement. A good craftsman seeks out the commonplace and tries to master it, knowing that "originality" comes of necessity, and not of searching.

CHAPTER XV
THE ROMAN ALPHABET & ITS DERIVATIVES

The Roman Alphabet

The Roman Alphabet is the foundation of all our alphabets (See Chapter I.). And since the full development of their monumental forms about 2000 years ago, the Roman Capitals have held the supreme place among letters for readableness and beauty. They are the best forms for the grandest and most important inscriptions, and, in regard to lettering generally, a very good rule to follow is: When in doubt, use Roman Capitals.

The penman may with advantage devote some study to a fine monumental type of Roman Capital (such as that of the Trajan Column Inscription: Plates I. and II.), and endeavour to embody its virtues in a built-up pen form for use in MSS. (p. 222).

Proportions Of Letters: Widths

The marked distinction between the "Square" and the "Round" forms, and the varying widths of the letters — as seen in the early inscriptions,[64] are characteristic of the Roman Alphabet. We may broadly distinguish Wide and Narrow letters thus —

WIDE {	O Q C G D M W H (U) A N V T (Z)	} "Round" "Square"
NARROW {	B E F R S Y (X) I J K L P	

---

[64] Such inscriptions contrast favourably with that Nineteenth Century style in which it was customary to make every letter occupy the same space and look as much like its neighbour as possible.

The "Round" Wide Letters. — O, Q, C ,G, D. — **O** may be regarded as the key letter of any alphabet. Given and O and an I of any alphabet, we can make a very good guess at the forms of the other letters.

In fine Inscriptions the external line of O is commonly an almost perfect circle (See Plate II.) — i.e. its height and width are equal. This may be regarded as the ideal shape, though a slight widening or narrowing of the letter (Fig. 157) is quite permissible.[65]

FIG. 157.

Q, C, G, and D follow the proportions of O very nearly, and, though C, G, D are a little narrower, they have the same effect of roundness and width.

The "Square" Wide Letters — M, W, and H, (U), A, N, V, T, (Z) —

---

[65] Note. — There is less danger of spoiling letters by narrowing them than by widening, because the limits to the possible narrowing of a letter are more obvious than the limits to its possible widening. Further, when letters are widened there is a tendency to thicken their parts and make them heavy and vulgar.

M & W Their mean width is properly about equal to their height.

H Width equal to, or a little less than, height (Fig. 158), but if made too narrow it would look heavy, being double-stemmed.

FIG. 158.

U (See pp. 287, 284) resembles H.

A, N, & V are double-stemmed, and have internal angles, moreover, which would become too sharp — and tend to close up — if they were made too narrow (Fig. 158).

T The cross-bar — the characteristic part of T — projects a fair way on either side of the stem.

Z Either wide or (moderately) narrow (Fig. 158).

The Narrow Letters, B, E, F, R, S, Y, (X) (See Fig. 159).

BERS X

B.E.R.S. width is approximately half the height.

narrow X

wide x.

FIG. 159.

There is a point of division in these letters about the middle of the stem or a little above (See p. 207), and we may argue that each being composed, as it were, of two little letters — which are half-height, they are proportionately half-width: and this will be found approximately correct. **B** may be said to consist of one little D on the top of another, averaging respectively half the height and width of a full-sized D.

E, F, & R follow the proportions of B (See also E, 4, p. 213).

S may be made of one little tilted O on the top of another — joined together and having the superfluous parts removed.

Y is like a little V upon a little I.

X Either narrow or wide (Fig. 159).

The Narrow letters, K, L, and P —

212

These forms are related to the B, E forms, but it is permissible to make them a little wider to give clearance to the angles of the **K** and force to the single arm and loop — the characteristic parts (See Fig. 149)— of **L** and **P**.

Upper & Lower Parts

In the letters B, E, H, K, X (A), F, R, P (S), Y there is generally a tendency to enlarge the lower part, the cross-bar — or division — being set above mid-height. This tendency may reasonably be accounted for as follows:—

The natural division of **B, E, H, K, & X,** regarded as abstract forms, would be symmetrical — i.e. at the centre of the stem.[66] In order that its apparent position may be central, however, it is necessary, for optical reasons, to make its actual position above the centre.[67] And further, by a reasonable enlargement of the lower part, these letters acquire a greater appearance of stability.

It would be well, I think, for the letter-craftsman to begin by making such divisions at the apparent centre (i.e. very slightly above mid-height; See E, F, X, Plate II.), so keeping most nearly to the essential forms (See p. 206). Later he might consider the question of stability (See B, Plate II.). The exaggerated raising (or lowering) of the division associated with "Art Lettering" is illegible and ridiculous.

A The lower part is essentially bigger, and the cross-bar is not raised, as that would make the top part disproportionately small.

---

[66] The primitive forms of these letters were vertically symmetrical, I believe.

[67] It is interesting to note in this connection that the eye seems to prefer looking upon the tops of things, and in reading, is accustomed to run along the tops of the letters — not down one stroke and up the next. This may suggest a further reason for smaller upper parts, viz. the concentration of as much of the letter as possible in the upper half.

F usually follows E, but being asymmetrical and open below it may, if desired, be made with the bar at — or even slightly below — the actual centre.

R In early forms the bow was frequently rather large (See Plate II.), but it is safer to make the tail — the characteristic part — more pronounced (See Plates III., XXIV.).

P The characteristic part of P is the bow, which may therefore be a little larger than the bow of R (See Plate III.).

S in the best types of this letter the upper and lower parts are approximately equal; there is a tendency slightly to enlarge the lower part. (In Uncial and early round-hands the top part was larger: See Plates IV. to VII.)

Y varies: the upper part may be less than that of X, or somewhat larger.

Essential Or Structural Forms

The essential or structural forms (See p. 177) are the simplest forms which preserve the characteristic structure, distinctiveness, and proportions of each individual letter.

The letter-craftsman must have a clear idea of the skeletons of his letters. While in every case the precise form which commends itself to him is matter for his individual choice, it is suggested in the following discussion of a typical form — the Roman B — that the rationale of his selection (whether conscious or unconscious) is in brief to determine what is absolutely essential to a form, and then how far this may be amplified in the direction of the practically essential.

The letter B reduced to its simplest (curved- bow) form — i.e. to the bare necessity of its distinctive structure — comprises a perpendicular item spanned by two equal, circular bows (a, Fig. 160).

In amplifying such a form for practical or aesthetic reasons, it is well as a rule not to exceed one's object — in this case to determine a reasonable (though arbitrary) standard essential form of B, having a distinctive and proportionate (f) structure. We may increase the arcs of the bows till their width is nearly equal to their height (b), make their outer ends meet the ends of the stem (c), and their inner ends coincide (d). Raising the division till its apparent position is at or about the middle of the stem entails a proportionate increase of width in the lower part, and a corresponding decrease in the upper part (e).

Suggested method of determining "Essential Form" of Capital B.

FIG. 160.

The very idea of an essential form excludes the unnecessary, and its further amplification is apt to take from its distinctiveness and legibility.

Where no limits are set, modification is apt to become exaggeration. And, though special forms and ornamental letters may be produced by "reasonable exaggeration" (k, l, m, Fig. 161), if the tool be kept under proper control, yet, generally, such structural changes do not improve the appearance of the plain letter forms.

ARBITRARY "Standard"
Essential = B = Form of B.
Having a "distinctive
and proportionate structure"
(a.)

The Dangers of a tendency to exaggeration of any feature

b. c. d. e.

are

f. g. h. i.

disproportion and indistinctness

k. l. m.

Note: a larger degree of exaggeration is permissible in Ornamental Forms.

FIG. 161.

We may test our "Standard" (a, Fig. 161) by considering the effects of further amplification.

1. Raising the division[68] slightly is permissible (b, Fig 161) — too much makes the top part disproportionately small (c).

2. Widening both bows, or separating their junction from the stem, tends to dissociate the bows from the stem, making the letter less distinctive (g and i, Fig. 161).

Widening and narrowing are both allowable and occasionally desirable, but assuming that a standard or ideal width can be approximately determined, it is well to keep to it for common and ordinary use.

Characterisation Of Forms
(See also Built- Up Forms, pp. 220-25, and pp. 177, 187)

That the tool[69] gives character and finish to the Essential Forms of letters, can easily be proved by a little practical experience of the natural action of a properly cut pen (See Figs. 142 to 148, and 162). And the penman — or indeed any other letter-maker — is advised to allow the pen to train his hand to make the proper strokes automatically: then he may begin to master and control the pen, making it conform to his hand and so produce which have every possible virtue of penmanship and are as much his own as his common handwriting.

Most of the letters in a good alphabet have specially interesting or characteristic parts (p. 184), or they exhibit some general principles in letter making, which are worth noting, with a view to making good letters, and in order to understand better the manner in which the tool — whether pen, chisel, or brush — should be used.

---

[68] The extremely beautiful and finished B in the "Trajan Alphabet" (Plate II.) has the division a little higher, and a marked enlargement of the lower part; until the letter-craftsman can approach the perfection of its execution he will find a simpler form more suitable for his "standard." A curious form, in which the top lobe has nearly or quite disappeared {comp. c, Fig. 161), is found in early Roman inscriptions. This form (which may have helped to give us the useful small b) is not suitable for a modern Capital, and would lack the distinctiveness of B.

[69] Chisel-made Roman Capitals (possibly influenced by brush, &c, pp. 221, 304), Plates I., II.: (modern), XXIV. Pen-made, Plates III., XVIII.: (modern), Figs. 147, 148, 167, 168, &c.

FIG. 162.

The characterisation of the Roman Capital Form. Note. — The large types below are indices — not models.

A 1. A pointed form of A, M, and N (See Plate II.) may be suitable for inscriptions in stone, &c., but in pen work the top is preferably hooked (Fig. 167), beaked (Fig. 147), or broken (Fig. 158), or specially marked in some way, as this part (both in Capital A and small a) has generally been (Fig. 189).

2. The oblique strokes in A, K, M, N, R, V, W, X, Y, whether thick or thin, are naturally finished with a short point inside the letter and a long, sharp point, or beak, outside (See serifs of oblique strokes, p. 219).

3. The thin stem may be drawn out below for an occasional form (See F, 3).

B 1. B, D, R, and P are generally best made round-shouldered (Fig. 162 & Addenda, p. 26).

2. B, D, E, F, P, R (and T) have generally an angle between the stem and the top horizontal, while

3. below in B, D, E (and L) the stem curves or blends with the horizontal.

4. See O, 2.

C 1. C, G, and S: the top horizontals or 'arms' may be straighter than the lower arms, or vice versa (See Figs. 167 and 206).

2. C, G, and S: the inside curve is best continuous — from the 'bow' to the ends of the 'arms' — not being broken by the serifs, and

3. it is best to preserve an unbroken inside curve at the termination of all free arms and stems in built-up Roman Capitals. In C, G, S, E, F, L, T, and Z the upper and lower arms are curved on the inside, and squared or slightly pointed outside (the vertical stems curve on either side) (Fig. 163).

4. 'Arms' are best shaped and curved rather gradually out to the terminal or serif, which then is an actual part of the letter, not an added lump (p. 219)

5. See O, 2.

D
1. See B, 1.
2. See B, 2 and 3.
3. The curve may be considered as springing from the foot of the stem, and may therefore for an occasional form be separated from the stem at the top (D, Fig. 177).

4. See O, 2.

E
1. See B, 2 and 3.
2. See C, 3 and 4.
3. The lower limb in E, L (and Z) is often drawn out: these, however, are properly to be regarded as occasional or special forms: the lower serif of this type commonly points out (See Figs. 206, 188).

4. E's three arms (& F's two) are approximately equal in length in the best early forms (Plate II., &c.).

F
1. See B, 2.
2. See C, 3 and 4 (and E, 4 above).
3. One or more (the development of the letter and tradition may decide which) of the free stems of A, F, G, H, I, J, K, L, M, N, P, R, T, V, W, X, Y may be drawn out for occasional forms (See Fig. 188).

4. The elongated stems of F, I, J, P, T, Y may hang below the line, or they may (occasionally) stand on the line and overtop the other letters.

G
1. See C, 1, 2, 3, and 4.
2. The stem may be drawn out below the line (F, 3).
3. The stem sometimes forms an angle with the lower 'arm' (this is safest: See Fig. 148), sometimes they blend (Fig. 147).

4. The point of the lower 'arm' may project a very little beyond the stem to mark the outer angle.

5. The wholly curved "gothic" G and also the other round letters: See p. 76) may be introduced occasionally among Roman Capitals.

6. See O, 2.

H 1. The left-hand stem is occasionally drawn out above (F, 3 & comp. Fig. 3), and

2. this form is sometimes associated with an ornamental cross-bar (Fig. 189).

3. H and N may slightly widen out above.

I 1. The stem may be drawn out above or below (F, 3 and 4).

2. See J, 2.

J 1. The stem or tail may be drawn out (F, 3 and 4).

2. Note. — With regard to the use of I for J (and V for U): this is associated so much with the Latin usage, that it is perhaps permissible still in Latin.[70] But for modern English, in which these letters are strongly differentiated, the tailed J and the round U are to be preferred. Besides the suspicion of affectation attaching to the other mode, its strangeness gives an appearance of awkwardness — almost amounting to illegibility — to common words, such as "A QVAINT IVG" or "IAM IAR." And, at the least,

---

[70] J. C. Egbert in an "Introduction to the Study of Latin Inscriptions" says, "J was not specialised as a letter until the 15th century." It would seem that in early inscriptions a tall I was frequently used for J between vowels, and for I at the beginnings of words: later, while the medial I remained straight, the initial form was curved to the left and used for both I and J; this curved initial form, J, at length became identified with the letter J.

Similarly, it appears that V was used for an initial, and U for a medial; and later, the V form became identified with the consonant.

In the words in Fig. 95, the initial I is curved like a J, while the medial i's are straight; the initial V has a v form, while the medial V in nativ (itatis) has a u form.

very careful discrimination is desirable: "IVBILATE" may pass, but "IVIVBE" is not really readable.

3. The tail of the J may be slight, provided it be distinct, and the second stem of the U may match the first (Fig. 158); the ugly **J** and **U** in common use need not be copied.

4. See also Tails, pp. 219-220.

K 1. The stem is sometimes drawn out above (F, 3).

2. Both arms are occasionally lengthened, and the width of the letter increased, by joining the thin arm to the stem lower down; the thick arm, or tail, then springs from the side of the thin arm (compare **R**). This tends away from the essential, and is therefore a less safe form.

3. The tail may be curved or drawn out occasionally (See Tails, pp. 219-220).

4. Serifs on arms. See A, 2.

L 1. See B, 3.
2. See C, 3 and 4.
3. See E, 3.

4. See F, 3.

M 1. The stems are commonly slightly spread out to give greater clearance for the inner angles. An occasional form is much spread out **M**.

2. Note. — There are inscriptional forms of M and N without the top serif (Plate II.). But the pen forms and others have top serifs, and these commonly extend outward — tending to beaks (See A, 1 and 2) — rather than in. (V, W, X, Y (and N) show a similar tendency — See p. 219.)

3. The thin stem of M is occasionally drawn out (F, 3).

N 1. See C, 3 and 4.
2. See H, 3.
3. See M, 2, and A, 1 and 2.

4. The first stem is drawn out below the line for an occasional form (most suitable for an Initial Letter): the right-hand stem is very occasionally raised (when a final letter) (F, 3).

5. Note. — The stems of N (the only vertical thins — not counting M's — in the Roman Capitals) tend sometimes to be thicker: See Plate II.

O 1. O is the key letter of the curved forms and, in a sense, of the whole alphabet (p. 203). The upright form — O — may be regarded as the ideal simple letter.

2. Very commonly, however, O is tilted — *O* — (See Fig. 163), and when this is the case, all the curved letters — B, C, D, G, P, Q, R, S, U — are correspondingly tilted (See Plate II.). The tilted form is more easily made, but both are good forms.

P 1. See B, 1 and 2.
2. See O, 2.
3. (P with stem below line (See Plate IV.) must not be allowed to confuse with D) (See F, 3 and 4).

4. The bow of P appears to be attached (to the stem) above: in certain forms it is slightly separated from the stem below: See Plate II.

Q 1. Q resembles O with a tail: See O.
2. There are many characteristic varieties of the tail: See Tails (pp. 219-220).
3. Note. — Q being always followed __ by U, it is convenient often to deal with the two letters together. (See Plate II.)

R   1. See B, 1 and 2.

2. See O, 2.

3. In the form nearest the essential, the junction of the Bow and the Tail touches the stem. If the tail springs from the curve of the bow (Plate II.) greater care in construction is necessary (compare K). The treatment of the tail is very important. It may end in a serif (See A, 2), or it may be curved and pointed (See Tails, pp. 219-220). It may be drawn out (See Fig. 50).

4. See F, 3 (& comp. Fig. 169).

S   1. See C, 1, 2, 3, and 4.

2. See O, 2 (and p. 273).

3. S very often leans slightly forward.

T   1. See B, 2.

2. See C, 3 and 4.

3. Drawing out of stem: See F, 3 and 4.

4. Note. — The right arm is occasionally extended — to fill a line — when T is a terminal letter (in this case it is generally made lighter, and the left arm heavier — somewhat as in the Uncial T, Figs. 56 & 188).

U   1. Note. — The curve — if it be modelled on the common tilted O (See O, 2) — is thin where it meets the second stem.

2 (V for U). See J, 2, 3, and footnote.

3. The foot of the second stem projects on the right only, and gives clearance to the angle of the curve on the left. Sometimes the second stem ends in a hook or beak, which (very occasionally) is drawn out below.

V 1. See M, 2, and A, 2.

2. The thick stem may be drawn up (F, 3), in which case the thin commonly curves over for strength (See Figs. 89, 95).

3. (See note on V for U, under J.)

W 1. See M, 2, and A, 2.

2. The best form is of two V's crossed, **W**.

3. The first or both the thick stems may be drawn up and the thins curved over (See V, 2).

X 1. See M, 2, and A, 2.

2. There is sometimes a slight curving in of the stems, especially the thin stem (See Fig. 80).

3. The thin stem is sometimes drawn out below (F, 3), and commonly curved.

Y 1. See M, 2, and A, 2.

2. See F, 3 and 4. (Y with stem below line (See Plate V.) must not be allowed to confuse with V.)

An occasional rather interesting form of Y has the arms curving out and ending in points (See Fig. 167).

Z 1. See C, 3 and 4.

2. The lower arm of Z is sometimes drawn out (See E, 3): it may be curved and pointed (or flourished).

General Remarks on the characterisation of the Roman Capitals and related forms (See Fig. 163).[71]

VERTICAL STEMS — (a, Fig. 163) Thick (excepting in the thin stemmed N (and M)).

(b) Slightly curved in on either side (See Fig. 116), or appearing so because of the outward curve of the serifs (See Figs. 204, 206).

(c) A fine effect is obtained when the stem is made wider above than below (See p. 76).

(d) Free stems occasionally are drawn out (See above, F, 3 and 4, and pp. 185, 193, 255).

OBLIQUE STROKES OR STEMS — Thick, to the left, thin to the right, (See A, K, &c.), otherwise like vertical stems (above) — (See also SERIFS (e) below).

HORIZONTALS, ARMS, BRANCHES, OR BARS — Thin: free ends sometimes drawn out and flourished (See Figs. 125, 188).

BOWS AND CURVES — Gradated, and following the O (See pp. 9, 78, 203, 216).

SERIFS OR FINISHING STROKES — (a) Note. — Serifs of some sort are practically essential to the proper characterisation of an alphabet (See Figs. 147, 148, 162), and should generally have a certain uniformity (p. 247).

(b) The serifs, &c., of simple-written forms are treated at p. 180 (See Fig. 145).

(c) In Versals and certain other forms the mode of making requires the serif to be a distinct addition Derivatives to the letter (See Figs. 116, 166).

(d, Fig. 163) In the finest built-up A B Cs serifs are treated as the actual finishing and shaping of the ends of the stems and branches, rather than as added parts (See C, 3 & 4, p. 212 and p. 177). This particularly affects the construction of the thin strokes (See Figs. 165, 167).

(e) The serifs of the oblique strokes in A, K, M, N, R, V, W, X, Y are commonly not placed centrally, but projecting in the direction of the

---

[71] The more ornamental treatment of Stems, Bows, Serifs, Tails, &c., is referred to at p. 331, and in Figs. 188, 189.

stroke (i.e. away from the letter, thus: ✗), branching out from the parent stem (See tails, below), and avoiding an acute angle (as ⊤). This has tended to produce hooks and beaks (See Fig. 163), which are often used for the oblique strokes, particularly of A and N (See Figs. 189, 158), and the tails of K and R (See below).

(f) There is a similar natural tendency to hook or flourish the terminals of vertical stems on the left, particularly of B, D, I, J, K, L, P, R; less often of E, F, H. A very interesting and beautiful effect may be obtained by delicately curving down the upper serifs on the left (like thin beaks). Such serifs are sometimes very slightly turned up on the right, and it may be noted that this tendency of the "horizontals" to curve up and forward ⁓ is natural and characteristic of freely made, vigorous lettering (See Uncial T, pen dashes, &c., Figs. 169, 125, &c.).

TAILS — (a) The tails of K, Q, R and J) — and the strokes in A, F, G, I, M, N, P, Y, &c., which may be drawn out tail-wise — play an important

FIG. 163.

part in the right construction, and the occasional decoration, of plain lettering. They may end either in serifs or in curves (See SERIFS (e), above, and Fig. 188).

(b) Note. — It is a characteristic of vigorous forms that branches, &c., stand out well from their stems (pp. 157, (e) 219, (N) 204), and a good tail should stand out well from the letter (K, Q, Fig. 167).

(c) An excellent form of tail for ordinary use, combining strength and grace, consists of a (strong) straight stroke ending more or less abruptly in a (graceful) finishing curve.

(d) An extraordinarily long tail requires a slight double curve to take off its stiffness.

(e) A good tail may be made by the addition of a double curved stroke on the underside of a straight tail (or of a single curve above).

(f) In treating the tail of J, or the drawn-out stems of A, F, G, I, M, N, P, Y, it is important to preserve the essential straightness of the stems. Therefore, if a finishing curve be used, its size is related to the length of the straight stroke, and, unless this be extraordinarily long, the curve is usually made rather small and abrupt. A curve which is too large is apt to weaken the form and "pull it out of the straight" (g, Fig. 163).

Built-Up Forms

Built-up Letters are composed of compound strokes (c, d, Fig. 164); Simple-written Letters of simple strokes (a, b).

The Pen being an instrument which produces definite thick and thin strokes on a smooth surface, is perfectly adapted to the construction of either simple or compound forms: other tools, such as the stylus, needle, graver, &c., produce various scratches, stitches, or cuts, generally of the nature of rather varying thin strokes, and to produce thick strokes a building-up process is required.

In making built-up forms the control exerted by the tool is less obvious, and more depends upon the craftsman, who must therefore use greater care and judgment. Not only is it possible, but, occasionally, it may be desirable to depart from the more obvious tool-forms: though generally the more simply and naturally tool-made a form is, the better it is.

The fine early inscriptions are supposed to have been first drawn or painted (in outline) and then cut into the stone. The chisel forms were doubtless affected in this way by brush (and indirectly by pen) forms, but these were of the simplest — nothing was sketched in that was unfitted for the chisel to make into a natural and true chisel-form.

The action of the brush or "pencil" to a certain extent resembles that of the pen, but their effects are really distinct. In contrasting pen-made and brush-made letters, we may observe that a pen form tends to abrupt changes from thin to thick: a brush form to gradation (Fig. 164). The pen particularly affects curved strokes (comp. a & b), generally making them more quick and abrupt (or even broken, See * * c). than brush curves. The brush will give more graceful and finished but less uniform letters (See p. 289).

The character of a pen-letter depends greatly on the nib-width (p. 247), and narrow, medium, or broad nibs are used according to the type of letter required.

+OXO
.a.   b.
Simple-written PEN curves

'Built-up' PEN-Letter (c.)   BRUSH=made (d.)

FIG. 164.

A narrow nib may be used for special (built-up) Initials and Capitals, which are drawn rather than written (a, Fig. 165). The horizontal arms (made by the pen held horizontally) are markedly affected, and if a very fine nib were used, the necessity of strengthening and thickening them would tend further to reduce the pen character.

A broad nib gives strong, uniform pen-letters (b).

For ordinary use letters are perhaps best made with a "medium" nib (c). The width of the ordinary writing-pen, or rather narrower, gives a good proportion for initials, &c. (See pp. 74, 156).

FIG. 165.

In MS. books the early built-up Capitals were commonly of a rather severe type — approaching the Roman Capital, but having the sharp contrast between the thicks and the thins characteristic of pen-letters (Fig. 166). They make very simple and effective "Versals."

FIG. 166.—Pen-capitals from a tenth-century MS. *(writing-lines dotted in fig. to show spacing method).*

A more highly finished type of pen-made Roman Capital may be made by blending the serifs and stems (d, p. 219): it is nearer to the inscriptional form, but it exhibits a more curved and supple outline, which comes of natural pen-strokes (Fig. 167).

AFGIJ KLM^N_O PQTY WY

Built-up, Pen Capitals (see also Figs. 157, 158, 159.) - Note tilted O.

FIG. 167.

The remarks in Chapter VII. on the treatment of the more elastic "Gothic" Versal (a free variety of the Roman) may be taken as applying generally to (Coloured) Built-up Capitals — due allowance being made for the characteristic differences of the various types.

Simple-Written Capitals

"Rustic Capitals" (Fig. 4) may be referred to here as typical, simple-written capitals. Though not a very practical form,[72] they are full of suggestions for a semi-ornamental lettering in which the pronounced treatment of the heads and feet might be a feature (comp. Fig. 203). They were used as ornamental letters for titles and the like (See Plates VIII, IX., &c.) for centuries after they had gone out of ordinary use.

---

[72] Their thin stems and heavy branches may tend to weakness and illegibility — e.g. such letters as E, F, I, L, and T (See Fig. 4) are not always easily distinguishable.

SIMPLE-WRITTEN ROMAN CAPITALS — (Examples: Plates III., XVIII., XIX., XXI, Figs. 147, 148, 168, 175, 179. See also pp. 182, 351.)

UNCIALS — (Examples: See p. 227.)

Simple-written Capitals ordinarily conform to the writing line — as set by the small text (p. 46). This applies even where several words in capitals have to be inserted in the small text, though in special cases where these might look too crowded such capitals might be written on alternate lines.

Used for Initial Words, headings, whole pages, or books, in black or colour, they are written with greater freedom and accorded more special treatment (See pp. 226-27).

Simple-written Capitals are best composed of sharp, clean, pen-strokes: they may be quite plain or more or less decorative (Fig. 168), subject to the general rule that the fewer the number of letters or the & its more ornamental their office, the more elaborate and fanciful may be the forms employed (See p.222).

ABCDEE
FGHILM
NOPQVR
RSTVX.

Simple-Written Capitals : roughly copied from Plate XVIII.

FIG. 168.

A freely used pen naturally produces occasional varieties for special or ornamental purposes: these tend to elegance and drawn out flourished strokes (p.252); they vary chiefly in being extra-large.[73] Several of these may be used with fine effect in a page of plain Capitals, their "weight" (and generally their colour) being the same as that of the text (See Plate V., and p. 251).

WHOLE BOOKS OR PAGES WRITTEN IN CAPITALS — A very grand effect may be produced by these at the expense of a little more time and material than a Small-letter MS. entails. The lines of writing are commonly made one-letter-height apart: this requires ordinary simple ruling — the capitals being written between every alternate pair of lines (See p. 324).

Such writing may conveniently be treated as "Fine Writing" (p. 195). It justifies the use of wider margins. It is generally more difficult (and less necessary) to keep the right-hand edge as straight as a small text permits. The irregularities of this edge may be balanced by setting out in the left margin the first letters of sentences, verses, and the like (See p. 197). Such initials may be written larger or more ornamentally as suggested above; or, if built-up Letters are required, plain, rather slender Roman Capitals are the most suitable: these look best in burnished gold.

Perhaps the finest and most beautiful work which the penman can produce, is a book written entirely in gold[74] capitals[75] on purple vellum (See pp. 113, 124). This is only possible in special cases, but a book rightly so made being illuminated from within, has an incomparable simplicity and grandeur, surpassing that of the finest post-decorated and illuminated manuscripts.

Examples: Plates IV., V.; Figs. 5, 169 (enlarged) ; (modified, Fig. 56).

---

[73] Increasing the size of letter affects the form as though the nib were narrowed (See p. 248).

[74] Some may be in "silver" (p. 114).

[75] In a very short book these might even be built-up capitals.

quae dicitur efrem
et ibi morabatur cum
Proximum autem er
pascha iudaeorum
Et ascenderunt mul
Lyma de regione ant

FIG. 169.—*Part of Plate V. (q.v.), enlarged three times linear.*

Unicals

Uncials are typical pen-capitals.[76] Though not of such practical use as the simple-written Roman Capitals, their great possibilities and their beauty make them worth practising. (See Round, Upright, Formal Hands, p. 229.)

Their use is limited by two considerations —

First: that while the round ծ. Є. h. ɱ. ᴜ, are essentially legible (p. 175), people generally are not accustomed to them, and may find them hard to read; and

Secondly: that ծ. ғ. Ģ. h. ȷ. ᴋ. ʟ. ᴘ. ǫ. ʏ. have ascending and descending strokes which are apt to become too pronounced and give an unpleasant appearance of "tailiness" to a page of Uncial Writing (in English, See footnote, p. 248).

The first difficulty may be met by keeping Uncials for special MSS. — for private use — and introducing them sparingly or not at all in Service Books, Placards, &c., where ease and quickness of reading are essential.

The appearance of "tailiness" (not so obvious in Latin) may be avoided by making the tails shorter and keeping the lines of writing well apart. Or freely made Roman Capitals without tails (See D, tail-less, Fig. 57) may be substituted for one or more of the chief offenders.

Uncials may be "round" (See Plate IV., Fig. 5, and p. 229), or "pointed" (See Fig. 169, and p. 325).

Capitals & Small-Letters

During the development of Small-Letters from Capitals but little distinction was made in their use, and such capital forms as N and R were freely and promiscuously used in the round minuscule writings, together with the small-letters n and r (See Plates VI., VII.). On the other hand, Small-Letter forms were frequently written larger and used as initials. In Irish and Anglo-Irish MSS. these were filled inside with green, yellow, or red, and

---

[76] Palaeographers call them "majuscules"(="large letters"), but distinguish them from "Capitals." For the purposes of the modern penman, however, they may be regarded as Round Capitals. (For their treatment, See pp. 225-6, and 229.)

surrounded outside with red dots, or otherwise decorated with colour (See Fig. 7, and Plate VI.).

In early MSS., therefore, one does not find an alphabet of Simple-Written Capitals, which is peculiar to a given small text. But we may employ a kindred capital — such as the round Uncial for the round Half-Uncial. And a fitting alphabet may always be constructed, from the "Roman" or "Uncial" types of Capitals (footnote, p. 229), by taking the same pen with which the small-letters have been made and using it in a similar manner: "straight" for "straight-pen" writing, and "slanted" for "slanted-pen" writing (See Figs. 147, 148).

When in doubt as to the type of Capital — for any purpose — use Roman Capitals.

Early, Round, Upright, Formal Hands

Examples: Half Uncials — Fig. 6 (Roman); Plate VI. (Irish), Plate VII. (English) Fig. 170 later; See also pp. 4, 8, 328-29. Uncials (Plate IV. and p. 3).

The main types are the "round" Uncial and Half-Uncial, commonly written with an approximately "straight pen."[77] They are generally treated as fine writing (p. 195), and written between ruled lines: this has a marked effect in preserving their roundness (See p. 329).

They are very useful as copy-book hands (See p. 35), for though the smooth gradation of their curves, their thin strokes, and their general elegance unfit them for many practical purposes, yet their essential roundness, uprightness, and formality afford the finest training to the penman, and prevent him from falling into an angular, slanting, or lax hand. Their very great beauty, moreover, makes them well worth practising, and even justifies their use (in a modernised form) for special MSS., for the more romantic books — such as poetry and "fairy tales" — and generally where speed in writing or reading is not essential.

With an eye trained and a hand disciplined by the practice of an Irish or English Half-Uncial, or a modified type, such as is given in Fig. 50, the

---

[77] The writing in Fig. 170 shows a slightly slanted pen. To make quite horizontal thins is difficult, and was probably never done, but it is worth attempting them nearly horizontal for the sake of training the hand.

penman may easily acquire some of the more practical later "slanted-pen" types.

duodea

potest

eicereh

lahguor

FIG. 170.—*Part of an English eight-century MS. (British Museum, Case C, No. 68), enlarged three times linear.*

"Slanted-Pen" Small-Letters

(Typical Examples: — Carlovingian ninth-century MS. — enlarged, Fig. 171):

English tenth-century MS. — Plate VIII. (enlarged, Fig. 172):

English eleventh-century MS. — Plate IX. (enlarged, Fig. 173):

Italian twelfth-century MS. — Plate X. (enlarged, Fig. 174)

The use of the "slanted pen" generally produced stronger, narrower, and stiffer letters. Its effects are detailed in pp. 8-11, and Fig. 11, and may best be studied in the tenth-century example (Fig. 172 — the letter forms are described on p. 333).

In the Carlovingian MS. — which does not show these effects in any marked degree — we may note the wide letter forms, the wide spacing, the long stems (thickened above by additional strokes), the slight slope of the letters, and the general effect of gracefulness and freedom (See Fig. 171). Carlovingian MSS. may be said to represent a sort of mediaeval copy-books, and their far-reaching influence on writing makes them of great interest to the modern penman, who would, moreover, find one of these hands an excellent model for a free "formal hand."

For practical purposes the "slanted-pen" letter is generally superior to the "straight-pen" letter. The "slanted-pen" letters have greater strength and legibility, due mainly to the presence of the thick horizontals — often equal in width to the verticals. Their use saves both space and time, as they are narrower, and more easily and freely written[78] than the straight-pen forms.

The real importance to us of these early types lies, I think, in their relation to the Roman Small-Letter (pp. 338-39 & 363-71), and their great possibilities of development into modern formal hands approaching the "Roman" type.

---

[78] Note. — Single-line ruling is commonly used — the writing being on, or a little above or below, the line: this allows of greater freedom than the double line (See p. 229).

Fig. 171.—*Part of fig. 8, enlarged three times linear (see p. 305).*

angeli dñi dño. ƀ
aquae omnes quae
κ dño. ƀ omnes
sol & luna dño.

FIG. 172.—*Fig. 12, enlarged twice linear (see p. 305 & Plate VIII).* Note: *top line is cut down.*

aunt . quae uer

gent conanua . 1

l . & idarco nobi

FIG. 173.—*Part of Plate IX. (Charter of CNUT), enlarged three times linear (see p. 340).*

if ihs xp̄
Veniad
'inconui
irgenſau
ixit a·D

Fig. 174.—*Part of Plate X., enlarged three times linear (see pp. 339–341).*

Roman Small-Letters

Ex.: (Italian) Plates XIX., XX. (15th century); Figs. 175, 176 (16th century): Figs. 147, 148 (modern MS.).

The Roman Small-Letter is the universally recognised type in which the majority of books and papers are printed. Its form has been in use for over 400 years (without essential alteration) and as far as we are concerned it may be regarded as permanent.

And it is the object of the scribe or letter-maker gradually to attain a fine, personal formal hand, assimilating to the Roman Small-Letter; a hand against the familiar and present form of which no allegations of unreadableness can be raised, and a hand having a beauty and character now absent or unfamiliar. The related Italic will be mastered for formal MS. work (p. 241), and the ordinary handwriting improved (p. 246). These three hands point the advance of the practical, modern scribe.

The Roman Small-Letter is essentially a pen form (and preferably a "slanted-pen" form; p. 230), and we would do well to follow its natural development from the Roman Capital — through Round Letters and Slanted-Pen forms — so that we may arrive at a truly developed and characteristic type, suitable for any formal manuscript work and full of suggestions for printers and letter-craftsmen generally.

A finished form, such as that in Plate XX. — or even that of Fig. 175 — would present many difficulties to the unpracticed scribe, and one who so began would be apt to remain a mere copyist, more or less unconscious of the vitality and character of the letter. An earlier type of letter — such as that in Plate VIII. — enables the scribe to combine speed with accuracy, and fits him at length to deal with the letters that represent the latest and most formal development of penmanship.

And in this connection, beware of practising with a fine nib, which tends to inaccuracy and the substitution of prettiness for character. Stick to definite pen strokes, and preserve the definite shapes and the uniformity of the serifs (p. 248): if these be made clumsily, they become clumsy lumps. It may be impossible always to ascertain the exact forms — especially of terminals and finishing strokes — for the practised scribe has attained a great uniformity and some *sleight of hand* which cannot be deliberately copied. But — whatever the exact forms — we may be sure that in the best hands they are produced by uniform and proper pen strokes.

Omnes ſcti apli et euangeliſte. orate:
Omnes ſcti diſcipli dñi orate:
Omnes ſcti inocētes. orate.
Sancte Stephane. ora.
Sancte laurenti. ora.
Sancte vincenti. ora.
Sancte fabiane. ora.
Sancte ſebaſtiane. ora.
Sancte blaſi. ora.
Sācti Ioā. et paule orate.
Sācti Coſma et damia orate.
Sācti geruaſi. et pthaſi. ora:

FIG. 175.—*Italian Prayer Book: 16th century (see opp. p. & p. 266).*

FIG. 176.—(*From same MS. as fig. 175, enlarged three times linear.*)

catorum contr

est salus super p

benedictio tua

Italics

Ex. Plate XXI. and Figs. 94, 177, 178 (enlarged).

Italics[79] closely resemble the Roman Small-Letters but are slightly narrowed, slightly sloped to the right, and very freely written (commonly

---

[79] It is convenient to use the term "Italics" for both the cursive formal writing and the printing resembling it. Italic type was first used in a " Virgil " printed by Aldus Manutius of Venice in 1500. The type was then called "Venetian" or "Aldine." It was counterfeited almost immediately (in Germany and

with a "slanted pen"). The serifs generally consist of slight natural terminal hooks, &c. — though in p and q a finishing stroke is sometimes added. Ascending and descending strokes (in b, d, f, h, k, l, g, j, p, q, y) are commonly rather long, and often end in curves, sometimes in flourishes (Fig. 177).

 The lines of writing are generally widely spaced — allowing for the long stems: the bodies of the letters being narrow are generally rather closely packed, and frequently the lines of writing appear as almost continuous light but compact writing, while the ascenders and descenders and parts of the Capitals may be flourished freely in the spaces between the lines — sometimes filling them with ornamental pen work, which contrasts strongly with the extreme plainness and regularity of the bodies.

 Italic Capitals are a variety of the Roman Capitals, slightly sloped (frequently less sloped than the accompanying small-letters), and sometimes much flourished (Fig. 177). The types modelled on the latter were called by printers in the seventeenth century, "Swash Letters."

bdhilmnruvpq
Simple-serif and flourished Jtalics
bbbp A B B
D E F L M v Z

FIG. 177.

Holland it was called "cursive"); Wynkin de Worde used it in 1524. It seems to have been originally intended for printing entire Classics, but was afterwards used to distinguish portions of the text (see also p. 283).

Tal, ch'a noia et disdegno hebb

Et se non fusse che maggior pau

Freno l'ardir; con morte acerba

A laqual fui molte fiate presso,

Fig. 178.—*Part of Plate XXI, enlarged, (approx.) four times linear (see p. 376).*

Use of Italics. — In printing they served at first to mark such portions of the text as —

| Introductions, Prefaces, Indexes, Notes, | } And subsequently were used for | { Quotations, Emphasizing, Words not part of the Text (e.g. chapter headings in the Bible, &c.). |

In MSS. when it is not desirable to alter the character, Red Writing (See p. 86) may be substituted for italics. Italics — either in black or red — go best with "Roman" characters.

Like the Roman Small-Letter, the Italic is a generally recognised and accepted form: this and other considerations, such as the peculiar elegance and charm of the letters, their formal relation to modern handwriting, their compactness and economy of space in the line, and the fact that they may be written easily and with extreme regularity — being indeed the most rapid of formal hands — are practical reasons for a careful study of the type, and justify the writing of certain MS. books entirely in Italics.

Semi-Formal Writing

Figs. 179, 180, and 181 are taken from a sixteenth-century Italian MS.[80] written in a semi-formal cursive hand in dark brown and red-brown inks (probably originally nearer black and red), on 150 leaves of fine paper.

The proportions of the Book,[81] together with the good writing, have a very agreeable effect, and are interesting as being used by a writer over 300 years ago. The extra width of the side margins may have been allowed for annotations — some notes were written in by the scribe himself.

Page = $11\,1/8$ inches high, 8 inches wide.

Margins   Inner ($7/8$ inch + $5/8$ inch allowed for Small Capitals) = $1\,1/4$ inch (approximate).

---

[80] The Book is a catalogue of early Roman inscriptions: apparently a written copy of a printed book.

[81] With a sheet of paper $11\,1/8$ inches by 16 inches the student might reconstruct these.

{ Top = 1³/₈ inch (constant).
Side = 2¾ inch (approximate).
Foot = 3 inch (approximate).

Writing-Line Space nearly ⁵/₁₆ inch high: length (varies), average 4 inches.
Text Column nearly 6¾ inches high, consisting of 22 lines of MS.

Jn Scā Katharina .   Jn uia prope Iriuui
    D M .   PERPETVAE SECVRITATI
F VNIAE   IVSTIAE NEPOTILLAE
SEVERAE   CONIVGI CASTISSIMAE BE
VIX·AN·XVI·   NEMERITAE ETIVSTIAE PRAE
L·IVNIVS   SIDIAE FILIAE AVR·SEVE
FELIX LIB·   Jn aede · S Petri
BENE ME ·   LIMINA RERVM ANNI
FECIT ·   D · M · XC · VI ·

FIG. 179.

CHARACTER OF THE WRITING — The good shapes of the letters, their great uniformity, and their easy yet formal arrangement, mark this MS. as the work of a skilful penman. But, while pen character of a sort is very evident, the writing approaches the stylographic (apparently a rather narrow blunt nib was used), and the absence of definite thicks and thins distinguishes it from all the formal hands hitherto discussed: it may conveniently be termed Semi-formal.

FECIT.   D · M · XC · VI ·

· Ibidem in Lapide corroso · ·

M · Sallus Domitiano AQ Tribus Firmifrono Sing
sing · digitos decem quin · supra foramen in
libr · qt nouae Dimidiamos Dimidium altum
digit · Dimidium · ccc ii · in non · noctis primę
ad hor · eiusdem · reliqua fora longa singula di ·
quo alta sing · Digt declar · qv primp sohan · AQ
Singul · foramina · D · tres et dimid · alta · acci
pret foraminib · ad horam decum ·

FIG. 180.

Delphis in Templo Pythy Apollinis ipsorum.

ΘΕΟΙΣ ΕΠΙ ΑΡΙΣΤΑΓΟΡΑ ΑΡΧΟΝΤΟΣ
ΕΝ ΔΕΛΦΟΙΣ ΠΥΛΛΑΙΑΣ ΗΡΙΝΗΣ ΙΕ'
ΡΟΜΝΙΜΟΝΟΥΝΤΩΝ ΑΙΤΩΛΩΝ ΠΟ'
ΛΕΜΑΡΧΟΥ ΑΛΕΞΑΜΕΝΟΥ ΔΑΜΩΝΟΣ.

Judam.

. ΠΥΘΙΝ ΜΑΝΤΙΣ .

Ν ΑΥΘΕΣΩ . ΑΥΚΟΕΡΓΕ ΕΜΟΝ ΠΟΤΙ ΠΙΟΝΑ
ΝΗΟΝ ΓΗΝ ΙΦΙΛΟΣ ΚΑΙ ΠΑΣΙΝ ΟΛΥΜ .

FIG. 181.

CONSTRUCTION — The rapidity and uniformity of this writing are largely due to an extremely easy zigzag movement of the pen, such as is natural in writing m, n, and u — the final upstroke usually running on into the next letter. Note particularly that the round letters c, d, e, g, o, q generally begin with a nearly straight down stroke — like the first part of u — to which tops are added (See Fig. 182).

FIG. 182.

In the case of a, the first stroke curves forward to meet the second.

In the straight-stemmed capitals B, D, E, F, H, I, L, M, N, P, R, and T, the first stroke is made rather like an ⌠ (showing the tendency to a zigzag) the foot of which is generally crossed horizontally by a second stroke making a form resembling 1 — on this as a base, the rest of the letter is formed (See Fig. 182). This tends to preserve the uniformity of the letters: and gives a fine constructive effect, as, for example, in the letter N.

GENERAL REMARKS — The semi-formal nature of such a MS. would seem to permit of a good quill — not necessarily sharp — being used with the utmost freedom and all reasonable personal sleight of hand; of soft tinted inks — such as browns and brown-reds; of an un-ruled page (a pattern page ruled dark, being laid under the writing paper, will, by showing through, keep the writing sufficiently straight), and of a minimum of precision in the arrangement of the text. And in this freedom and informality lie the reasons for and against the use of such a hand. There is a danger of its becoming more informal and degenerating because it lacks the effect of the true pen in preserving form.[82] But, on the other hand, it combines great rapidity and freedom with beauty and legibility: few printed books could compete in charm with this old "catalogue," which took the scribe but little longer to write than we might take in scribbling it.

Many uses for such a hand will suggest themselves. Semi-formal documents which require to be neatly written out, and Books and Records of which only one or two copies are required, and even Books which are worthy to be — but never are — printed, might, at a comparatively low cost, be preserved in this legible and beautiful form.

It suggests possibilities for an improvement in the ordinary present-day handwriting — a thing much to be desired, and one of the most practical benefits of the study of calligraphy. The practical scribe, at any rate, will prove the advantages of being a good all-round penman.

Of Formal Writing Generally

ON COPYING A HAND — Our intentions being right (viz. to make our work essentially readable) and our actions being expedient (viz. to select and copy the simple forms which have remained essentially the same, leaving the complex forms which have passed out of use — See pp. 138-9), we need not vex ourselves with the question of "lawfulness."[83]

Where beautiful character is the natural product of a tool, any person may at any time give such character to a useful form, and as at this time a properly cut and handled pen will produce letters resembling those of the early MSS., we may take as models such early, simple pen-forms as have

---

[82] Practising a more formal hand as a corrective would prevent this.

[83] The Law fulfils itself: that which we must not copy is that which we cannot copy.

remained essentially the same,[84] and copy them as closely as we can while keeping them exact and formal.

Finally, personal quality is essential to perfect workmanship, but that is the natural and gradual — sometimes scarcely visible — departure from a model, that comes of practice and time.

FORMS OF LETTERS: COMPONENT PEN-STROKES — In a good hand the chief component strokes — stems, bows, and serifs — are repeated again and again (See pp. 180, 188) — this is essential to the uniform character and the quickness of the writing. When substituting a new for an old letter a naturally used pen will produce such common pen-strokes, giving the desired "family likeness" to the new letter[85] (b, Fig. 183).

PROPORTION[86] OF THICK STROKES — The broader the thick stroke is in proportion to the height of a letter, the more the form of the letter is controlled and affected by the pen (c, Fig. 183). For training and practice, therefore, the wide nib is the most useful. A narrower nib (d or e) allows of more freedom and variety, and there is a great charm in slender lettering — this the trained scribe may essay (See Plate XX., and p. 368).

PROPORTION OF STEM HEIGHT — The character of a writing depends very much on whether the stems are short, medium, or long. The stems of b and p may be as short as half the height of the bodies (f, Fig. 183); a medium stem for ordinary use might be two-thirds of, or equal to, the height of the body (g). Stems may be drawn out to almost any length, and may constitute a decorative feature of the writing, as in the Anglo-Saxon[87] MS., Plate IX. (See p. 331, and Fig. 188.)

---

[84] E.g. the letters in the tenth-century English hand — Plate VIII.: excepting the archaic long f and round Z (b, Fig. 183).

[85] The propriety of the actual form of the new letter will largely depend on the scribe's knowledge of the development of that particular letter and its component parts (comp. the interesting development of g, sketched in Figs. 3 & 183, but note correction of Ex. 173 in Addenda, p. 15).

[86] The proportions of the thick strokes, stem heights, &c., in a given hand need not be exactly followed, but it should be recognised that any alteration in these will inevitably alter the forms and the character of the letters (Fig. 183, and p. 47).

[87] In English so many ascending and descending letters are used, that it might be the best and most natural treatment of these to make them a marked feature of the writing (See also "Fine Writing," pp. 194-95). Note, in this connection, that our a b c has been developed as a Latin alphabet, and that the evenness of Latin MS. is largely due to the infrequence of tailed letters.

FIG. 183.

DISTINCT LINES OF WRITING — The line — especially in MS. books — is really a more important unit than the page; and the whole question of the arrangement of Lettering hinges on the right treatment of the lines. One is particularly struck by the distinctness of the lines of writing in the old MSS., due mainly to —

(a) The binding together of the letters in the line — commonly by strong serifs or heavy "shoulders" and "feet" (See Figs, n, 184, and p. 414).

(b) Packing the letters well together (See pp. 40, 195).

(c) Spacing the lines sufficiently apart (See pp. 195-98).

It is a good rule (especially when practising) to space the lines fairly widely. Really fine writing shows generally to greater advantage if not too much crowded, and there is more danger of making reading hard by crowding the lines, than by crowding the words (See Fig. 156).

Whatever mode of treatment be followed, each line should be written with as much freedom as possible, the simplest straightforward writing being preferable to that which is over-arranged.

excute *vij.*

laudate *x.*

regredere: dns *xv.*

catorum *xvi.*

FIG. 184.

Decorative Contrasts

The decorative treatment of lettering generally involves contrasts of size, weight, colour, or form — that is, of large and small, heavy and light, variously coloured, or variously shaped letters. As a general rule, marked contrasts are best; a slight contrast may fail of its effect and yet be sufficiently notice- able to give an unpleasant appearance of irregularity.

CONTRASTS OF COLOUR (See pp. 97, 127) — Note that, while it is convenient to distinguish "colour" — as red, blue, green, &c. — weight strictly involves colour: built-up or heavy letters in black show extra black beside lighter writing, while the latter appears grey in comparison (See Figs. 139, 131); in red writing the heavy letters appear red, the lighter letters, pink (See Fig. 90).

CONTRAST OF SIZE — The simplest decorative contrast is that of LARGE[88] letters with SMALLER letters (Fig. 185); the strokes being of equal, or nearly equal, weight, there is a harmonious evenness of tone throughout. Where the large letters are very much larger, their parts are made somewhat heavier to keep their apparent "weight" approximately equal (See p. 376). This is one of the most effective treatments for inscriptions generally (See p. 226, and Plates V. and XXIV.).

SIMPLE CONTRAST OF SIZE: HARMONY OF FORM, WEIGHT AND COLOUR

FIG. 185.

CONTRASTS OF "WEIGHT" AND SIZE — In simple writing these are obtained by using two sizes of pen — the small, light letters being used for the bulk of the text, the larger heavier letters being used for occasional words or lines (or vice versa). This is a very effective simple treatment for MSS. (Fig. 186). The occasional letters may be more decoratively treated (See Responses and Rubrics, p. 265) by introducing the further contrasts of colour (p. 97) or form (p. 258).

---

[88] Where there is only a slight difference in size, the effect is improved by using a different form or colour (See pp. 86, 265).

a few lines of much larger Writing gives an agreeable, simple contrast of size & colour. The larger writing is conveniently written between every other pair of writing-lines. It may be more decoratively treated. (a.)

FIG. 186.—(*See also fig.* 191.)

CONTRASTS OF FORM, "WEIGHT" AND SIZE — These are generally obtained by the use of large built-up Capitals, together with a simple-written (or ordinarily printed) text (Fig. 187).

Contrast of form, weight and size; & (usually) colour

FIG. 187.

A marked contrast usually being desirable, the built-up capitals (especially if black) are kept quite distinct from the rest of the text (See Fig. 197): if they are scattered among the other letters, they are apt to show like blots and give an appearance of irregularity to the whole. As a rule, the effect is improved by the use of red or another colour (See Figs. 91, 93).

Contrast of form — for decorative purposes — is usually combined with contrast of weight (e.g. "Gothic," heavier, p. 258) or size (e.g. Capitals, larger, p. 281).

Ornamental Letters

(See Chaps. VII., VIII., X., XII.,& Fig. 1 & p.185)

To give ornament its true value we must distinguish between ordinary occasions when simplicity and directness are required, and special occasions when elaboration is desirable or necessary.

The best way to make ornamental letters is to develop them from the simpler forms. Any plain type may be decoratively treated for special purposes — some part or parts of the letters usually being rationally "exaggerated" (p. 186). Free stems, "branches" tails, &c., may be drawn out, and terminals or serifs may be decorated or flourished (Fig. 203).

BUILT-UP FORMS — Even greater license (See Fig. 161) is allowed in Built-Up Letters — as they are less under the control of the tool (p. 221) — and their natural decorative development tends to pro- duce a subordinate simple line decoration beside or upon their thicker parts (Fig. 189). In MSS. the typical built-up, ornamental form is the "Versal" (See Chap. VII.), which developed — or degenerated — into the "Lombardic" (Fig. 1). Here again it is preferable to keep to the simpler form and to develop a natural decorative treatment of it for ourselves.

"Black Letter" or "Gothic" still in use as an ornamental letter (Fig. 190), is descended from the fifteenth-century writing of Northern Europe (Plate XVII.). A better model may be found in the earlier and more lively forms of twelfth and thirteenth century writing (Fig. 191).

Rightly made, and used, it is one of the most picturesque forms of lettering — and therefore of ornament — and besides its ornamental value, there is still in the popular fancy a halo of romance about "black letter," which may fairly be taken into account. Its comparative illegibility, however, — due mainly to the substitution of straight for curved strokes — debars it from ordinary use.[89] Though its distinction in form and colour (p. 249) from ordinary small lettering, make it useful in arresting attention; as in a legal document, where the clauses are marked by 𝔴𝔥𝔢𝔯𝔢𝔞𝔰 &c.

Its most effective use, however, is as pure ornament — when it does not matter whether the words are easily read or not. For mottoes, &c., painted or carved on walls or furniture, and for ornamental borders round tapestry hangings, tombs, book-covers, bowls, flagons, plates, &c., bands of such ornamental lettering are extremely decorative (See footnote (2), p. 189, & also p. 279).

---

[89] Compare **monotone** and monotone. For general purposes, therefore, and particularly for forming a good hand, the earlier scripts are to be preferred (or the late Italian): even twelfth- century "Gothic" writing is hardly readable enough for "practical" purposes.

bdfhkl ISflll Drawn-out stems: The serifs are usually more strongly marked to shew the termination of the strokes.

fggjpqkxyzz Wider spacing: OR the top line of writing may have ascenders flourished into top margin, while in the foot margin the descenders of the foot-line are flourished equally

Exodus Chapter xx

FJPTYG KRQ
E
KRMN L T
A H v W Z A

FIG. 188.—(*See also figs.* 125 *and* 150.)

Early Decorated Letters

Thin parts strengthened with knobs and 'buttress' strokes.

conf.
I, T, E, F.
curious links & cross-BARS.

Varied forms of Aa

Forms Illustrative of the origins of Simple Ornamental LETTERS.

FIG. 189.—(*See also Plates VI., XI., XXII., figs. 79 and 84, and p. 420.*)

FIG. 190.—*Ordinary Modern "Black Letter" Type (see p. 331).*

FIG. 191.—*MS. written by an English Scribe, in 1269, at Mons, in Hainault—Part of Colophon in large text.* (B. M. Egerton, MS. 2569. *Reduced five-sixths Scale.*)

FIG. 191 a.—*Shield of Arms of Earl de Warrenne, Castle Acre Priory, Norfolk (Gold and blue chequers, diapered—see p. 215): reproduced, by permission, from Boutell's " English Heraldry," No. 68.*

APPENDIX A

CHAPTER XVI
SPECIAL SUBJECTS

Divers Uses Of Lettering

The following list of some of the uses of handmade lettering, though necessarily very brief, will perhaps suggest possibilities both to the student and the craftsman: —

MS. BOOKS, &c. (See pp, 98, 341, & Author's Preface)

Fine Literature:	(1) Preferably "the best."
	(2) That which is worthy of calligraphy.
	(3) That which is the "favourite" of the owner of the book.
	Poetry is differently treated from prose (See pp. 55, 196, 281, 91), and should have extra wide side margins when possible (p. 369).
Single Poems, &c.:	Poems, cards, hymns, &c. (See pp. 89-90, & Poetry, above), preferably in the form of small books.
Tracts or Treatises:	Copies might be preserved (p. 239) in good writing (instead of Typewriting),
Church Services:	Prayers, Communion, Marriage, &c. (pp. 93, 97, 265).
Gospels & Psalters:	Note. — The Psalms, &c., may be treated as poetry (as in the "Revised Version") or as prose (as in the "Authorised Version"), See Fine Literature above.
Almanacks:	These may be very varied; containing vacations, terms, sessions; public, church, or family festivals, personal memoranda or topical quotations. They offer great opportunities for heraldic or symbolic ornament (such as coats-of-arms, astronomical signs, &c.).
Dedications, &c., in Books: (Lettering on Architects' Plans: See Maps & Plans, p. 262)	These may be on a parchment leaf inserted and securely glued into the beginning (preferably bound up with book), or be written on a fly-leaf. Annotations, extracts, &c., may be written in colour in printed books (p. 97).
"Copy-Books":	(See below).

BROADSIDES: Sheets printed (or written) on one side: See p. 268.

Notices:	(Posters, Placards, Hand-bills, &c.).
Quotations:	(Texts, Mottoes, &c.) (See p. 258).
Church Texts, &c.:	(The Creed, Commandments, &c.).
Family Trees & Pedigrees:	These may be very decorative — in plain black and red, or with coats-of-arms or other ornament. They might also be made in book form.

WALL INSCRIPTIONS Carved or painted: See pp. 268, 288-297, & Chapter XVII.

Public Notices: Lettering in Churches, &c.:	Note: on walls, plastered, or unsuited for carving, sgraffito might be used with fine effect. Letters may also be painted upon tiles, which (after baking) are cemented into the wall (p. 290)

Lettering in & upon public buildings:	
(ILLUMINATED) ADDRESSES, &c.: (Petitions, &c.) (See p. 271)	
MONOGRAMS & DEVICES: (See p. 277 These are frequently designed for stenciling or other mechanical reproduction).	

LETTERING FOR REPRODUCTION: (See p. 280). See also BROADSIDES, above.	
Printer's types and Ornamental letters:	(in woodcut and metal: pp. 280, 282).
Title Pages:	(See p. 279).
Paper and other Book covers:	(Magazines, Newspaper-Headings, Music, Catalogues, &c.).
Maps & Plans:	Good, clear lettering may be used in these with fine effect.
Book Plates:	(preferably simple, with Arms, Crest, or Symbol, and suitable lettering).
Letter-paper Headings, Cards, &c.:	(preferably in copper-plate "Roman" and "Italic").
Bill Heads, Receipt Forms, &c.:	(preferably in copper-plate or type: see p. 280).
Certificates:	(Testimonials, &c.) The plainer these are made, the better.
Programmes, Menus, Cards, &c.:	(Christmas cards, &c.).
Almancks:	(see above).
MS. Books and "copy-books":	Possibly might be reproduced by copper-plate if written well enough (p. 282).
Advertisements, &c.:	Better lettering in these would not only mitigate many eyesores, but would probably attract by its novelty (See p. 270).

ENGRAVING, &c.: (See pp. 279, 280, 288).	
Brasses, &c.:	("Brasses," Name-Plates, Doorplates, &c.).
Punches:	(for naming, numbering, &c.).
Utensils:	(Bowls, flagons, plates, &c.).
Ornaments:	(Jewellery, &c.).
Die Sinking:	(for coins, medals, &c., and for embossed letter-paper headings, &c.).

INSCRIPTIONS IN STONE & WOOD: (See pp. 288-297, & Chap. XVII.).	
On Monuments & Buildings:	Also on mile-stones, boundary stones, bridges, &c.
Tombstones:	
Foundations Stones:	
Memorial Tablets:	

"SIGN WRITING": (See pp. 268, 289).	
Signs:	(for stations, inns, shops, &c.)
Shop Fascias, &c.:	
Names, &c.:	(on doors & on carts, coaches, &c.).
Notice Boards:	
"Ticket Writing":	

EMBROIDERY, &c.: See remarks on built-up forms, p. 221: and Chapter XII. [on Lettering, &c..] of "Embroidery and Tapestry Weaving," by Mrs. A. H. Christie, in this Series.

Decoration for hangings, (p. 258): Marking clothes, &c.

All the arts employ lettering directly or indirectly, in fine decoration or for simple service.

The following list of ancient uses is interesting:[90] —

"I. TITULI

1. Dedicatory and Votive Inscriptions (Tituli Sacri).
2. Sepulchral Inscriptions (Tituli Sepulchrales).
3. Honorary Inscriptions (Tituli Honorarii).
4. Inscriptions on Public Works (Tituli Operum Publicorum).
5. Inscriptions on Movable Objects (Instrumenium).

II. INSTRUMENTA

1. Laws (Leges et Plebi Scita).
2. Decrees of the Senate (Senatus Consulta).
3. Imperial Documents (Instrumenta Imperatorum).
4. Decrees of Magistrates (Decreta Magistratuum).
5. Sacred and Public Documents (Acta Sacra et Publica).
6. Private Documents (Acta Privata).
7. Wall Inscriptions (Incriptiones Parietariae).
8. Consular Diptychs (Diptycha Consularia)."

MS. Books, &C.

Books in the making — as compared with ordinary inscriptions — are capable of great compression or expansion, and may be said to have a quality of elasticity. Nearly all other ordinary inscriptions are set inscriptions (p. 350), requiring a given number of words to be set out in a given space. But in books, while it is convenient that the treatment of the text should

---

[90] p. 224, J. C. Egbert's "Introduction to the Study of Latin Inscriptions,"— 1896.

conform generally to a chosen size of page (p. 63), the contents of the page may vary according to the letter-form and the spacing (pp. 65-66, 195), and the number of the pages is not definitely limited, so that another page, or a number of additional pages, may always be taken to complete the text.

The size of page, margin, and writing having been settled (See Chap. VI.) — and the pages ruled — the penman writes out the text with the utmost freedom, not stopping to make fine calculations, but leaving such spaces and lines, for Initials, Headings, &c., as his fancy and common-sense dictate, and letting the text — or its divisions — smoothly flow on from page to page till a natural termination is reached. And if the terminal page has only one or two lines on it, it is not necessary to attempt a balance with the previous page — the book or chapter[91] ends just there, for the good reason that there is no more of it.

COLOPHONS, TAIL-PIECES, &c. (See p. 95), make a pleasant finish, and may complete the page or not as convenient.

PLANNING: SECTIONS AND PAGES — Calculations of the amount of text, of the number of sections or pages required, and so on, are useful, and planning the pages may be convenient — for example, one or more of the verses of a poem, or a given number of words, may be allotted to the page — provided always that the scribe preserves his freedom, and treats each case on its merits. If he think it most suitable to devote a complete page to each paragraph, he may do so in spite of its resulting in the pages all being of different lengths.

The one general limitation which it is proper to observe is that of the Writing-line — its length[92] and spacing — and to this may be added the desirability of beginning the text of every page on the first or head line.[93] For most of us it is not practically possible to do without the aid of the writing-

---

[91] If there is sufficient room left on the terminal page for a clearly marked beginning (such as a decorative initial), the next chapter may begin there, and so fill the page — but generally there is no objection to leaving blank what the text has failed to fill.

[92] The line need not always be filed by the writing (p. 351).

[93] It would not be necessary for the first page of a chapter to have the ordinary dropped head and blank upper space if a fine initial or decorative heading were used to mark it.

lines — which really lead, through uniformity, to greater freedom — though a book written without them[94] might be as beautiful as any ruled manuscript.

MARGINAL LINES — These, the terminals of the writing-lines, are frequently made double, with about ¼ inch between (See Plates XX. and XV.). On the left this space is utilized for marginal capitals, or is left blank; on the right the first line acts as a warning mark and the normal termination of the text, the second as a barrier beyond which the writing should not go. The double lines, in being more obvious than single lines, are also more effective in "straightening" the page (p. 67): presumably for this reason the two upper and two lower writing-lines were often ruled from edge to edge of the page (See Plate XL).

RULING — Marginal and writing-lines, once ruled, are to be left intact, and may be regarded as actual component parts of the finished pages. They are best made with a hard blunt point (p. 66) — the furrows so made give an interesting character, almost a "texture," to the smooth surface of the page. But they may be ruled with a fine lead pencil, or with a fine pen and faint black or

Special coloured inks. Inked or coloured lines, however, Subjects are not generally written upon (See footnote, p. 230), but between (See Plates XIII., XVII., XX., &c.).

CORRECTING MISTAKES — A neatly made rather small letter above and a "carat" below (as in ordinary writing) may be used for an omission (Fig. 192). A superfluous letter may be neatly struck out. Erasures are usually unsatisfactory, and a simple, unostentatious correction, besides

FIG. 192.

---

[94] Some of the books engraved by William Blake suggest possibilities of such unconventional treatment, both of writing and "illumination" (See also Preface).

disarming criticism, is in accordance with the proper freedom of the craft (See p. 122).

Annotations, &c., preferably in smaller coloured writing, are very decorative in the broader margins (pp. 97, 241).

SPECIAL BOOKS — A MS. book is necessarily unique, and some special or personal interest — either of the craftsman (See p. 95) or his "client"— inevitably attaches to it. This may affect its size and form, the treatment of the text, and the decoration and construction generally (See p. 60). Every legitimate opportunity of adding to its individual character should be taken by the scribe and illuminator.

Fig. 175 and Plate XX. are both taken from Special private prayer books or psalters: in each the name Subjects of the owner (e.g. "Euanzelista famulo tuo" Plate XX.) is frequently inserted. Plates XV. and XXII. are also taken from specially commissioned MSS., and many evidences of their ownership, such as portraits or coats-of-arms, form part of the decoration of such books.

CHURCH SERVICES, &c. — (For a special church or person.) Church uses are so varied, that it is most important to ascertain the custom, use, or taste of the persons concerned — especially as to the order of, and the introduction or omission of, certain words, paragraphs, or parts, the colours used in the text, the notation of the music — and the manner in which the book will be used.

A service book for the use of a priest gives prominence to the parts in which he is concerned — the responses[95] may be smaller, and different in form or colour. The rubrics — in red (See pp. 93, 97) — are kept quite distinct, and may form a very decorative feature. For a private person the other parts — such as are said by the congregation — might be specially marked. In either case a certain amount of planning — e.g. completing prayers, &c., in an openings to avoid turning over — may be justified by its convenience to the reader. Should very careful planning ever be required, a pattern-book may be made, having the contents of each page roughly indicated in it.

---

[95] The distinction in the Prayer Book between "Amen" and *"Amen"* — used as a response — is best marked by the sign R (for Responsum) in red, placed before the latter, as: R Amen (See pp. 97, Preface).

WEDDING SERVICE BOOKS, &c. — The interest and value is enhanced if the book is specially prepared — containing the proper names and dates, and only the special psalms, hymns, prayers, homilies, &c., which will be used. Dated pages may be provided at the end of the book for the signatures of the "friends and neighbours" of the principals.

Binding MSS.

MSS. should be bound without delay in order to complete and protect them.

To bind books in stiff boards, in leather, requires considerable practice and skill, but a very effective limp vellum cover can be made by the scribe himself, who, in binding his own books, will learn to think of the binding as a part of the book, and to allow for it in the writing and planning (See p. 65).

Head Kettle Stitch

Tail Kettle Stitch

FIG. 193.

The following note[96] on covering books in limp vellum is specially contributed by Mr. Douglas Cockerell: —

"How to cover a book in a limp vellum cover without using special appliances.

"Cut four strips of stiff vellum $3/8$ inch wide and about four inches long. On these slips you will sew the sections of your book.

"Add to your book, a plain section at either end;[97] vellum for a vellum book, paper tor a paper book. Knock up the backs of the sections squarely, keeping the heads level, and across the back mark with a soft pencil guided by a square, lines to show the position of the slips. The positions of the four slips should leave the space between the slips the same as that between the top slip and the head of the book; the space between the bottom slip and the tail should be a little longer than the spaces between the slips. At about $1/2$ inch from either end make an additional line across the back for the "kettle" or catch stitch. These lines will show as dots on the back of single sections. Each individual section should now have at the back a dot at either end for the kettle stitches, and four pairs of dots $3/8$ inch apart to show the position of the slips, ten dots in all.

"To sew the book, fold the vellum slips about $1½$ inch from one end and bend to a right angle. Place your front end-paper outside downwards, with the back even with the edge of a table or board, and place your folded slips with their shorter ends under it. Then insert your needle from the outside, at the head "kettle stitch" mark, into the centre of the section and bring it out at the first band mark; put the slip in position and reinsert your needle at the mark on the other side of the slip, and so on to the end of the section, coming out at the tail kettle stitch. This should leave your section with a thread,[98] passing alternately along the centre fold inside and across the slips outside, with a loose end hanging from the kettle stitch mark where you began, and a thread with the needle hanging from the other kettle stitch mark (Fig. 193).

---

[96] Figs. 195 and 196 are from Mr. Cockerell's "Bookbinding and the Care of Books," in this Series.

[97] These form the fly-leaves (p. 68).

[98] Thread should be unbleached. Silk of the best quality is better than thread.

"Lay on your next section and sew it in the same way but in the reverse direction, tying up with the first loose end when you come to it. Sew the whole book in the same way, tying on a new needleful of thread as each is exhausted, making practically a continuous thread going backwards and forwards inside the sections and across the slips from end to end of the book. Each succeeding kettle stitch should be caught up by a loop (Fig. 194), and it is well to catch together the loose threads crossing the slips.

FIG. 194.

"When the book is sewn, the back may be covered with thin glue and lined with a piece of leather, but as this is a little difficult to manage neatly, and as the book will hold together without it, for a temporary binding the sections may be left without glue.

"For the cover cut a piece of covering vellum[99] (vellum with a surface) large enough to cover the book and to leave a margin of 1½ inches all round. Mark this with a folder on the underside, as shown at A, Fig. 195. Spaces (1) and (2) are the size of the sides of the book with the surrounding "squares,"[100] space (3) is the width of the back, and space (4) the width for the overlaps on the foredge.[101] Cut the corners as shown at (5), and fold the edges over as at B, and

---

[99] Forrel may be used as a cheap substitute for vellum.

[100] "Squares" = "the portion of the boards projecting beyond the edges of the book."

[101] "Foredge" = "(fore edge) the front edge of the leaves."

then fold over the overlaps and back as at C. Be sure to make all folds sharp and true.

"To avoid mistakes it is well to make a cover of stiff paper first, and then, when that fits exactly, to mark up the vellum from it.

FIG. 195.

"On the inside of the vellum cover, mark faint lines about ¾ inch from, and parallel to, the creases of the back, and further lines about ¼ inch from these. Place your book in the cover and mark the places where the slips cross these lines. Make slits in the cover there, and lace the slips through them (Fig. 196), first putting a piece of loose, toned paper inside the cover to prevent any marks on the

278

book from showing through the vellum. Then lace pieces of silk ribbon of good quality[102] *through the cover and end-papers, leaving the ends long enough to tie."*

Broadsides, Wall Inscriptions, &c.

SET INSCRIPTIONS — Ordinary inscriptions generally consist of a given number of words to be set out in a given space. Careful planning may sometimes be required to fit in the words suitably, or to adapt the lettering to the space. But setting-out (p. 192) becomes much simpler after a little practice, and the good craftsman avoids over-planning.

THE PLACE OF THE INSCRIPTION — The actual space for a wall inscription is commonly suggested by an architectural feature — a stone, a panel, or a niche — of the wall; but in choosing a suitable space for a given inscription, or suitable lettering for a given space, we must take into account—

1. The office of the inscription,
2. How it is to be read —
   a. "At a glance" or
   b. by close inspection.
3. The distance from the reader.
4. The lighting of the space.
5. The character of the surroundings.
6. Any special features.

THE SIZE OF THE LETTERS — The all-important question of readableness may be settled thus: the inscription having been planned suitably to fill the space, one or two words are written or painted (the exact size) on paper — smoked or otherwise coloured if necessary to resemble the background. This is stuck upon the chosen part of the wall, and then viewed from the ordinary position of a reader. When the inscription is high up, the thin parts — especially the horizontals of the letters — must be made extra thick to be seen properly from below.

---

[102] A good, rather dark green ribbon looks well — such as that known as "Church lace," used for the "tyers" in some of the Kelmscott books. Very good ribbons may be obtained from a bookbinder, at 6d. to 1s. 6d. a yard.

FIG. 196.

MARGINS — Wide margins are only required for comparatively small lettering which demands the close attention of the reader,[103] and generally a set inscription looks best if the lettering be comparatively large — covering most of the given surface, and leaving comparatively narrow margins. The frame or moulding, or the natural edge or environment of the circumscribed space, is very often sufficient "margin" (See Plate XXIV.).

The margins vary, however, according to circumstances: especially the foot margin, which may be very narrow if all the space is required for the lettering (See Fig. 211), or very large[104] if there is plenty of space (See Fig. 210). And, as in special pages or terminal pages of books, so in single sheets, panels, &c., the "foot margin" may show — as it really is — as the space which did not require to be filled, and was therefore "left over."

NUMBER OF DIFFERENT TYPES — While in a book of many pages considerable diversity is allowed, it is essential to the strength and dignity of a single sheet or set inscription to limit the number of types employed in it. Three or four ordinary types will generally give sufficient variety, and if it be necessary — as in notices and placards — that Important Words be put in special types to catch the eye, let two — or at most three — special types suffice, and let the remainder of the text be as quiet and reserved as possible. "Display Types" commonly defeat their object by being overdone. A simple contrast is the most effective (Fig. 197).

---

[103] E.g. all ordinary written and printed matter intended to be read at a short distance (See pp. 63-65).

[104] As much as two-thirds, or more, of the whole space.

> # CAPITALS
> in the head-line, large and spaced wide, are contrasted with a mass of smaller lettering below (see p. 330). NOTE.—Generally a finer—though less striking—effect is obtained by keeping large capitals rather slender—contrasting *size* rather than *weight* (p. 328).
>
> FIG. 197.

Illuminated Addresses, &C.

FORMS OF ADDRESSES, &c. — The writer should be prepared to advise his "clients" on the form which the address may take, on special features in its writing and illuminating, and on its general treatment. Ordinarily an Illuminated Address is prepared either as a Framed Parchment (p. 273), a Parchment Scroll, or sheet (p. 273), or a small bound MS. (i.e. in book form: p. 274).[105]

The wording commonly consists of three parts: the Heading (usually the name of the addressee), the Text (usually divided into paragraphs), the Signatures (or a list of names) of the subscribers.

An address is commonly in the 1st or 3rd person, and in case of any confusion of these, any slip of the pen, or other oversight in the draft, the penman should, if possible, call attention to it before the document is put into permanent form.

A very convenient and agreeable style of "address" is a formal letter, beginning "Dear Mr. A — B — ," and ending in the ordinary way. This is a form which may be drawn up more simply, and which reads more naturally, than the ordinary 1st or 3rd personal statement.

---

[105] The addressee's taste and convenience ought to be considered: e.g. to one the framed inscription might be an embarrassment, while by another it might be preferred.

An "address" is sometimes in the form of a resolution passed by a public or private body or committee. For municipal or other important corporations, such an extract from their minutes, neatly and "clerkly" written out on parchment, and duly attested by the signatures of their "head" and their secretary, and without ornament save their seal — on a dependent ribbon — or their coat-of-arms, or badge, would not only be the most natural, but possibly the most dignified and effective shape which might be given to the formal presentation of their compliments.

An "address" accompanying a present is frequently little more than a list of names with a brief complimentary or explanatory statement. If possible, such an inscription should be written or engraved on the article itself, or be specially designed to accompany it. In some cases, this is very simple: when a volume, or set of volumes, is given, the inscription may be written in the first volume — or on a parchment which may be inserted — or it may be prepared in book form, in a binding to match. A silver or other ornament sometimes has a little drawer provided to hold a narrow scroll of names. A portrait may have an inscription on the frame — or even in a corner of the picture — or be accompanied by a simple, framed parchment.

SIGNATURES — A neatly written out list of subscribers — especially when their number is large — is very convenient: it does not require individual personal appointments, nor involve risks of damage to the address. The actual signatures of subscribers, however, are of greater interest and sentimental value, and on such grounds are preferable to a mere list of names.

To avoid risks (or with a view to incorporating the signatures in the decorative scheme) the decoration, gilding, &c., may sometimes be deferred until after the signing of the address.

When the exact number and the names of the subscribers are known beforehand, lines may be provided for their signatures, marked with letters in alphabetical order (the proper number of lines under each). This method solves any difficulty in regard to precedence in signing.

Note. — Ordinary signatures require about ½ inch by 3 inches space each. If there are many, they may be conveniently arranged in two or more columns, according to the space available.

Directions for Signing[106] —

- Edges of parchment not to project beyond desk or table, lest they be creased.
- Paper to be provided to cover the address, with flaps to raise when signing.
- When lines for signatures are grooved (p. 66), signatories to face the light (this makes the lines more evident).
- Ink of one colour to be used if possible.
- Clean, ordinary pens to be provided, and pieces of paper for trying them on.

SPECIAL FRAMED PARCHMENTS — The parchment may have — beyond the top and foot margins — spare pieces which (after the writing and illuminating is finished) are bent over the ends, and glued to the back, of a stout, white card, or millboard — covered with white or light coloured paper. Or — extra margin being allowed all round — the edges of the parchment are cut into tags or "scallops," and folded over an ordinary canvas stretcher, and well tacked at the back with small brads. The wedges are carefully adjusted till the parchment lies flat.

A parchment glued to the surface of a millboard is more convenient for framing, but has a less natural surface, and is not so easily managed by the penman as the plain, flexible parchment.

Frames should be gold, black, or white; very plain, and generally without mounts. The parchment, however, must be framed so that there is no danger of any part of it coming into contact with the glass (as that, being damp, would lead to cockling).

PARCHMENT SCROLL — The foot edge of the parchment may be folded over twice,[107] a strong, silk ribbon (See footnote, p. 268) is laced along through slits in the folded part (a, Fig. 198), so that the two ends come out again at the centre — where they may be knotted together — and are ready to tie round the scroll when it is rolled up (b). A rather narrow, "upright" parchment is most convenient (c). An "oblong" parchment may be

---

[106] To be given to the person in charge of the address.

[107] The original intention of this fold, in deeds, was to provide for the attachment of the seal, and, perhaps, to prevent any addition being made. If the folded part be fairly wide, say, f to 1 inch, little or no foot margin need be allowed.

very effectively arranged in long lines of writing (d). If a special casket or case is not provided, a neat japanned tin case may be obtained for a few shillings.

A small Bound MS. is certainly the most easily handled form in which an address may be prepared — its convenience to the penman, the signatories, the reader, and the addressee, is strongly in its favour. A lengthy address, or a very large number of names, may be contained in a comparatively small book.

FIG. 198.

METHOD OF PLANNING OUT ADDRESSES, &c. — If in the book form, the address is treated much as an ordinary book (See Chap. VI., and Binding, p. 266). The framed or scroll address is planned similarly to a single sheet (p. 52). The following notes of a working method were made during the planning out of an address: —

284

(1) Decide approximately the general form, shape, and decorative treatment of address.
(2) Count words in TEXT (leaving out HEADING and SIGNATURES) = 130
    a. Count paragraphs . . . = 3

(Decide whether first or last paragraph is to be in a different form or colour.)

    b. Decide approximate width . . . = 12 inches.
    c. Decide approximate tide margins (2½ inches each) . . . =5 inches
    d. Hence length of writing-line = . . . 7 inches
    e. Allow ½ inch lines, and approximately eight words to the line.
(3) 130 words TEXT, approx. . . . 16 lines = 8 in. deep
    a. Allow extra (on account paragraphs) .... 1 line = ½ in. deep
    b. (Roughly sketch out HEADING on lines each ½ inch by 7 inches.) Allow for HEADING . . .6 lines = 3 in. deep
    c. Allow for two SIGNATURES, &c. . . . . . .3 lines = 1½ in. deep
    d. Total depth of Writing, &c. . 26 lines = 13 inches.
    e. Allow for Top margin . . . 2 inches
    f. Allow for Foot margin . . . 3 inches
    g. (Note. — This was a "scroll," and the foot margin was folded up to within an inch of the SIGNATURES. A plain sheet would have required about 4 inches foot margin.)
    h. Length of Parchment . .18 inches.
(4) Cut a paper pattern, 12 inches by 18 inches. Rule (in pencil) Side margins (2½ inches and 2½ inches), and Top margin (2 inches), and 26 (½ inch) lines. On this write out the address in ordinary handwriting, using ordinary black and red (or coloured) inks: make approximately eight words to the line, and write as fast as possible; this helps to keep the spacing uniform.

This written pattern should not take more than twenty-minutes for its entire preparation: it is intended to be used as a check on the previous calculation (not as an exact plan), and as a copy, it being easier to copy from your own, than from another's, handwriting.

If the original draft is typewritten, it is hardly necessary to make such a pattern.

(5) Check this copy very carefully with the original to See that the words, &c., are correct.

(6) Cut, rule, and pounce the parchment (pp. 264, 122).

(7) On some scraps of parchment, ruled with a few similar lines, and pounced, try one or two lines of writing, both in vermilion and black, to see that all goes well.

This enables you to get the pens and inks into working order, and will very likely save the carefully prepared parchment from being spoilt.

(8) Write out the address, leaving suitable gaps for gold or special letters.

(9) Put in special letters, decorative capitals, and any other decoration.

(10) Check the finished address very carefully with the original draft (See (5) above) and look it over for mistakes, dotting i's, and putting in commas, &c., if left out. It is important that such a formal document should be accurate.

GENERAL REMARKS — The above simple mode of planning out can be further simplified in custom and practice. By the penman keeping to regular shapes, proportions,[108] and modes of treatment for regular occasions, the addresses, &c., will practically "plan themselves" (p. 61), and better workmanship is the natural result.

Generally, the simpler the form and the treatment of an Illuminated Address, the better the effect. The most effective decoration is the plain coloured or gold capital, and the finest ornament is a coat-of-arms (See "Heraldry" below ; and for general, simple Illumination, See Chapters VII. to XIII.). A symbolical mark, such as a crest, badge, monogram, cypher, or other device (p. 278), boldly and decoratively treated, may be used in place of a coat-of-arms.

There is too much "Illumination" in the conventional "Address," which looks like a "piece of decoration" with a little writing. A really reasonable and effective Illuminated Address is a piece of writing suitably decorated.

HERALDRY — A reliable handbook must be consulted, for accurate "blazoning" is essential. Early examples should be studied (See p. 300). The diagram, Fig. 199, is given as an example of how a charge was

---

[108] E.g. to keep to ½ inch writing-line spaces (except for extra small addresses, or small books). This being approximately the right space for ordinary SIGNATURES, results in further simplification of ruling and arrangement.

evenly arranged on the shield (See balanced background, p. 339). Another example — showing a diapered chequer — is given on p. 258.

Shields in Illuminated borders may be coloured before the border, lest the brilliant mass of colour of the shield clash with the border. The shield, if large, may with advantage set the tone of the whole colour scheme.

Diagram shewing the arrangement of the charges in the earliest form of the English Coat of Arms: Rd.I. to Ed.III.

FIG. 199.

Monograms & Devices

A Monogram consists of two or more letters combined in one form, as the diphthong Æ, and the ampersand[109] & for ET: its legibility may be helped by compound colouring. A Cypher consists of linked or interlaced letters, as ⅏, and may be repeated and reversed if desired (See Subjects Fig. 200).

---

[109] In the common form &, the letters e c (See Plate VI.) are now barely traceable.

Monograms and cyphers may be very decoratively employed as ornaments, and may be used to mark a man's goods, or as a signature on his work: something easily recognised — either very legible or characteristic — is therefore desirable. The two modes may be combined, and there is no limit to the effective devices and ornaments which may be composed of letters. Simple and straightforward devices, however, are generally preferable to very ornate or intricate designs.

C. repeated and reversed.

Device used by Charles the Great: KAROLVS.

1651. A.D.

IL repeated & reversed.

IN planning this sort of Cyphers, the letters may be written on a piece of paper, which is folded, so that the letters reverse symmetrically, while the ink is still wet.

FIG. 200.

CHRONOGRAMS — A chronogram consists of a word or words in which the numerical letters indicate a date. The following is from a very fine memorial inscription at Rye (See Fig. 207): —

Ioannes ThreeLe MeDIo Laetae aetatIs fLore obIIt.

It expresses the date I+L+M+D+I+L+I+L+I+I (or 1+50+1000+500+1+50+1+50+1+1)=1655. As every letter having a numerical value (i.e. C, D, I, (J), L, M, (U), V, (W), X) may be counted, a proper chronogram is not easily composed.

288

The letter-craftsman will discover many ways of "playing" with letters, and of expressing — or concealing — names and numbers in other words, and he may take every liberty he chooses in his private pleasure, provided it does not clash with public convenience.

Title Pages

If large capitals be used, the Name of the Book, the Author, &c., above; the Name of the Publisher, the Date, &c., below,[110] may together fill the page. Ordinary capitals (as used in the text) leave a space in the centre (See Title Page of this book): often pleasantly filled by a small woodcut — a symbolical device, monogram, or printer's mark.

Generally, the fewer and simpler the types, the better: though contrasts of size, form, or colour see p. 249) — such as printing one or two words in large **CAPITALS**, or in 𝕭𝖑𝖆𝖈𝖐 𝕷𝖊𝖙𝖙𝖊𝖗 (p. 252), or part in red — may sometimes be used with good effect. When the types are rather varied, single or double framing lines (called "rules") placed round the page have the effect of binding the whole together. The page may also be divided into parts by transverse "rules" — these further solidify it. Black rules are preferable to red (p. 97): if they are double, the outer line may be thicker than the inner.[111]

RELATION OF TITLE PAGES, &c., TO THE TEXT — Generally, the practical part of the book is to be considered and settled before the ornamental and the decorated Title page conforms to the treatment of the text pages, and should be clearly related to them by the character of its letters or its ornaments. Its margins (especially the top margin) should be approximately the same as those of the text pages, though framing borders may occupy part of, or nearly all, the marginal space. Without doubt the artless, ordinarily printed title page is preferable to those specially designed "title pages" that have little or no relation to the rest of the book.

WOOD ENGRAVING (See pp. 280, 284) — Of all the "processes," wood engraving agrees best with printing. The splendid effect of Title and Initial pages engraved in wood may be seen in the books of the Kelmscott Press. In early printing, woodcut ornaments or borders were commonly used to decorate the printed title page. An example of this

---

[110] Other particulars may be put in the colophon (p. 142).

[111] The use of "rules," though quite legitimate, will be found misleading if it be depended on to "doctor" and "pull together" any weak arrangement of lettering.

combined method — of which unfortunately the greater part of the borders have to be left out — is shown in Fig. 201 (from a 16th century book).[112]

INITIAL PAGES AND OPENINGS — The claim of these to decorative treatment should be considered (p.84). We generally look at the outside of a book for the title — which should be clearly stamped on the cover. But inside the book we look rather for its actual beginning than for its name, and, while something in the nature of the "sub-title" might be used, it would be quite reasonable to revive the ancient fashion — especially in the case of MS. Books — of making the actual beginning the most decorative part of the book. Or a very fine effect may be obtained by the decoration of the entire initial opening — the title on the verso (left page), the beginning of the first chapter on the recto (right page).

---

[112] More, Sir Thomas: *"Utopia, et Mori et Erasmi Epigrammata"*: 4to, Froben, Basle, 1518. Woodcut borders and Title pages by Holbein. (The reproduction is from the title page to the Epigrams.) Note. — The exceptionally fine type of capitals (See p. 283) here shown is used throughout the book, for headings. &c.

EPIGRAM-
MATA CLA
RISSIMI DI
SERTISSIMI-
QVE VIRI
THOMAE
MORI BRI-
TANNI, PLERAQVE E GRAE
CIS VERSA.

FIG. 201 (*see footnote*, p. 365)

Lettering For Reproduction

Where it is possible, it is generally best to make use of ordinary typography. A good fount of type and a natural setting-up or arrangement of it, are more effective than many special designs (See pp. 279, 200).

WOOD AND METAL ENGRAVING — If special forms or arrangements of letters are required, for which type is lacking or unsuited, they are best cut in wood or metal. The engraver leaves the mark of his tool and hand upon, and so gives character to, such lettering; while, if he has some knowledge of letters, he may give fresh beauty to their forms.

The Zincotype Process reproduces, either in facsimile or on a reduced scale, the "design" made by the craftsman in "black and white." This it does more or less exactly according to the pains taken by the zincographer, the quality of the paper employed, &c. The literalness and facility of this process, however, seem to have had a prejudicial effect on the work of the designer. Unless he conscientiously determines that his design shall stand without "touching-up," the knowledge that he may blot out or trim a faulty line with white, that he may fill out or finish a deficient stroke with black, that he may work large and zincograph small, is apt to result in carelessness combined with over-finishing — or a sort of perfection without character.

If zincography be used, a strong, rather type- like letter, or a built-up letter — arranged to give a general effect of richness of mass, would appear more natural than the doubtful "reproduction" of delicate writing or fine pen-lettering.[113]

ETCHING — Calligraphy might be reproduced with very fine effect, retaining its natural delicacy and on a plane surface, if a process of etching writing in facsimile were possible.

Printing

The general question of fine printing and its relation to calligraphy can only be briefly referred to here. A proper study of the art of typography necessitates practice with a printing press, and probably the help of a trained assistant.

---

[113] Doubtful, because, unless unusual care be taken, its delicate quality may be lost in the process, and also because of the type-like impress of the block on the paper.

To would-be printers, printers, and all interested in typography, the easily acquired art of writing may be commended as a practical introduction to a better knowledge of letter forms and their decorative possibilities.

In this connection I have quoted in the preface (p. 1) some remarks on Calligraphy by Mr. Cobden-Sanderson, who, again, referring to typography, says —[114]

"The passage from the Written Book to the Printed Book was sudden and complete. Nor is it wonderful that the earliest productions of the printing press are the most beautiful, and that the history of its subsequent career is but the history of its decadence. The Printer carried on into Type the tradition of the Calligrapher and of the Calligrapher at his best. As this tradition died out in the distance, the craft of the Printer declined. It is the function of the Calligrapher to revive and restore the craft of the Printer to its original purity of intention and accomplishment. The Printer must at the same time be a Calligrapher, or in touch with him, and there must be in association with the Printing Press a Scriptorium where beautiful writing may be practised and the art of letter-designing kept alive. And there is this further evidence of the dependence of printing upon writing: the great revival in printing which is taking place under our own eyes, is the work of a Printer who before he was a Printer was a Calligrapher and an Illuminator, WILLIAM MORRIS.

"The whole duty of Typography, as of Calligraphy, is to communicate to the imagination, without loss by the way, the thought or image intended to be communicated by the Author. And the whole duty of beautiful typography is not to substitute for the beauty or interest of the thing thought and intended to be conveyed by the symbol, a beauty or interest of its own, but, on the one hand, to win access for that communication by the clearness and beauty of the vehicle, and on the other hand, to take advantage of every pause or stage in that communication to interpose some characteristic and restful beauty in its own art."

Early Printing was in some points inferior in technical excellence to the best modern typography. But the best early printers used finer founts of type and better proportions in the arrangement and spacing of their printed pages: and it is now generally agreed that early printed books are the most beautiful. It would repay a modern printer to endeavour to find out the real

---

[114] "Ecce Mundus (The Book Beautiful)," 1902.

grounds for this opinion, the underlying principles of the early work, and, where possible, to put them into practice.

*Diagram shewing arrangement of pages (about ⅓ size).
Note · Inner columns of Commentary narrow (Text cols. equal)*

FIG. 202.

FREEDOM — The treatment or "planning" of early printing — and generally of all pieces of lettering which are most pleasing — is strongly marked by freedom. This freedom of former times is frequently referred to now as "spontaneity" — sometimes it would seem to be implied that there was a lawless irresponsibility in the early craftsman, incompatible with modern conditions. True spontaneity, however, seems to come from working by rule, but not being bound by it.

For example, the old Herbal from which Figs. 135 to 141 are taken contains many woodcuts of plants, &c., devoting a complete page to each.

When a long explanation of a cut is required, a smaller type is used (comp. Figs. 135 & 138); when the explanation is very short, it does not fill the page.

This is a free and natural treatment of the greatest convenience to the reader, for illustration and text are always in juxtaposition. And though the size of the type and the amount of the text are varied, yet the uniform top margins, and the uniform treatment and arrangement of the woodcuts, harmonise the pages, and give to the whole book an agreeable effect of freedom combined with method. An old way of treating a text and its commentary is indicated by the diagram (Fig. 202). The text is printed in large type, the commentary, in smaller type, surrounds it; such portion of the text being printed on each page as will allow sufficient surrounding space for the accompanying commentary on that portion. The proportions and treatment of every page are uniform (note, particularly, the uniformity of the upper parts of the pages, five lines of commentary being allowed to enclose the text, or bound it above, on every page) with the exception that the height of the text-column varies — one page having as few as three lines of text to the column, another having fifty-nine lines. This free treatment of the text gives a charming variety to the pages.

POETRY — A broader and freer treatment is desirable in the printing of poetry. The original lines and the arrangement of the verses should be more generally preserved. And though the opening lines of a poem may sometimes be magnified by printing them in capitals — which necessitate their division — to sacrifice the naturally varying line to the "even page" is questionable, and to destroy the form of a poem in order to compress it is a "typographical impertinence" (See p. 55).

DECORATION OF PRINT ✠ MUCH MAY BE DONE BY ARRANGING IMPORTANT TEXT IN "ITS OWN" CAPITALS; OR BY THE OCCASIONAL USE OF EXTRA LARGE CAPITALS.

For special letters or ornaments, woodcuts are best (See p. 279). The early printers generally had little, simple blocks of ornamental devices which might be used separately, or be built up into a frame border for a whole page — a simple method and effective, if used reasonably. The judicious use of colour, especially of red (See pp. 82, 97), is very effective. The extra printings required for additional colours may make it worthwhile (in the case of limited editions) to put in simple initials, paragraph marks, notes, &c., by hand (See pp. 137, 70). The earliest printed books, being modelled on the MS. books, employed such rubrication freely, in spaces specially left in the text or in the margins. There are still great possibilities in the hand decoration of printed books.

The following note on printing, reproduced here by the permission of Mr. Emery Walker, appeared in the Introductory Notes of the Catalogue of the first exhibition of The Arts and Crafts Exhibition Society, in 1888.

"Printing, in the only sense with which we are at present concerned, differs from most if not from all the arts and crafts represented in the Exhibition in being comparatively modern. For although the Chinese took impressions from wood blocks engraved in relief for centuries before the wood-cutters of the Netherlands, by a similar process, produced the block books, which were the immediate predecessors of the true printed book, the invention of movable metal letters in the middle of the fifteenth century may justly be considered as the invention of the art of printing. And it is worth mention in passing that, as an example of fine typography, the earliest dated [115] book, the Gutenberg Bible of 1455, has never been surpassed. Printing, then, for our purpose, may be Special considered as the art of making books by means of movable types. Now, as all books not primarily intended as picture-books consist principally of types composed to form letterpress, it is of the first importance that the letter used should be fine in form; especially, as no more time is occupied, or cost incurred, in casting, setting, or printing beautiful letters, than in the same operations with ugly ones. So we find the fifteenth and early sixteenth century printers, who were generally their own type-founders, gave great attention to the forms of their types.

"The designers of the letters used in the earliest books were probably the scribes whose manuscripts the fifteenth-century printed books so much resemble. Aldus of Venice employed Francesco Francia of Bologna, goldsmith and painter, to cut the punches for his celebrated italic letter. Froben, the great Basle printer, got Holbein to design ornaments for his press, and it is not unreasonable to suppose that the painter may have drawn the models for the noble Roman types we find in Froben's books. With the decadence in handwriting which became marked in the sixteenth century, a corresponding change took place in the types: the designers, no longer having beautiful writing as a model and reference, introduced variations arbitrarily. The types of the Elzevirs are regular and neat, and in this respect modern, but they altogether lack the spirit and originality that distinguish the early Roman founts of Italy and Germany: Gothic characteristics inherited from their mediaeval predecessors. In the seventeenth century type-founding began to be carried on as a craft apart from that of the printer, and although in this and

---

[115] [It was dated 1456 by a rubricator, not by the printer. — E.W.]

the succeeding century many attempts were made to improve the "face" (as the printing surface of type is called), such examples as a rule reflect only too clearly the growing debasement of the crafts of design.

"Notable among these attempts were the founts cut by William Caslon, who started in business in London as a letter-founder in 1720, taking for his models the Elzevir types. From this time until the end of the century he and his successors turned out many founts relatively admirable. But at the end of the eighteenth century a revolution was made, and the founders entirely abandoned the traditional forms of their predecessors, and evolved the tasteless letters with which nearly all the books published during the first sixty years of the present century are printed, and which are still almost universally used for newspapers and for Government publications. Particularly objectionable forms are in everyday use in all continental countries requiring Roman letter. (The last two sentences are set in a type of this character.)

"In 1844 the Chiswick Press printed for Messrs. Longmans' 'The Diary of Lady Willoughby,' and revived for this purpose one of Caslon's founts. This was an important step in the right direction, and its success induced Messrs. Miller & Richard of Edinburgh to engrave a series of 'old style' founts, with one of which this catalogue is printed. Most other type-founders now cast similar type, and without doubt if their customers, the printers, demanded it, they would expend some of the energy and talent which now goes in cutting Japanese-American and sham seventeenth-century monstrosities in endeavouring to produce once more the restrained and beautiful forms of the early printers, until the day when the current handwriting may be elegant enough to be again used as a model for the type-punch engraver.

"Next in importance to the type are the ornaments, initial letters, and other decorations which can be printed along with it. These, it is obvious, should always be designed and engraved so as to harmonise with the printed page regarded as a whole. Hence, illustrations drawn only with reference to purely pictorial effects are entirely out of place in a book, that is, if we desire seriously to make it beautiful.

—EMERY WALKER."

INSCRIPTIONS ON METAL, STONE, WOOD, &c. — As the material naturally modifies the shapes of the letters cut or formed on its surface, and as the object bearing the inscription affects their arrangement, it is essential that the inscription cutter make himself familiar with various stones, metals, woods, &c., with the various chisels and gravers which are properly employed on them, and with fine inscriptions or examples of good pieces of lettering (See pp. 301, 176).

A knowledge of penmanship will be found useful, and the pen may be appealed to decide questions of abstract form in regard to letters which have come from pen forms (e.g. Roman Small-Letters, Italics, &c). And in this connection, it may be noted again that the "slanted-pen forms"(pp. 230, 8) are generally the most practical.

ENGRAVING ON METAL — Letters incised in metal may most nearly approach pen forms, as the fine grain of the metal and the comparatively small scale of the work allow of fine "thin strokes." The engraver, however, while following generally the "thicks" and "thins" of the penman, allows the metal and the tool and, to a large extent, his own hand, to decide and characterize the precise forms and their proportions.

INSCRIPTIONS IN STONE (See Chap. XVII., Plates I., II., and XXIV., and pp. 221, 2). — The grain of stone does not generally allow of very fine thin strokes, and the "thicks" and "thins" therefore tend to differ much less than in pen-work. Their origin, moreover, is much less easily traced to the tool — i.e. the chisel — and the difference was less in the Special early inscriptions (See Plate II.) than we are now accustomed to (See Plate XXIV.): perhaps it may be explained as a fashion set by penmanship (See p. 178).

Inscriptions on Wood are frequently in relief (See raised letters, p. 290), matching the carved ornament. Incised letters may be painted or gilded to make them show more clearly.

SIGN-WRITING AND BRUSH-WORK — Inscriptions, such as shop signs, notices, &c, painted on wood or stone, require — besides a practical knowledge of materials — a considerable facility with the brush or "pencil." Directness and freedom of workmanship are most desirable.[116]

A suitable brush will make letters closely resembling pen letters. But the pen automatically makes letters with a uniform precision, which it is neither desirable nor possible for the brush to imitate: and greater skill is required to control the brush, which in the hand of a good "Writer" will be

---

[116] This is recognised in the Sign-writing profession, where, I understand, an applicant for work is sometimes given a blackboard or a piece of American cloth, on which he writes out a short inscription in "sharp white." It is not necessary to watch the writer; good, direct workmanship shows itself, and also every hesitating stroke or fault, every patch or "touching-up" or "going over," is made evident.

permitted to give its own distinct character to the lettering (See also p. 221, and Fig. 164).

The brush is properly used for temporary inscriptions, especially on the surface of painted wood or stone, but, for more important work, incising or carving (painted if desired) are to be preferred as being more permanent[117] and preserving the original form[118] of the lettering.

Of Inscriptions Generally
(See also Chapter XIV. and pp. 268-271)

ALPHABETS — For practical purposes the best letters are the Roman Capitals, Roman Small-Letters, and Italics. These are susceptible of very decorative treatment without loss of legibility. And there are many varieties of the pure Roman Capital (See Figs. 203 - 207), besides the "Gothicised" Roman and the simple "Gothic" Capitals, which are all essentially readable.

Different Sizes of Capitals in inscriptions in wood, stone, metal, &c., are generally kept approximately equal in "weight" (See p. 251). Note. — A downward decrease in height of the letters is common in early inscriptions (p. 318).

Incising is generally the most simple, and therefore the most natural, method for making an ordinary inscription. The letters should be large rather than small, and be deeply cut. Note, however, an incised stamp or die produces an impression in relief on clay, &c. This may be seen in the lettering on Roman pottery.

RAISED LETTERS — From the earliest times letters in relief (or litterae prominentes) have been used for special purposes. They are generally rather more legible than the incised letters, and the difference between "thicks" and "thins" tends to disappear.

It is quite possible to make a beautiful and characteristic alphabet of equal-stroke letters, on the lines of the so-called "Block Letter" but properly proportioned and finished (such letters may be Raised, or Incised ox Painted: See incised form, p. 304).

---

[117] Brush lettering may be used very effectively on Tiles and China, &c. (See p. 261-2), when it is of course rendered permanent by baking.

[118] The original form of a painted inscription (not carved) is inevitably spoilt by re-painting.

TI·CAESARIS
DIVI·AVG·AVGVSTI
MILES·MISSICVS·ENIVS
FES·TVS·MILITAVIT·ANNOS·XXV

FIG. 203.—Hübner's *Exempla*, No. 187 (¼ scale of inscription), "*Rustic Capitals*" (see p. 297) *between* A.D. 14-37.

SPENDONTI
C·STATI·PATERCLI
Q·STATIVS·MVRANVS
SODALI
IAMBIS·VOCIONOS·SPENDON·COMPLEVERAT·ANNOS
RAPVSQVE·FATIS·CONDITVS·HOC·TVMVLO·ST

FIG. 204.—Hübner's *Exempla*, No. 384 (one-fifth scale of inscription). 1st or 2nd Century, A.D.

IIII·NON·SEPTEMBR·IN·CVRIA·TEMP
Q·GRANIVS·AITICVS·M·SIIACCVS·A
QVOD·AVFIDIVS·HR·A·SEAICLAVDIVS·A
CVM·M·AEIIVS·AIIMVS·VIR·P·ROBISSIMVS
AEDIFICIO·QVOD·EXTRVIT·IN·TRANSITO
POTESTAS·QVE·AEDIFICIES·VI·AD·SEP·ERTINERE·PC
ADMIIII·REMIITQVE·ISOLARIVM·CVM·P·IVS·E

FIG. 205.—Hübner's *Exempla*, No. 1084 (one-fourth scale of inscription). 2nd Century, A.D.

FIG. 206.—(*Two portions*) From a Rubbing of a Florentine marble dated MCCCCLXVII, slightly reduced (scale twelve-thirteenths). Note the interlinear spaces are 1⅜ inch.

FIG. 207.—From a Rubbing of a Slate at Rye, dated 1655 (see p. 363). Exact size.

FIG. 208.—From a Rubbing of a Stone at Oxford (by A. E. R. Gill, 1905). Reduced, two-thirds scale.

Raised letters, if exposed to wear or damage, may be protected by being on a sunk panel or having a raised frame or ornament. The background also may be left in raised strips flush with the letters, between the lines of the inscription.

PUNCTUATION — In early inscriptions the words were separated by points: in the more ancient they are square shaped ■, ■, —, in the more elaborate, triangular ▶, ▲, ◀, sometimes with curved-in sides ▲ (Plate I.). These developed later into the ivy leaf 🙶 🙷 , or "hederae distinguentes." Such points may be used occasionally in modern work with fine effect, but should seldom be used between every word, unless the words are necessarily so close that distinguishing marks are required.

PHRASING AND ARRANGEMENT — An inscription may be arranged in sentences or phrases, and occasionally, by the use of larger letters, greater prominence is given to a word or phrase (See Figs. 197, 204, 211). This method is particularly adapted to the nature of a set inscription (p. 197), and may help both its readableness and its appearance, but it must be borne in mind that to lay stress on any one statement or word may pervert its meaning or attract too much attention to it.

Any confusion of sense, or accidental word (p. 193) or phrase, appearing in the setting-out is avoided, if possible, by a slight rearrangement of the part, or, if necessary, of the whole inscription. Great care is taken that the spelling is accurate: a pocket dictionary should be carried.

Reading is further facilitated by avoiding, where possible, the dividing of words at the ends of lines. It may be observed that in the more ancient inscriptions words were generally kept entire.

Exercises in letter form and arrangement, more profitable than mere paper "designing," might be devised by the craftsman. Inscriptions might be cut — on a small scale — in gesso or chalk, or inscriptions might be variously spaced and arranged on a properly coloured surface — such as a drawing-board covered with light or dark cloth — in letters cut out of sheet-lead or card.

BIBLIOGRAPHY, &C.

The few books and pamphlets given below are generally, of recent date, practical, and inexpensive. The prices quoted are, I believe, those at which the books are generally sold (not necessarily their published prices). They are all illustrated, except Nos. *9, 10, 11, and 19.

Writing, &c.

(See also Nos. 8, 12, 14, 19, 28, 29, and 31.)

1. The Story of the Alphabet: Edward Clodd, 1900. 9d.
2. Greek and Latin Palaeography: Edward Maunde Thompson. 3s. 9d. (The extracts in these pp. 36, 41, 416, &c, are from the 2nd edition, 1894.)
3. The Journal of the Society of Arts, No. 2726, Feb. 17, 1905 ; Papers on Calligraphy and Illumination: Edward Johnston and Graily Hewitt. 6d.
4. Fac-similes de Manuscrits Grecs, Latins et Francais du V e au XIV e Siecle exposes dans la Galerie Mazarine: Bibliotheque Nationale Departement des Manuscrits. 5s.
5. "A Guide to the Manuscripts" in the British Museum, 1906 (30 plates). 6d.
6. Bible Illustrations: Oxford University Press, 1896. About 2s.

Illumination, &c.

(See also Nos. 3, 4, 5, 12, 14, 29, and 31.)

7. Illuminated Letters and Borders: John W. Bradley, 1901 (19 plates). (Price at South Kensington Museum) is. 8d.
8. English Illuminated Manuscripts: Sir E. M. Thompson, 1895. [Now out of print.)
9. The Journal of the Society of Arts, No. 368, April 8, 1898 ; a Paper on English Art in Illuminated Manuscripts: Sir E. M. Thompson. 6d.
10. The Book of the Art of Cennino Cennini (a contemporary practical treatise on 14th- century Italian painting): Translated by Christiana J. Herringham, 1899. 6s.

11. Some Hints on Pattern Designing: (lecture, 1881), William Morris, 1899. 2s. 6d.

    (11a. "Books for the Bairns. — No. 50," contains 55 reproductions of Bewick's Birds, id.)

Books — Manuscript & Printing.

(See also Nos. 2 to 9, and 29 and 31.)

12. Books in Manuscript: Falconer Madan, 1893. 6s. (Frontispiece draw <n from this by permission.)
13. The Story of Books: Gertrude Burford Rawlings, 1901. 9d.
14. The Old Service - Books of the English Special Church: Christopher Wordsworth and Subjects Henry Littlehales, 1904. 7s. 6d.
15. Early Illustrated Books: Alfred W. Pollard, 1893. 6s.
16. Facsimiles [in colour] from Early Printed Books in the British Museum, 1897. 7s. 6d.
17. A Guide to the Exhibition in the King's Library (illustrating the History of Printing, Music Printing, and Bookbinding): British Museum, 1 90 1 (36 illustrations). 6d.
18. "Arts and Crafts Essavy by Members of the Arts and Crafts Exhibition Society "— Printing: William Morris and Emery Walker — (1st pub. 1893), 1899 2s. 6d.
19. "Ecce Mundus," containing The Book Beautiful: T.J. Cobden-Sanderson, 1902. 2s. 6d.
20. Printing (a technological handbook): Charles Thomas Jacobi, 1898. 3s. 9d.
21. Bookbinding and the Care of Books (The Artistic Crafts Series of Technical Hand-books), 1901: Douglas Cockerell. 5s.
22. A Note on Bookbinding: Douglas Cockerell, 1904. id.

Heraldry, Symbolism, &R.

(See also Nos. 1, 12, 15, 29, and 31.)

23. The Journal of the Society of Arts, No. 2309, Feb. 19, 1897; A Paper on The Artistic Treatment of Heraldry: by W. H. St. John Hope. 6d.

24. English Heraldry: Charles Boutell, 1867. 6th ed. 1899, aDout 3s 9.

25. The Stall Plates of the Kniehts of the Garter, 1348-1485: W. H. ^St. John Hope (90 coloured plates, Imp. 8vo). About £3.

26. Didron's Christian Iconography (or the Subjects History of Christian Art in the Middle Ages): 2 vols. 3s. Cjd. (each).

Lettering, &c.

(See also Nos. 1 to 8, and 12 to 20.)

27. Lettering in Ornament: Lewis F. Day, 1902. 5s.

28. Alphabets: Edward F. Strange (1st ed. 1895). 4th ed., 3s. 9d.

29. The Pa Ideographical Society's Publications (out of print), containing hundreds of fac- similes (chiefly of MSS.), are of great interest. They may of course be seen in the British Museum Library. The New Pa Ideographical Society publishes a selection of facsimiles annually.

30. Hiibner's Exempla Scripturae Epigraphicae Latinae a Caesaris dictatons morte ad aetatem Justiniani (Berlin, 1885, price 46s.) contains many fine outline drawings of ancient Roman inscriptions (See Figs. 203-5). It is kept with the books of reference in the Reading Room at the British Museum.

31. Photographs of fine pieces of lettering may be obtained at the Book Stall in South Kensington Museum (See. footnote, p. 409). Original MSS. or Inscriptions — from which we can learn much more than from photographs or drawings — may be found in most parts of the country, and in London especially in the British Museum, South Kensington Museum (See p. 391), the Record Office (Rolls Chapel, See p. 11), and Westminster Abbey (MSS. in the Chapter-House).

APPENDIX B

CHAPTER XVII
INSCRIPTIONS IN STONE

(By A. E. R. Gill)

Treatment & Arrangement

Treatment. — Inscriptions are carved in stone for many uses: for Foundation Stones and Public Inscriptions, for Tombstones and Memorial Inscriptions, for Mottos and Texts, for Names and Advertisements, and each subject suggests its own treatment.

Names and Advertisements should be easily read, and usually entirely unornamental. The Treatment of Texts, Memorial Inscriptions, Foundation Stones, &c., may, according to the needs of the case or the opportunities of the carver, be either simple or elaborate.

Colour and Gold may be used both for the beauty of them and, in places where there is little light, to increase legibility,

ARRANGEMENT — There are two methods of arranging Inscriptions: the "Massed" and the "Symmetrical." In the former the lines are very close in together, and approximately equal in length, and form a mass. Absolute equality is quite unnecessary. Where the lines are very long it is easy to make them equal; but with lines of few words it is very difficult, besides being derogatory to the appearance of the Inscription. In the "Symmetrical" Inscription the length of the lines may vary considerably, and each line (often comprising a distinct phrase or statement) is placed in the centre of the Inscription space.

Short Inscriptions, such as those usually on Tombstones or Foundation Stones, may well be arranged in the "Symmetrical" way, but long Inscriptions are better arranged in the "Massed" way, though, sometimes, the two methods may be combined in the same Inscription.

The Three Alphabets

The Roman Alphabet, the alphabet chiefly in use today, reached its highest development in Inscriptions incised in stone (See Plate I.), and it became absolutely suited to the material.

Besides ROMAN CAPITALS, it is necessary that the letter-cutter should know how to carve Roman small-letters[119] (or "Lower case") and Italics, either of which may be more suitable than Capitals for some Inscriptions.

Where great magnificence combined with great legibility[120] is required, use large Roman Capitals, Incised or in Relief, with plenty of space between the letters and the lines.

Where great legibility but less magnificence is required, use "Roman Small-Letters" or "Italics," or Roman Capitals, either small, or close together, or both.

All three Alphabets may be used together, as, for instance, on a Tombstone, one might carve the Name in Capitals and the rest of the Inscription in Small-Letters, using Italics for difference.

Beauty of Form may safely be left to a right use of the chisel, combined with a well-advised study of the best examples of Inscriptions: such as that on the Trajan Column (See Plates I., II.) and other Roman Inscriptions in the South Kensington and British Museums, for Roman CAPITALS; and sixteenth and seventeenth century tombstones, for Roman small-letters and Italics.[121] If the simple Inscriptions elementary form of the letter be cut firmly and in Stone directly, it will be found that the chisel will suggest how that form may be made beautiful. This may be shown, for example, by an attempt to carve a quite simple Incised letter with no Serifs and with all the strokes equally thick. In making the ends of the strokes nice and clean it will be found that there is a tendency to spread them into Serifs, and the letter is at once, in some sort, beautified (See Fig. 209).

---

[119] With which we may include Arabic numerals.

[120] It should be clearly understood that legibility by no means excludes either beauty or ornament. The ugly form of "Block" letter so much in use is no more legible than the beautiful Roman lettering on the Trajan Column (See Plates I., II.).

[121] Roman small-letters and Italics, being originally pen letters, are still better understood if the carver knows how to use a pen, or, at least, has studied good examples of manuscripts in which those letters are used.

FIG. 209.

Size & Spacing

DRAWING OUT — Take paper and pencil, or what you will, and write out the words of the Inscription in Capitals, or small-letters (or both), without any regard to scale or the shape of the space the Inscription is to go in. The carver will then see easily of what letters and words his Inscription is composed. Next draw the shape of the Inscription space (say to 1 inch or 1½ inch scale), and in that space set out the Inscription, either "Massed" or "Symmetrical" as has been decided. The drawing should be neither scribbled nor elaborated. A good plan is to cut the lead of the pencil to a chisel shape. The natural thicks and thins of the letters (See p. 8) may then be produced easily and quickly. The carver will thus be able, after a little experience, to calculate quite easily what size he will be able to carve his letters, what space he will be able to leave between the lines, and what margins he can afford.[122]

The Size of Lettering depends on where it is to go (i.e. outdoors or indoors, far away or near), the material to be used, and the space at the carver's disposal.

Out of Doors letters should not, as a rule, be less than 1¼ inch high, more if possible.[123]

Indoors smaller lettering may be carved, but even then 1 inch is quite small enough, and that only in marble, slate, or the finest stones.

---

[122] Some advice from the letter-cutter might be useful to the client as to the number of words and the space they will occupy in cases where it is possible to adapt the one to the other.

[123] Small lettering is less convenient to read out of doors, and is apt to get filled with dirt or moss.

In such stones as Ancaster or Ham-Hill it is not possible to carve good letters less than 3 inches high.

More than one size of letter may be used in the same Inscription to give emphasis to certain words, thus: on a Foundation Stone the Date (See Fig. 210), and on a Tombstone the Name (See Fig. 211), may be made larger than the rest.

This Stone was Laid on the 4-th of July 1904

Fig. 210.

SPACING — Proper spacing is essential to a good Inscription. As a general rule, Roman letters should not be crowded together. Space should be left between each, varying according to the letters — a narrower space between two O's, for example, and, generally, a wider space between two straight letters. The lines may be about the height of the lettering apart (See Plate I.) or pretty close together (See Plate XXIV.).

MARGINS — If the Inscription is to be carved in a panel, the surrounding mouldings take the place of margins, and the lettering may fill the panel (See Fig. 211). If any space be left, let it come, as it naturally will, at the bottom. If the lettering is not to be in a panel, the margins depend primarily on what the carver can afford, and where the Inscription is to go. Every case must be treated on its own merits, but as a general rule one may say that the bottom margin should be the widest and the top margin the narrowest.

> To the dear memory of
> ELIZABETH ✝
> Daughter of John &
> Elizabeth Smith of
> this parish.. She died
> August 14, 1901, Aged 16.

FIG. 211.

The Material

The best quality a stone can have, from a letter-cutter's point of view, is fineness or closeness of texture, combined with freedom from holes and flints or occasional shells, and the letter-cutter will do well to choose the stone himself, if possible, having regard to this quality.

The following is a list of a few of the best stones for outdoor and indoor use: —

Outdoors or Indoors.

Portland. — Especially good for lettering on account of its fineness and its excellent weathering qualities, for it not only hardens on the surface, but also becomes quite white if exposed to wind and rain, thus showing very clearly any differences of light and shade.

Hoptonwood Slate. — Fine and hard: good weathering qualities. Great delicacy may be attained in these.

Amcaster Ham-Hill Ketton. — Only suitable for large lettering.

Indoors Only.

Clunk Chalk. — Very fine and delicate work may be done in these.

Bath. — A cheap stone, and easily carved; but unsuitable for small lettering.

Marbles and Alabasters. — Excellent for Inscriptions indoors, but much colour or veining tends to confuse lettering.

Setting Out

The stone being ready for the setting out, i.e. smoothed and cleaned, lines are ruled on it for the lines of lettering and margins with a pencil or point. If the Inscription is to be arranged "Symmetrically" a centre line is ruled from top to bottom.

The carver should rule and set out one line and carve that before ruling another, as pencil marks are liable to be rubbed off by the hand in carving.[124]

In "Setting Out" the spacing of the letters is thought of rather than their forms. And though the beginner may find careful drawing helpful, the forms which may best be produced with the chisel are found only by practice and experience (p. 311).

The chisels needed for simple work are flat chisels of the following sizes: —

1/16 inch, ¼ inch, ³/₈ inch, ½ inch, 1 inch.

The shanks should be about 7 inches long.

It will be found useful to keep a few "Bull-nosed" chisels (See 7, Fig. 212) for use in cutting curves, and a few "skewed" chisels (8, Fig. 212) for use in cutting the background of Raised letters, as a chisel of that shape is more easily used in a corner.

The chisels are either Hammer-headed or Mallet-headed, or they may have wooden handles (See Fig. 212, and pp. 311-12). The Hammer-headed are the most used, and a good number should be procured. The best are made with cupped ends, to prevent them from slipping on the hammer (See 5, Fig. 212).

---

[124] Whenever it is possible the carver should not be bound to follow a drawing strictly, but should do his work in the straightforward manner described above. Unfortunately, he is often obliged to set out the whole Inscription exactly before carving it, and in such a case it is usual to carve the bottom line of letters first and to work upwards, cutting the first line last.

FIG. 212.

1 Wooden-handled
2 Section of No. 1
3 Straight Hammer-headed
4 Enlarged section of No. 3
5 Section of Hammer-head enlarged to show cup
6 Mallet-head
7 'Bull-nosed'
8 'Skewed'

TEMPER AND SHARPNESS — Above all things the chisels must be of the right temper, and sharp.[125]

They may be tempered by a smith or tool-maker — if the craftsman can do it for himself, so much the better. They are sharpened on a piece of Grit-stone (hard York stone, for instance) with water. The Temper of a chisel may be seen by the colour (blue shows a soft or low-temper, straw colour a hard or high temper), and felt by the way it rubs on the Grit-stone (a hard tool will slide easily over the stone, while a soft one will seem to stick or cling).[126]

---

[125] Really sharp, i.e. sharp enough to cut a piece of paper without tearing it.

[126] The harder the stone to be carved, the more highly tempered will the chisels need to be.

MALLETS — A wooden mallet or Mel, a Zinc mallet or Dummy, and an iron or steel hammer are required (Fig. 213).

The Mell is made wholly of wood, and should, for letter cutting, be about 5½ inches in diameter.

The Dummy has a head of zinc and a wooden handle. It should be about 2½ inches in diameter.

The hammer should be about the same size and weight as the Dummy.

Mallet or Mell   Dummy

Hammer

FIG. 213.

A Right Use Of The Chisel

The workman must find out, for himself, how best to use his tools. In the ordinary way, it is best to hold the chisel at an angle of about 45° with the surface of the stone — in the manner shown in Fig. 214 — in cutting both straight stems and curves. The chisel is held firmly (usually in the left hand, with the little finger about an inch from the cutting end of the chisel) and tapped rather than banged, and lightly rather than heavily.

FIG. 214.

The best way to cut a letter is to start at the extreme left-hand point of the bottom Serif, and, working upwards, to cut the left side of the stroke first. Then start similarly at the extreme right-hand point of the bottom Serif, and cut the right side of the stroke. Then finish the Serifs.

When cutting a curve, cut the inside first (Fig. 214), and start as near the narrowest part of the curve as possible.

In Incised letters unnecessary junctions of the parts may be avoided (See Fig. 215). Where they are necessary, as in a capital E, or in a small y, cut away from the junction or down on to it, rather than towards it.

KR
mg

Note points 'A' showing how junctions may be avoided in stone.

FIG. 215.

The Mallet-headed and wooden-handled chisels are used with the Mell for large work and for cutting surfaces.

The Hammer-headed chisels are used with the hammer for ordinary work, and with the Dummy for small and delicate work.

A Mallet or Dummy is not used in carving chalk, but the chisel is pushed; the right hand doing the pushing, and the left hand guiding and steadying the chisel (See Fig. 216). If the chisel were struck, the surface of the chalk would flake off.

FIG. 216.

    In cutting an Incised Inscription with the ordinary "V" section (See Fig. 217), use one size of chisel throughout. The width of the chisel should generally be about the width of the letter stem required. More elaborate sections necessitate the use of several sizes of chisels.

Incised Letters & Letters In Relief

    Inscriptions may be Incised or in Relief: that is, sunk or raised.[127] The modus operandi and the time spent in carving the actual letters are the same in either case, but whereas when the Incised letter is carved there is nothing more to be done, after the carving of the Raised letter there is still the stone surrounding it (i.e. the background) to be dealt with, and this may

---

[127] In learning to cut Inscriptions one would naturally begin with Incised letters.

simply be carved smooth,[128] or, if our imagination be strong enough, and our hand have the cunning, it may become under the tool a field of roses and lilies in which the letters are set.

Other things being equal, it becomes a question of economy which form of lettering one will cane, as the necessity of dealing with the background of a Raised Inscription, while more than doubling the opportunities of the carver, at least doubles the time spent in carving.

1 For ordinary work.

2
3 } For large work

4 For gilding

5 For ordinary work.

6
7 } For large work

FIG. 217.

---

[128] Where the ground between the letters is left plain, an absolute flatness and evenness is not necessary, The common method of jabbing or "pecking" the background is objectionable.

Raised lettering will show out more clearly than Incised lettering where there is little light.

Roman Capitals are more adapted for carving in Relief than are Roman small-letters or Italics, which are directly derived from the pen.

Raised lettering is more allied to ordinary carving, while Incised lettering may be thought of as writing in stone.

The Sections Of Letters

For Incised letters, a "V" section (i, Fig. 217) of about 60° is best for regular use; deeper rather than shallower. The letters may with advantage be cut a little deeper towards the Serifs (See Fig. 218).

Although the simple "V" section is the most useful, other sections may be used for large letters (i.e. letters more than 6 inches high), or letters in a very fine material (2 & 3, Fig. 217).

FIG. 218.

If the lettering is to be gilded, and the stone will permit of it, Section 4 (Fig. 217) is a good one to use. Only the curved part is to be Gilded, and not the small beveled sides.

For Raised letters, the best and most useful section is No. 5; the slightly beveled sides tell as part of the letter. Experience, and the weathering conditions, will suggest the amount of Relief to be given. For letters 1½ inch high, out of doors, $^3/_{16}$ inch of relief is ample, and if there be good light $^1/_8$ inch is enough. Excessive relief looks clumsy.

Sections Nos. 6 and 7 are suitable only for large letters: and elaborate sections should as a rule be used only for letters standing alone.

Working In Situ

If possible, the carver should work in situ. When that is impracticable,[129] he should consider most carefully where his Inscription is to go.

---

[129] E.g. Tombstones and Memorial Slabs are not usually fixed until finished.

In an Inscription which is much above the eye in Stone level, the letters may be narrower in proportion to their height, and the horizontal strokes extra thick to allow for foreshortening. (See also pp. 269, 203)

The advantages of working in situ are great, for by so doing the carver sees his job as he works under the same conditions of light and environment that it will finally be seen under, and the work is more likely to become a part of the place because it has grown there.

And it is good to carve an Inscription on the actual wall of a fine building, and better still to work in the inspiriting atmosphere of building in progress, or to work in the open air where the artificial notions of workshop or studio are dissipated and the feeling of life and freedom gained.

COLLOTYPE PLATES AND NOTES

(Note. — In order to make the illustrations [whether of facsimiles or enlargements] as large and as full as possible, I have sacrificed "appearance" to use and allowed most of the collotype plates, and many of the diagrams in the book, to encroach on the margins. — E. J.)

GENERAL NOTE — All the plates are in facsimile as to size (or nearly so, allowing for errors in reproduction) except I., II., XXIL., and XXIV., which had to be reduced, and therefore only portions of the MSS. can be shown. Note. — All the MSS. are on "Vellum" (See p. 122). In order to get a better impression of the size and general proportion of a MS., the student might reconstruct it — or at least mark off the margins, text, — on paper, from the measurements given. Or a sheet of paper might be cut to the size of the given page or opening, with an aperture (in its proper place) through which the plate might be viewed.

The plates are arranged in chronological order as nearly as possible. They are intended briefly to illustrate the Development of the Formal Book Hands from the Roman Capital and the General Development of the Illuminated MS.: I hope, moreover, that, fragmentary as they are, they will prove usefully suggestive in regard to the Arrangement of Text and Lettering and Ornament. The wonderful effect of the colouring cannot be given here, but, in any case, the illuminator should look at some original MSS. Several of the MSS. from which the plates are taken are exhibited in the British Museum.

PLATE I

— Portion of Inscription on base of Trajan Column,[130] Rome, circa 114 A.D. Scale approx. 1/9th linear.

THE STONE (within the internal line of the moulding): 3 feet 9 inches high, and 9 feet ¾ inch long.

THE BORDERS — The lettering practically fills the panel (See p. 270): the surrounding moulding is approx. 4 inches wide.

THE LETTERS (for their forms see next note).

Approximate Heights
{
First two lines: 4½ inches high
Second two lines: $4^3/_8$ inches high
Fifth line: $4^1/_8$ inches high
Last line: $3^7/_8$ inches high
}

THE SPACES (between Lines) decrease from 3 inches to 2¾ inches. A decrease in the height of the letters from the top to the foot line is common in early inscriptions (See Figs. 203-205). Several reasons for this suggest themselves: (a) (Sometimes the beginning words, being farther from the reader, may require to be larger), (b) The architectural beauty of a large heading (comp. stem heads, p. 218). (c) The importance of beginnings generally (there is very often a marked difference between the upper lines containing important words and the rest of the inscription: comp. Figs. 197, 91).

Note. — The WORDS are separated by triangular points (p. 296).

---

[130] There is a cast (No. 1864-128) in the Victoria and Albert Museum, South Kensington, where also the photograph of the inscription is obtainable, from portions of which Plates I. and II. are reproduced.

Plate I.—Portion of Inscription on base of Trajan Column, Rome, circa 114 A.D. Scale approx. ⅛th linear. (*See also Plate II.*)

PLATE II

— Alphabet from Trajan Inscription. {Circa 114 a.d.) Scale approx. 1/6th linear. (See note above.)

THE "TRAJAN" ALPHABET — Very fine letters for inscriptions in stone: possibly painted before incision (See p. 221); See also remarks on Roman Capitals, pp. 200-225, and note: —

SERIFS — Small and carefully curved.

THIN PARTS about half the width of the thick stems (pp. 375, 285).

A (M and N), pointed (p. 210).

B — a very beautiful form, with large lower bow (p. 209).

C, G, and (D) — Upper parts rather straight (p. 212).

E and F — mid arm slightly shorter than upper arm.

E and L — lower serif pointed out (p. 213).

LO (shown sideways in collotype) and LT show L's arm projecting under next letter.

M — pointed: slightly spread (p. 215), distance apart of points above equal to inside distance of stems below.

N — pointed: practically no difference in thickness of vertical and oblique parts (p. 216).

O — very beautiful: width slightly less than height (p. 203); slightly tilted (as are all the other curved letters: See p. 216).

P — Bow not joined to stem below (first P rounder topped).

Q — tail carried under V (U).

R — large bow: straight tail, with finishing-curve (p. 220).

S — leans forward slightly (p. 217).

Proportions of widths to heights (comp. with pp. 269-273)	OCDGMNQA	width slightly less than height,
	ARTV	width approx. 1/6th less than height,
	BX	width rather more than half height,
	P	width approx. equal half height,
	LS	width slightly less than half height,

330

{ EF   width approx. 3/7ths of height.

H, (J), K, (U), W, Y, Z are not present in the inscription. A rough diagram (Fig. 219) is given below showing approximately suitable forms for these (Rejunction of U in stone; See p. 311, & Fig. 215).

HJKU
WYZ

FIG. 219.

Plate II.—Alphabet from Trajan Inscription (*Circa* 114 A.D.) Scale approx. ⅓ linear. (*See also Plate* 1). *Note.*—L and O are shown sideways in the 2nd line.

PLATE III

— Written Roman Capitals, Fourth or Fifth Century. (Virgil's "Æneid"). (From a facsimile in the Palaeographical Society's Publications, 1st Series, Vol. II., Pl. 208, of a MS. in the library of S. Gall, Switzerland. See also "Greek and Latin Palaeography," p. 130.)

LETTERS — Simple-written (slanted-pen) Roman "Square Capitals."

WORDS in early MSS. were not separated (p. 69).

LINES ruled with a hard point (p. 264). The letters appear to have been written between every alternate pair (p. 226), but slightly over the line.

A very handsome writing which might still be used for special MSS. (See pp. 229, 227, 226).

Plate III.—Written Roman Capitals, Fourth or Fifth Century.
(Virgil's "Æneid").

PLATE IV

— Uncial Writing, probably Italian Sixth or Seventh Century. (Latin Gospels). Brit. Museum, Harl. MS. 1775. (Shown in Brit. Mus. Department of MSS., Case G, No. 11.)

THE VOLUME contains 468 leaves (7 inches by 4¾ inches).

MARGINS, Approx.: Inner ⅝ inch, Head ⅞ inch, Side ⁹/₈ inch, Foot ⁸/₈ inch. (They may have been cut down by the binder.)

WRITING — A fine round Uncial MS. (pp. 2, 228), arranged in long and short lines.

Note. — On many of the letters there are fine hair-line curved tails and flourishes, which are scarcely visible in the photograph. (These tails were also used in the earlier Uncial shown in Fig. 5 — See also Addenda, p. 14.)

SECTIONS — Marked by built-up letters of an Uncial type, and numbered, MR cxxiiii to MR cxxvi (with references to "Harmonies"). The passage is S. Mark xi. 21-25.

ecce ficus cui male-
dixisti aruit
Et respondens ihs
ait illis
habete fidem di
amen dico uobis
quicumque dixerit
monti huic tol
lere et mitte
in mare
et non hesitauerit
in corde suo
sed crediderit
quia quodcumque
dixerit fiat
fiet ei.
Propterea dico uobis
omnia quaecumque
orantes petitis
credite quia accipietis
et euenient uobis
Et cum stabitis ad
orandum dimit
tite si quid habe
tis aduersus aliquem

Plate IV.—Uncial Writing, probably Italian Sixth or Seventh Century.
(Latin Gospels). Brit. Museum, Harl. MS. 1775.

PLATE V

— Uncial Writing, probably Continental Seventh Century. (Gospel of S. John). Ex libris Stonyhurst College. (See also enlargement, Fig. 169.) Plates (From a facsimile in the Palaeographical Society's Publications, 1st Series, Vol. II., Pl. 17.)

THE VOLUME contains 90 leaves, approx. $5^3/_8$ inches by $3^5/_8$ inches. The Inner margin is approximately ½ inch wide.

WRITING — A very beautiful pointed (slanted-pen) Uncial. The "pointed" character of the letters, which yet retain their typical roundness, give this writing a peculiar charm. Note the top of the P has a marked angle, and the **M** and **H**, and even the **O**, have this slightly or strongly.

RULING — Single lines, rather wide (p. 230).

ARRANGEMENT — Certain of the lines are indented one letter (p. 197).

LARGE LETTERS — On verso Col marking a "Chapter" is built-up in red, on recto the three large letters (marking sections) are simply written with the text pen (p. 226). (The passage is S. John xi, 46-56.)

et dixerunt eis quae fecit ihs
Colligerunt ergo pontifices
et pharisaei concilium
et dicebant quid facimus quia hic
homo multa signa facit
si dimittimus eum sic
omnes credent in eum
et uenient romani et tollent
nrm et locum et gentem
unus autem ex ipsis caiaphas
cum esset pontifex anni illius
dixit eis uos nescitis quicquam
nec cogitatis quia expedit nobis
ut unus moriatur homo
pro populo
et non tota gens pereat
hoc autem a semetipso non dixit
sed cum esset pontifex anni
illius prophetauit
quia ihs moriturus erat pro gente

et non tantum pro gente
sed et ut filios dī qui erant dispersi
congregaret in unum
Ab illo ergo die cogitauerunt
ut interficerent eum
ihs ergo iam non in palam
ambulabat apud iudaeos
sed abiit in regionem iuxta
desertum in ciuitatem
quae dicitur efrem
et ibi morabatur cum discip suis
Proximum autem erat
pascha iudaeorum
et ascenderunt multi hieroso
lyma de regione ante pascha
ut sci ficarent se ipsos
quaerebant ergo ihm
et con loquebantur ad inuicem
in templo stantes
quid putatis quia non ueniṫ ad die

Plate V.—Uncial Writing, probably Continental Seventh Century (Gospel of S. John). Ex Libris Stonyhurst College. (See also enlargement, fig. 169.)

PLATE VI

— Half-Uncial (Irish), Seventh Century. "Book of Kelts" (Latin Gospels). Ex libris Trinity College, Dublin.

(From a facsimile — part of Pl. XLVII. — in "Celtic Ornaments from the Book of Kells," by the Rev. Dr. T. K. Abbott.)

THE LEAVES — which are cut down and much damaged — measure 13 inches by 10 inches.

WRITING — A beautifuland highly finished (approx. straight pen) Half- Uncial (pp. 4, 229), tending to ornamental and fanciful forms whenever opportunity offered. (Note the treatment of INde.)

ARRANGEMENT — Long and short lines: wide spacing.

THE LETTERS combine extreme gracefulness with an unusual appearance of strength. This is mainly due to the ends of all the strokes being finished; the thick strokes have large, triangular heads (p. 250) on the left, and bases broadened by an additional stroke below on the right (thus '*l.*). And the horizontal thin strokes are either finished with a triangular terminal (p. 181), or run on into the next letter — joining the letters together.

The extreme roundness of the letters is contributed to by their being written between DOUBLE LINES (pp. 229, 50), the upper line of which tends to flatten the tops. The pen not being quite "straight" (See footnote, p. 229), together with a tendency to pull the left hand curves, gives a characteristic shape to the letters a,c,b,e,q,t.

THE ILLUMINATION throughout the book is most elaborate and beautiful. Each division has an entire Initial page occupied with the first few letters. The COLOURS were "paled green, red, violet, and yellow, intense black, and white, but no gold": See description of Celtic MSS., p. 4, Bradley's "Illuminated Letters and Borders," and also the Palaeographical Society's 1st Series, Vol. II., Pl. 55-58, 88, 89.

This notable book may be taken as an example of the marvellous possibilities of pen-work and complex colour-work (See p. 155).

In considering the value of the writing as a model, it may be noted that its highly finished nature demands practised skill on the part of the copyist, and that though modern Irish writing (for which it would be an excellent model) still employs ᚐ, ᚇ, ꝼ, ᚷ, ӏ, ꞃ, ꞇ. these letters would be apt to look peculiar in English. The Kells MS. ɑ, c, e, h, m, ƞ, o, p, q, ꞃ, s, u. however, however might be used, and a very beautiful ornamental hand (p. 229) might be founded on this writing.

Plate VII.—Half Uncial (English), circa 700 A.D. "Durham Book" (Latin Gospels). Brit. Mus., Cotton MSS. Nero D. IV.

PLATE VII

— Half-Uncial (English), circa 700 A.D. Notes on the "Durham Book" (Latin Gospels). Brit. Mus., Collotype Cotton MSS. Nero D. IV. Plates

THE VOLUME contains 258 leaves (13½ inches by $9^7/_8$ inches).

THE WRITING is an English — or rather Anglo-Irish — Half-Uncial, written at Lindisfarne (Holy I.) under Irish influence (p. 4).

ARRANGEMENT — two columns of 24 lines — long and short — to the page (note how **eis** is got into the fifth line): wide spacing.

The writing bears a strong resemblance to that of the "Book of Kells," but is generally much plainer; it is also less graceful, being heavier and wider in proportion. The "Book of Kells" O is a circle, while the "Durham Book" O is considerably wider than its height, and all the other letters are correspondingly wide. The RULING in both books consists of double lines, ruled with a hard point on both sides of each leaf.

THE ILLUMINATION also resembles that of the "Book of Kells" (See opposite), but a small amount of gold is employed in it. (See also Palaeographical Society's 1st Series, Vol. II., Pl. 3-6, 22.)

Note. — The "Gloss," or interlinear translation, is in the Northumbrian dialect, and was put in in the tenth century, more than 200 years after the book was written.

A hand founded to some extent on the "Durham Book" hand is given in Chap. IV. as an easy copy: See Figs. 49, 50.

sicut ethnici faciunt
  hia poenas ꝥðon ðaðo
putatur enim qui
  inmonig fald ꝡnðc   hir
inmulta loquio suo
  bið gehenoð
exaudiantur
  nallarge ðonne ꝡora gelic
nolite ergo assimila**ri**
  pat ꝥðon   faðon   iunne   **es**
Sat enim pater uester
  opðom ðeunꝥ ꝥiotir iuh
quid: opus sit uobis
  aeꝥ ðon
antequam
  giebidde   hino
petatis eum
  ꝡug ðon iuih giebidge
Sic ergo uos orabitis
  faðen upen   ðu anð t.
pater noster qui es
heo in heoꝡnu ꝡie gehalgud
ar in caelis sꝧ ꝡictair
     noma   ðin
nomen tuum
 to cymeð   ꝡic   ðin
adueniat regnum tuum

Plate VII.—Half Uncial (English), *circa* 700 A.D. "Durham Book" (Latin Gospels). Brit. Mus., Cotton MSS. Nero D. IV.

PLATE VIII

— English Tenth-century Writing. (Psalter). Brit. Mus., Harl. MS. 2904. (See enlargement, Fig. 172). (Shown B. M. Grenville Lib. Case 2, No. 9.)

THE VOLUME contains 214 leaves (13¼ inches by 10 inches), 18 lines to the page; probably written at Winchester in late tenth century. (Pl. reduced scale 8/9ths.)

WRITING — An extremely good, formal, "slanted- pen" writing, having great freedom (note the very slight slope forward) and simplicity. This type of letter may be regarded as a link between the Half-Uncial and the Roman Small-Letter (See p. 237).

THE RULING: single lines (See footnote, p. 232).

THE LETTERS show very strongly the effects of the "slanted pen" (See pp. 4, 232). Note the heavy shoulders and feet in n, b, &c., and the thick horizontals in r**c**. The curved tops or arches are flattish and strong: the thick strokes end in points and are hooked below, thin strokes scarcely appear except as the finishing strokes of **a, c, e, l, c,** while **d, (h), i, m, n, u** end in small heavy hooks. Note generally the tendency to internal angles and external roundness (examples, **f** and **o**).

Note particularly the junctions and accidental crossings of the strokes (seen best in the enlargement, Fig. 172) as bearing on the mode of construction of the letters (See p. 84).

Note the fine shape of the ampersand (**&**: 3rd line).

THE ILLUMINATION (See Characteristics of Winchester Illumination, or "Opus Anglicum," pp. 82, 83, Bradley: "Illuminated Letters and Borders"). All the CAPITALS beginning the verses are in raised, burnished gold, in the margin. The titles are in red in fancy "Rustic Capitals" (p. 225). The Line-Fillings consist of groups of red dots, in threes (∴ ∴ ∴).

This extremely legible MS. would form an almost perfect model for a modern formal hand (**s** being substituted for long *f*, and the straight **t** for the curved **c** (See Fig. 183): the removal of the **e** flourish would also help readableness). And though it is somewhat large and heavy for ordinary use, it is good for practising, and might be developed into a form resembling any of the more difficult later forms (Plates IX., X., XX.).

hymnus trium puerorum.
Benedicite omia opera dni dno
Laudate & super exaltate
eum in sæcula
B en angeli dni dno. b cæli dno
B en aquae omēs quae sup cælos
sunt dno. b oms uirtutēs dni dno

Plate VIII.—English Tenth-century Writing. (Psalter). Brit. Mus., Harl. MS. 2904. (See enlargement fig. 172.)

PLATE IX — English Writing, dated 1018. Two portions of a Charter of CNUT. Brit. Museum. (See also enlargement, Fig. 173.) [Pl. reduced scale 11/12ths] (Shown in Brit. Mus., Department of MSS., Case V., No. 3.)

THE WRITING resembles that in Plate VIII. (see above), but is more slender and rounder — the pen being a little less slanted, and the arches more curved, and showing more of the thin stroke. The ascenders Plates and descenders are longer, the heads are more marked, and there is a general elegance and distinction, due perhaps to the MS. being a charter. Charter-hands are generally more showy and less legible than Book-hands, but in this hand there is great legibility, and a very few changes (similar to those suggested above) would make it quite suitable for modern use. Its relation to the Roman Small-Letter is obvious.

Notes. — The (black) ✠ V and u were probably built- up with the writing pen.

The forms of **a, e, g, (h), r,** may be noted as differing considerably from the tenth-century hand.

The combined **ra** (in the 4th line) is curious: and the **r** in Anglorum — this r (which represents the Bow and Tail of R) commonly follows the round letters b, o, p, in "Gothic" writing: there is another curious form in the linked **rt** in cartula (last line).

The word CNUT and several other names are in ornamental "Rustic" Capitals (See p. 225).

The two lines of English from another part of the charter have very long stems and ornamental serifs, giving a very decorative effect (See footnote, p. 248).

Plate IX.—English Writing, dated 1018. Two portions of a Charter of CNUT. Brit. Museum. (See also enlargement, fig. 173.)

PLATE X

— Italian (first half of) Twelfth-century Writing. (Homilies and Lessons). Brit. Mus., Harl. MS. 7183. (See also enlargement, Fig. 174.) (Shown in Brit. Mus., Department of MSS., Case C [lower part], No. 101.)

THE VOLUME — Homilies and Lessons for Sundays and Festivals from Advent to Easter Eve — contains 317 leaves (approximately 21½ inches by 15 inches); two columns, each of 50 lines, to the page. The MARGINS are, approximately, Inner 1¼ inch, Head 1 ¼ , Side 3¼ inches, Foot 4¼ inches (between columns 1 ⅛ inch: See Plate). The portion of a page, shown in Plate X., consists of the last eleven lines, second column, of folio 78.

WRITING — This has all the qualities of good writing (p. 175) in a marked degree, and I consider it, taken all round, the most perfect and satisfactory penmanship which I have seen.

Its simplicity and distinctiveness are very marked, so also are its character and freedom. There is an almost entire absence of artificial finish — the terminals are natural hooks, beaks and "feet" made with a fine sleight of hand (p. 237) — and its very great beauty of form is the natural outcome of good traditions and eminently satisfactory craftsmanship.

Notes. — The letters are very wide, and the inside shapes differ considerably from those of the tenth-century MS. (above) — with which, however, there is a considerable affinity (See p. 333).

The **f** is longer than the **f**, the **g** has a very fine form with a closed loop, the **r** is sharpened, the **t** straight.

Small (Uncial) CAPITALS **um** follow the Versal; the serifs on the **S** and **E** are made with dexterous movements of the nib (p. 181), and resemble those on the Versal **C, V** and **U** are both used for the consonant (**V**).

There are very few VERSALS in this book: the **C** shown is in red (which has been smudged).

The large "ILLUMINATED INITIALS" in the book are in yellow, blue, and red, and appear to me to be comparatively poor, at least, to fall short of the perfection of the MS.

Of this writing, Sir Edward Maunde Thompson ("Greek and Latin Palaeography," pp. 271-2) says: —

"The sense of grace of form which we perceive in the Lombardic writing of Italy is maintained in that country in the later writing of the new minuscule type, which assumes under the pens of the most expert Italian scribes a very beautiful and round even style. This style, though peculiarly Italian, extended its influence abroad, especially to the south of France, and became the model of Spanish writing at a later time. We select a specimen from a very handsome MS. of Homilies of the first half of the 12th century (Pal. Soc. ii. pl 55), written in bold letters of the best type, to which we shall find the scribes of the fifteenth century reverting in order to obtain a model for their MSS. of the Renaissance. The exactness with which the writing is here executed is truly marvellous, and was only rivalled, not surpassed, by the finished handiwork of its later imitators.

"It will of course be understood that this was not the only style of hand that prevailed in Italy. Others of a much rougher cast were also employed. But as a typical book-hand, which was the parent of the hands in which the greater proportion of carefully written MSS. of succeeding periods were written in Italy, it is to be specially noticed."

(P. 284) — *"we give a specimen of a hand of the Italian Re naissance, a revival of the style of the eleventh or twelfth century, and a very successful imitation of a MS. of that period. It was this practice, followed by the scribes of the Renaissance, of reverting to that fine period of Italian writing (See p. 272) to find models for the exquisitely finished MSS. which they were compelled to produce in order to satisfy the refined taste of their day, that influenced the early printers of Italy in the choice of their form of type."**

(P. 285) — *"in the comparatively small number of extant literary MSS. of a later date than the close of the [fifteenth] century it is noticeable that a large proportion of them are written in the style of the book-hand of the Italian Renaissance — the style which eventually superseded all others in the printing press. The scribes of these late examples only followed the taste of the day in preferring those clear and simple characters to the rough letters of the native hands."*

**The specimen hand given is of date 1466. Plate XVIII. may here be taken as an example of the Renaissance revival; Plate XX. and Fig. 175 as examples of later MSS.*

Plate X.—Italian (first half of) Twelfth-century Writing. (Homilies and Lessons). Brit. Mus., Harl. MS. 7183. (See also enlargement. fig. 174).

PLATE XI

— English (late) Twelfth-century Writing, with flourished Capitals. (Breviary). Brit. Mus., Royal MS. 2. A. x. (Shown in Brit. Mus., Department of MSS., Case D, No. 111.)

THE VOLUME — sometimes called the St. Albans or Albanus Psalter — contains 200 leaves ($6^7/_8$ inches by $4^7/_8$ inches); twenty-seven lines to the page, some pages have two columns. MARGINS, approximately, Inner $5/_8$ inch, Head under ½ inch (See Plate), Side 1¼ inch (part occupied by Versals), Foot $1^1/_8$ inch.

THE WRITING is fairly legible, but approaches Black Letter (p. 252) too nearly to be of use to us for ordinary purposes. Note the ornamental Semi-Rustic Capitals in text. Note the RULING of the two head lines and of the foot line is carried into the margin.

THE VERSALS — The main interest lies in the varied forms of the Versals, which are most beautifully made in red and green alternately. There is one elaborate gold initial in the book, and several Versals in blue and white (hollow: See p. 148).

The five ծ' s — and the D in the text — on this page (folio 85b) by no means exhaust the varieties of **D** alone, and there are very many varieties of the forms of the other letters. On some pages each line begins with a small Versal, while the more important Initials are much larger, varying in size and ornament.

THE CONSTRUCTION of the Versals is unusually slender, curved, and gradated. A rather fine pen seems to have been used (p. 221), and though the letters are upright, the natural tendency to slant the pen can be detected in the thickening of the thin parts — above, on the right, and below, on the left — giving the suspicion of a *tilt* to the O.

The O-part of each ծ was made first, and the tail \ added. This is very obvious in the D in the text, where a stem | was added to O to make D.

Note the dots inside the Versals, one above and one below. Originally these may have been intended to effect — or hide — the junction of the thin strokes, by a twirl of the pen at the end of the first stroke and the beginning of the second, thus (. ·). Their use is very common in Versal forms (See Fig. 189), and besides being decorative in the ordinary sense, they may be said to strengthen the thin parts (much as the weakest part of the loop in an old key was thickened for strength). Note the right hand Bows of the O's are made thinner, as though the Rubricator had been afraid of running into the text in making their last curves — such an expert, however, may well have had a better reason for it.

Plate XI.—English (late) Twelfth-century Writing, with flourished Capitals. (Breviary). Brit. Mus., Royal MS. 2. A.X.

PLATE XII

— Illuminated Initial in a Flemish MS. A.D. 1148. (Latin Bible). Brit. Museum, Addl. MS. 14790. (Shown in Brit. Museum, Department of MSS., Case C, No. 91.)

THE VOLUME — the third, and most interesting, of this MS. Bible (Numbered 14788-89-90) — contains 223 leaves (17 inches by 11 $7/8$ inches). MARGINS, approximately, Inner 1 $1/8$ inch, Head (cut) 1 inch, Side 2 $3/8$ inches, Foot 3½ inches. (Between columns $15/16$ inch.)

THE WRITING is a not very legible "Gothic." The zig-zag tendency exhibited, especially by the word niniuen (Niniveh), second line, is unsuited for such formal writing (See p. 375). The rapid placing of the Heads of the letters is such that they appear broken and partly detached from the stems. The VERSALS are of a good type.

THE INITIAL is a monogrammatic **ET**. The arms of the round **E** terminate in leaves folded back, its form is hollow and inwoven (p. 148), and gives rise to foliage, which fills the interior — passing over the fish and behind Jonah. Note also how the jaws of the fish are interlaced, and how compactly all the parts are put together.

The close application of the background to the curves adds to the general compactness, and together with its spacing from the straight front balances the masses (p. 349): it may be compared to the even spacing of curved and straight strokes (See Fig. 53). There is an extension of the background to hold the fish's tail.

THE COLOURS-

Initial, Foilage, Fish: Jonah:	Red: Black:	} Outlined & lined	Parchment left plain
Bands on Initial, Hollows in Initial, Backs of folded leaves:	}	Gold, outlined red	
Outer background:		Paled green	
Dots on outer ground:		Red	
Inner background:		Paled blue	

354

We may not, I think, attempt to imitate the complex 12th-century decoration of this initial (See p. 139), but the treatment of the elements of form and colour is very suggestive, and the whole piece of lettering is characteristic of the grand style in which a book was at that time begun.

The ARRANGEMENT of the letters themselves is very simple, and might be made good use of (Fig. 220).

INCIPIT·JONAS⸗PPHĀ:
(*propheta*)

F
A
C
T
U
M.
(*ET*)
E
S
T.

verbum d(*omi*)ni ad jonam filiu(*m*) amathi dicens. Surge & vade in niniven civitatem magnam. & pr(*a*)edica in ea.

FIG. 220.

INCIPIT IONAS PPHA:

FACTVM ESC

uerbum dni ad ionam filiu amathi.
dicens Surge & uade in niniuen ci
uitatem magnam. & predica in ea.

Plate XII.—Illuminated Initial in a Flemish MS. A.D. 1148 (Latin Bible). Brit. Museum, Addl. MS. 14790.

PLATE XIII

— English (2nd half) Thirteenth-century Writing and Illumination. (Latin Bible). Ex libris Collotype S. C. Cockerell.

THE VOLUME — probably written at York — contains 427 leaves (8 inches by 5½ inches): two columns to the page: MARGINS, approx.: Inner ⅝ inch, Head ⅝ inch, Side ⅞ inch, Foot 1^{7}/$_{16}$ inch. (Between the columns ⅜ inch.) The pages have been cut down.

THE WRITING is very small, and there are many contractions.[131] In the thirteenth and fourteenth centuries the whole Bible, written in this fashion, was often small enough to be carried in the pocket. Note the closed a and the 7 form of &. The page is RULED with 50 lines: the 49 lines of writing lie between these, so that in each case the ascenders touch the line above, and the descenders, the line below. Note the double lines in the Foot margin (See p. 264).

VERSALS — A very narrow type is used in the narrow margins: the example shown is in red, flourished blue; it begins the second chapter [Er angelo ephesi, &c.), which is also marked by coloured Roman Numerals at the side (II). The page heading is "APOCA" in small red and blue Versals.

THE ILLUMINATED INITIAL is "historiated" — i.e. it contains a picture illustrating the text, viz. a representation of S. John writing to the Seven Churches — purely conventional forms, or rather symbols, for the most part, are used and beautifully fitted into the available space. The greater size and more careful drawing of the human figure (the centre of interest) is characteristic of a fine convention. The slope of the vellum page on which S. John is writing, and even the manner in which the quill is held, are such as would naturally be employed by a scribe (See frontispiece, & p. 31).

The capitals of the pillars mark the position of the cross-bar of A. The top serif is carried up and forms a bud, which gives rise to leaf-like flourishes: the free thin stem runs down forming a grotesque, which gives out a leaf-like tongue. In either case the object — in every sense recreative — is a renewal of interest in the designed, elongated, growth of the forms.

---

[131] The Apocalypse here begins "Apocalipfis iнu x^{1}"(for IHU XP, derived from the Greek and used as a mediaeval Latin contraction for Jesu Christi).

358

Note the curved thickening of A's left stem ends nearly level with the foot of the right stem. This gives balance to the letter (See R, Fig. 81 & A, Fig. 189), and preserves the essential form, which suffers no distortion by the thinner continuation below.

Note the balancing of the background mass on the straight and curved sides of the Initial (as in Plate XII., See above); also the extension and shape of the background accompanying the drawn out parts of the letter.

COLOURS of Initial—

Right stem:	red	} With white lines and patterns
Left stem and serif:	blue	
L. Stem, lower half, & dragon		Pale "lake"
The background (counter-charged)	{ Outer	Pale "lake"
	Inner:	Blue
	Lower extension:	Blue
	Final flourish	Pale "lake"
Band (dark) down left side, dragon's wings, 6 "berries," halo, seat, tops of pillar caps:	{	Burnished gold
Leaves (dark) & pillar caps:		Red
Small stems & leaves:		Green

Here again no natural work would come of a modern attempt to imitate so complex a "design" — natural and even inevitable 600 years ago. But the spirit of delicacy and fantasy, the ingenious contrivance, and the balancing and disposal of form and colour shown by the antique art, may well be matter for imitation by the modern draughtsman-illuminator, and even by the mere penman.

Plate XIII.—English (2nd half) Thirteenth-century Writing and Illumination (Latin Bible). Ex. Libris S. C. Cockerell.

PLATE XIV

— Thirteenth-century Line-finishings: Pen-work. (Psalter). Brit. Museum, Royal MS. i. D. x.

THE LINE-FINISHINGS (see p. 145), of which there are very many throughout the book, all in red or blue pen-work, are very varied. Nine kinds are shown in the plate (which represents about a quarter of a page), and three others from the same MS. are given in Figs. 87 (3) and 126 (f, g).

The directions of the thick and thin strokes indicate a pen held at right angles to its usual position (almost "upside down," in fact: See Fig. 126, g), and the penmanship exhibits great speed and lightness of hand — the rapidity and skill are indeed quite remarkable (e.g. in the Lion in the eighth line).

Note that, though the writing occasionally runs into the margin, the line-finishings stop at the marginal-line.

The photograph shows red dark and blue light: e.g. the Bird is red, the Lion and the Fish are blue. The fifth Line-finishing is a red filigree with blue "berries" — it can hardly be described as a "floral growth," as the "branching" is reversed: the rubricator gained speed and uniformity by the simple repetition of the whorls all along the line — the upper branches were probably put in afterwards, and the "berries" were added later when he was making the blue Line-finishings.

The more complex decoration (not shown in the plate) in this MS. is inferior to the penmanship: the small background Capitals with which the verses begin — presumably put in by a different hand — are more pretentious, and do not match the Line-finishings.

GENERAL NOTE — When a space occurs at the end of a line of writing, it is often best to leave it, and in a plain MS., if it be "well and truly" written, there is no objection to varying lengths of line (See pp. 196, 281). But a book, such as a Psalter, divided into many short verses — in which the last line usually falls short of the marginal line — offers a fair field for such simple and effective decoration. (See also pp. 359, 376, Fig. 130, and Plates Plate XXIII.)

igantcs ea tepibunt p̅ diuiu

icantur abste

erere deo bonū est & ponere in

eam

nes predicationes tuas: in portas

repulisti in fine iratus est furor

oues pascue tue

sto congregationis tue quā

io

eredicasti tue mons hjon in

eo

in superbias eoū in fine quanta

minicus in s̅c̅o

Plate XIV.—Thirteenth-century Line-finishings: Penwork. (Psalter).
Brit. Museum, Royal MS. 1, D.X.

363

PLATE XV — English Writing and Illumination, circa 1284 A.D. (Psalter). Brit. Museum, Addl. MS. 24686.

THE WRITING is a fine, freely formed, "Gothic" (p.252). Note, the i's are "dotted." Note the double MARGINAL LINES (p. 264).

THE SMALL INITIALS are of the "Lombardic" type (p. 150), in which the Serifs are much thickened and ornamented. Note the tails of the Q's are turned to the left to clear the writing. The LINE-FILLINGS match the small initials (p. 135).

THE LARGE INITIAL, &c. — The plate shows the end of the fourteenth and beginning of the fifteenth Psalm (𝔇omine quis habitabit) Note "Arabic" numerals (15) in margin.

The tail of the Initial O is formed of a dragon, the head of which rests on the O-part: its wings project into the inner margin (and these in the plate, which shows a fragment of a verso page, run into the fold between the pages): the tail (together with the background) descends till a convenient point is reached from which the lower scroll-work springs. The tail, wing, and claws above, belong to a magpie which is perched on the initial.

THE DRAWING: See reference to this at p. 143, and below.

Sir Edward Maunde Thompson (p. 39, "English Illuminated MSS.") says of this —

"*—the Additional MS. 24686 in the British Museum, known as the Tenison Psalter, from its having once formed part of the library of Archbishop Tenison. This psalter is one of the most beautiful illuminated English manuscripts of its time, but unfortunately only in part, for it was not finished in the perfect style in which it was begun . . . in the first quire of the text the ornamentation is of peculiar beauty . . .*"[132]

"*— the progress of the art [since the earlier part of the thirteenth century] . . . is . . . manifest. There is more freedom in the drawing, the stiffness of the earlier examples is in great measure overcome; and the pendant has thrown out a branch which has already put forth leaves. A great variety of colours, blue, rose,*

---

[132] It is supposed that the book was at first intended as a marriage gift for Alphonso, son of Edward I.

vermilion, lake, green, brown, as well as burnished gold, is employed in the composition of the large initial and its accompanying pendant and border, and the small initials are of gold laid on a ground of blue or lake, and filled with lake or blue; while the ribbons which fill up the spaces at the ends of the verses are alternately of the same colours and are decorated with patterns in silver on the blue and in gold on the lake."

"The group of the dismounted knight despatching[133] a gryphon, which has proved too much for the horse, upon whose dying body the expectant raven has already perched, is tinted in lighter colours. It is an instance of the use to which marginal space was put, particularly by English artists, for the introduction of little scenes, such as episodes in romances or stories, games, grotesque combats, social scenes, &c., often drawn with a light free hand and most artistic touch. Without these little sketches, much of the manners and customs, dress, and daily life of our ancestors would have remained forever unknown to us."

---

[133] The characteristic over and under arrangement of the gryphon's upper and lower bill, makes this doubtful.

Plate XV.—English Writing and Illumination, *circa* 1284 A.D. (Psalter). Brit. Museum, Addl. MS. 24686.

PLATE XVI

— Italian Fourteenth-century MS., Brit. Mus., AM. MS. 28841.

THE VOLUME: one of two (the other numbered 27695), a Latin treatise on the Virtues and Vices (The miniatures, drawings, &c., probably by "the Monk of Hyeres," Genoa). The vellum leaves have been separated, and are now preserved in paper books. The leaf illustrated shows a margin of vellum of less than $^3/_{16}$ inch all round (the plate).

The decorative borders are much more naturalistic in form and colouring than any other old illumination that I have seen (See reference to Plate XVI., p. 143).

The foliage is a delicate green, the berries are dark purple, the single fruits plain and pale orange-red; the two beetles in crimson and brown are made darker and too prominent in the photograph. The bands of small "Lombardic" Capitals are in burnished gold.

Note how skillfully and naturally the upper corners of the border are managed, and also the beautiful way in which the branches run into and among the text (See p. 152).

Plate XVI.—Italian Fourteenth-century MS, Brit. Mus., Addl. MS. 28841.

PLATE XVII

— French Fifteenth-century Writing, with Illuminated Borders. Ex libris E. Johnston.

THE PAGE 9½ inches by 6 $^{1}/_{8}$ inches: MARGINS, approx.: Inner 1 $^{1}/_{8}$ inch, Head 1 $^{3}/_{8}$ inch, Side 2 $^{3}/_{8}$ inches, Foot 2 $^{7}/_{8}$ inches (the edges have been slightly cut down).

The marginal lines (from head to foot of the page) and the writing lines are RULED in faint red.

THE WRITING is a late formal "Gothic" — the thin strokes have evidently been added (p. 14). The written Capitals are blotted with yellow (See p. 93).

The ILLUMINATED INITIAL Q is in blue, white lined, on a gold ground, contains a blue flower and five ornaments in "lake." The LINE-FILLINGS are in blue and "lake," separated by a gold circle, triangle, or lozenge.

THE FILIGREE ILLUMINATION springs from the initial in the narrow margin, and from a centre ornament (See "knot," Fig. 127) in the wide side margin. The side margins are treated similarly on either page (See p. 152); the inner margins are generally plain. This repetition gives to the pages a certain sameness — which is a characteristic rather than a fault of the treatment.

The border on the recto of the vellum leaf shows through on the verso or back of the leaf. The main lines of the first border, however, are freely traced and followed on the verso (and so nearly hidden) by the second border. This is also suggestive of the more rapid methods of book production in the 15th century.

COLOURS—

Stems, tendrils, &c.:		black			
Leaves	{	Ivy shaped Lanceolate	{	Burnished gold, outlined black (p. 187)	} Plain furred
Flowers, buds, centre ornaments, &c.: (See p. 182.)	{	Blue, "lake", or green tempered with white, and shaded with pure colour; white markings; the forms not outlined			

This type of illumination is discussed in pp. 139-142. Its chief points are its simplicity and rapidity. A penman or a novice in illuminating can, by taking a little pains, beautify his MSS. easily and quickly; and he may perhaps pass on from this to "higher" types of illumination.

Plate XVII.—French Fifteenth-century Writing, with Illuminated Borders. Ex. Libris E. Johnston.

PLATE XVIII

— Italian Fifteenth-century Writing and Illumination. (Perotti's translation of Polybius). Ex libris H. Yates-Thompson.

THE VOLUME consists of 174 leaves (13 $1/8$ inches by 9 inches); 35 lines to the page. The plate shows a portion of the upper part of the Initial (recto) page.

THE WRITING — The Capitals are simple-written, slanted-pen "Roman" — slightly ornamental — forms. They are freely copied on a large scale in Fig. 168: see p. 225. The Small-letters match the Capitals — they are "Roman" forms with a slight "Gothic" tendency. Both these and the Capitals would make very good models for free Roman hands.

THE INITIAL is a "Roman" **A** in burnished gold. Note the exceedingly graceful shaping of the limbs, the ornamental, V-shaped cross-bar, and the absence of serifs (See Fig. 116).

The "White Vine Pattern" (See p. 142), most delicately and beautifully drawn, interlaces with the letter and itself, and covers the BACKGROUND very evenly. The interstices of the background are painted in blue, red, and green, and its edge is adapted to the slightly projecting flowers and leaves. There are groups (∴ and ...) of white dots on the blue parts of the background.

THE BORDER (of which a small part is shown) is approximately ½ inch wide in the narrow margin at the side of the text — it is separate from the Initial. It extends above and below the text, where its depth is greater, matching the greater depth of the margins. Its treatment is similar to, though perhaps a little simpler than, that of the Initial decoration.

Plate XVIII.—Italian Fifteenth-century Writing and Illumination (Perotti's translation of Polybius). Ex libris H. Yates-Thompson.

PLATE XIX

— Italian MS., dated 1481. Ex libris S. C. Cockerell.

"Part of a [verso] page from a book containing the Psalter of St. Jerome and various Prayers, written and decorated by Joachinus de Gigantibus of Rotenberg in 1481 for Pope Sixtus IV. Joachinus was employed at Naples by Ferdinand I., and there are other fine examples of his work at the British Museum and the Bibliotheque Nationale, Paris. In each of these, as well as in the present book, he states that he was both scribe and illuminator." — [S. C. C]

THE VOLUME contains 31 leaves (6½ inches by 4¾ inches): MARGINS, approx.: Inner ⅞ inch, Head ⅞ inch, Side 1½ inch, Foot 1¾ inch. (The head margin, together with the edge of the book-cover, is shown in the plate.)

THE WRITING — Very clear, slightly slanted-pen "Roman." Note the blending of **b** and **p** with **e** and **o** (See Fig. 76, & p. 40). The CAPITALS are quite simple and plain, made (in (A)NIMA CHRISTI and in text) in black with the text pen. Note the long, waved serifs (See p. 219). The last two lines of the preceding prayer are made in burnished gold with a larger pen.

THE INITIAL A, its frame, the frame of the Plates border, and the "furred" berries (∴) are all in burnished gold, outlined black. The "white vine pattern" is rather simpler, and has a rather thicker stalk (in proportion) than that in the previous plate (See above). Its treatment is very similar, but it may be noted that the border is in this case attached to the Initial, and the pattern has almost an appearance of springing from the Initial. The pattern — save one escaped leaf — is straitly confined, by gold bars, throughout the length of the text, but at the ends it is branched out and beautifully flourished in the free margins above and below. These terminals of the pattern having a broad blue outline (dotted white) may be said to carry their background with them.

The (recto) page opposite that shown in the plate has an initial D and a border similarly treated, and each one of the Psalms and Prayers throughout the book is begun in like manner.

Fme dulcissima maria mater
dei & misericordie. Amen.
ORATIO AD DOMINVM
NOSTRVM IESVM XPM

ANIMA CHRISTI
sanctifica me. Corpus christi salua me.
Sanguis christi ine-
bria me. Aqua lateris christi
laua me. Sudor uultus xpi
defende me. Passio christi
conforta me. Mors christi
libera me. Sapientia christi
doce me. O bone iesu exau
di me. In tua uulnera absco
de me. Et ne permittas me

Plate XIX.—Italian MS. dated 1481. Ex libris S. C. Cockerell.

PLATE XX

— One page of an Italian (late) Fifteenth-century MS. Ex libris S. C. Cocherell.

"From a book containing the Penitential Psalms in Italian, the Psalter of St. Jerome, and various prayers. Written with great delicacy by Mark of Vicenza for someone named Evangelista [See 11th line] in the last quarter of the fifteenth century. Other works of this accomplished scribe are known."— [S. C. C]

THE VOLUME — of which a complete (recto) page is shown — contains 60 leaves (5½ inches by 3¾ inches): MARGINS, approx.: Inner ½ inch, Head ⁷/₈ inch, Side 1 ³/₁₆ inch, Foot 1 1³/₁₆ inch.

This very fine WRITING is typical of the practical style and beautiful workmanship which should be the aim of a modern scribe (See pp. 14, 237).

It is written with a very narrow nib, hence the pen-forms are not so obvious as in some early formal hands; and for this reason alone it would be better to practise such a hand as the tenth-century MS. (Plate VIII.) before seriously attempting to model a hand on the above (See pp. 333, 237, 247).

The use of a fine pen is apt to flatter the unskilled penman, and he finds it hard to distinguish between delicate pen-work which has much character, and that which has little or none. And he will find, after some knowledge of penmanship gained in practice with a broad nib, that the copying of this fine Italian writing — while in reality made much more feasible — may even appear more difficult than before.

CONSTRUCTION — The pen has a moderate slant — See thin stroke in e. The letters are very square, the tops flat (especially in m, n, and r), and the lower parts flat (as in u). This shows the same tendency that there is in the tenth century and other hands to avoid thin or high arches in the letters.

The feet in some of the letters (in i, for example) are in the nature of stroke-serifs, but the pen probably made these with an almost continuous movement — from the stem.

- Note — the fine form of the a;
- that b and l have an angle where the stem joins the lower part;

- that f was made something like t, and the upper part was added: this was a common mode — See Fig. 180 (the f shown in plate is unfortunately not a good specimen);

- that g — a very graceful letter— lacks the coupling serif;

- that i, p, u have triangular heads, and m, n, r hooks:

- that the ascenders have triangular heads, and the descenders p and q, stroke-serifs:

- that the ascending and descending stems are longer than the bodies, and the writing is in consequence fairly widely spaced.

Like most of the finest writings, this bears evidences of considerable speed (See pp. 47, 237). Besides the great uniformity of the letters, the coupling strokes are occasionally carried over the succeeding stroke, the arches of b, h, m, n, p, r (and the heads of the ascenders) frequently are separated from the stems, and the o and b occasionally fail to join below. These broken forms are the results of speed, and are not to be imitated except as to that which is both a cause and a result — their uniformity (p. 254).

The RULING is in faint ink: there are two vertical marginal lines on the left and one on the right of every page.

The DECORATION of the MS. is very simple. The Initial (here shown) is in green and powder-gold, on a lake ground, with white pattern: there is a very fine brownish outline, probably drawn first. The two upper lines of writing and ‖oro are in red.

cantent hoc psalterium: et
possidebunt regnum eternū.
Vscipe digneris do Oro
mine deus omnipotens
istos psalmos consecratos q̄s
ego indignus decantare cu
pio in honore nominis tui
domine: beate marie uirgi
nis et omnium sanctorum
tuorum prome miserrimo
Euanzelista famulo tuo: et p
genitore meo et genitrice mā.

Plate XX.—One page of an Italian (late) Fifteenth-century MS.
Ex. libris S. C. Cockerell.

PLATE XXI

— Italian (early) Sixteenth-century "cursive" or "Italic" MS. Ex libris S. C. Cockerell. (See enlargement, Fig. 178.)

"From the Poems of Cardinal Bembo, a fine example of the cursive writing perfected in Italy in the first half of the sixteenth century. The book measures 8½ by 5¼ inches, and contains 79 leaves."— [S. C. C.]

THE MARGINS of the page from which the plate is taken are approximately: Inner ⅝ inch, Head ¾ inch, Side 2 inches, Foot 1½ inch. Note. — The lines of writing begin as usual at the left margin, but do not extend to the (true) margin on the right, hence the latter (the side margin on the recto, and the inner margin on the verso) would appear unnaturally wide, but the effect is carried off by the (true) side margins being already exceptionally wide (and by the writing on the backs of the leaves showing through the semi-transparent vellum and so marking the true margins).

This mode is very suitable for a book of poems, in which the lengths of the lines of writing may vary considerably, because the writing-line being longer than the ordinary line of writing allows room for extraordinarily long lines, and any appearance of irregularity is carried off by the extra wide side margins.

THE WRITING is very beautiful, clear, and rapid — made with a M slanted pen (See "Italics," p. 311, and Fig. 178). Note the slightness of the slope of the letters (especially of the Capitals), and the length of the stems and the wide spacing.

Note, also, the flatness of the curves in a c d e g q and the horizontal top stroke in a d g q, oblique in e c (giving angular tops). The branching away from the stem of the first part of the arch in **bhmnpr** (seen also reversed in a **d g q u**), and the pointed, almost angular, quality of the arch. This, which is apt to become a fault in a more formal upright hand (See note on Plate XXII.) is helpful in a more rapid running hand, and gives clearance to the junctions of the strokes (*r i*) — See Fig. 182.

The heads, simple or built-up, hooks tending to become triangular.

The letters in this MS. are rarely coupled.

The very graceful g has a large pear-shaped lower loop touching the upper part.

Per tutto, ouel suo mar sospira et piagne,
Percosse in uista oltra lusato offesa;
Tal, ch'a noia et disdegno hebbi me stesso,
Et se non fusse che maggior paura
Frenò l'ardir; con morte acerba et dura,
A l'aqual fui molte fiate presso,
D'uscir d'affanno harei corta uia presa.
Hor chiamo; et non so far altra difesa;
Pur lui; che l'ombra sua lasciando meco
Di me la uiua et miglior parte ha seco.
Che con l'altra restai morto in quel punto
Ch'io senti morir lui, che fu'l suo core:
Ne son buon d'altro, che da tragger guai.
Tregua non uoglio hauer col mio dolore
In fin ch'io sia dal giorno ultimo giunto:
Et tanto il piangerò, quant'io l'amai.
Deh perche inanzi a lui non mi spogliai
La mortal gonna; s'io men' uesti prima?
S'al uiuer fui ueloce; perche tardo
Sono al morir? un dardo
Almen hauesse et una stessa lima
Parimente ambo noi traffitto et roso:
Che si come un uoler sempre ne tenne
Viuendo; cosi spenti anchor n'hauesse
Vn'hora, et un sepolcro ne chiudesse.
Et se questo al suo tempo, o quel non uenne;

Plate XXI.—Italian (early) Sixteenth-century "cursive" or "Italic" MS.
Ex. libris S. C. Cockerell. (See enlargement, fig. 178.)

PLATE XXII

— "Communion Service" written and illuminated by E. Johnston, 1902 A.D. ("Office Book" Holy Trinity Church, Hastings). Reduced (nearly ¾ scale).

The MS. on 160 leaves (15 inches by 10 inches) of fine parchment ("Roman Vellum," See p. 122), contains the Communion Service and many collects, epistles, and gospels for special festivals, &c. MARGINS: Inner 1 $^{1}/_{8}$ inch, Head 1¾ inch, Side 2¾ inches, Foot 3¾ inches.

THE WRITING — after tenth century model (See Plate VIII.) — has the fault (referred to at p. 344) of showing too much thin line (running up obliquely), the upper and lower parts of the letters are not flat enough. The tail of the g is inadequate, and the lines of writing are too near together. The writing is readable, however, and fairly regular. The CAPITALS are Uncials (after Plate V.) and occasional "Romans."

The RUBRIC ("¶ Then shall be said or sung") is in red, fitted in beside the round initial and marking the top left-hand corner of the page (See footnote, p. 150).

The word "GLORY"(and decoration) — and also the F and T, showing in recto page — are in raised burnished gold, which, it will be seen, has cracked considerably in the G (See p. 164).

The STAVES are in red (p. 93), the notes above GLORY in raised gold, those in the lower stave, black.

The BOOK was of a special nature (See pp. 265-6), being intended for use in a certain church and on certain special festivals: hence a considerable degree of ornament and a generally decorative treatment was permitted (p. 251). The Prayer of Consecration, together with a miniature, occupied a complete opening, the eight margins of which were filled with solid, framing borders (p. 152) in red, blue, green, and gold. Coats-of-arms and other special symbols and devices were introduced on the Title page and in other places.

Plate XXII.—"Communion Service" written and illuminated by E. Johnston, 1902 A.D. ("Office Book," Holy Trinity Church, Hastings). Reduced (nearly ¾ scale).

PLATE XXIII

— The Story of Aucassin and Nicolette, written and illuminated by IV. H. Cowlishaw, 1898 A.D.

THE VOLUME consists of 50 + leaves of "Roman Vellum" (7½ inches by 5½ inches).

MARGINS, approx.: Inner ¾ inch, Head $^{15}/_{16}$ inch, Side 1 $^{3}/_{8}$ inch, Foot 2 inches.

THE WRITING, very legible, rather "Gothic-Roman."

THE CAPITALS are illuminated throughout the text in gold on blue and red grounds. The backgrounds are square, with edges pointed or indented, outlined blacky and lined inside white. The INITIAL II is in gold on blue: the moon and stars are in white and gold and white.

THE LINE-FINISHINGS, mostly in black pen-work, consist of little groups (sometimes of sprays) of flowers, &c. Sprays from the border separate the "Song" from the "Tale."

THE MUSIC — Staves black; Clefs, gold; Notes, red.

THE BORDERS (in the opening from which the plate is taken) frame the text on both pages — nearly filling the margins (See p. 152): the side and foot edges of the (verso) page are shown in the plate. The main pattern is a wild rose, flowers and all, outlined with a rather broad blue line: the stalks and leaves (lined white) are apple-green, the flowers are painted white with raised gold hearts, the thorns are red. Through the wild rose is twined honeysuckle and woody nightshade: stalks — (h) red, (wn) black; and flowers — (h) red with yellow spots, (wn) purplish red with gold centres.

The whole effect is very brilliant and charming. The freedom and naturalness of the "design" remind one of a country hedgerow (p. 152), and show that vital beauty which is the essence of true illumination.

but he bestired himself as well;
tied his horse up with his other
and turned over on his side, so
on his back into the bower. In
through a chink in the bower, a
in the sky; and he saw one there
the rest, and he began to say:
ow it is sung.

Little star, I see thee plain,

That the moon draws to her tra
Nicolette is with thee there,
love, of the golden hair.

Plate XXIII.—The story of Aucassin and Nicolette, written and illuminated by W. H. Cowlishaw, 1898 A.D.

PLATE XXIV

— Inscription cut in Stone by A. E. R. Gill, 1903 A.D. Reduced ($3/_{16}$ scale). Note. — To view these incised letters have light on the left of plate (or cover with thin tissue-paper).

The STONE — a slab of "Hopton Wood" (p. 306), 30 inches by 18 inches by 2 inches, is intended to go over a lintel. It has a simple moulding. Note how the INSCRIPTION occupies the space (pp. 270, 307): the LETTERS have approximately the same apparent weight (p. 251) — the large stems are more than twice the height of the small; they are only $1/_3$ wider.

Note the strongly marked and elegantly curved serifs; the straight-tailed R; the I drawn out (marking the word IN); the beaked A, M, and N; the Capital form of U.

The letters DEO would be rather wide for ordinary use (p. 203), but as special letters, occupying a wide space,[134] are permissible.

Even in the collotype, I think this inscription shows to what a high level modern inscription cutting might be raised by the use of good models and right and simple methods.

---

[134] Letters in early inscriptions separated as these are indicated each a word (contracted), as S. P. Q. R. (Senatus PopulusQue Romanus).

Plate XXIV.—Inscription cut in Stone by A. E. R. Gill, 1903 A.D. Reduced ($\frac{3}{16}$ scale). *Note.*—To view these incised letters have the light on the left of the plate (*or cover with thin tissue paper*).

Made in the USA
Coppell, TX
08 June 2023

17860972R00239